Dearest Ida,   4/27/16

CROSSING THE EUPHRATES

You shine right
through the phone
and into my heart.
Thank you for all
your support.

With love & gratitude
Shara Arion

and into my heart.
your support.

ABOUT THE AUTHOR

Dr. Shoghagat Sharon Aroian (shown here with her grandfather) is a first-generation Armenian-American and has dedicated her life to the pursuit of knowledge and helping children and their families overcome trauma and adversity. She was a licensed marriage, family and child therapist and child development specialist for decades and practiced in Beverly Hills, California. She has lectured extensively on parenting, child development, and adoption. She has appeared on radio shows to promote better parenting insights and address questions from listeners. She has also helped countless children who suffer from autism and their families while they adjust and learn to love the uniqueness of each child. Her story would not be complete without the ongoing integration of her Armenian heritage and the complexity of a heritage that was destroyed with such violence yet never spoken about throughout her formative years. She had to face this unutterable violence and make peace by writing this book that is written with utter and complete honesty. She lives with her beloved husband in California. He was her *Gagad a Ger* ('Destiny is written on your forehead') as she worked in war-torn Armenia after the devastating earthquake of 1988.

SHOGHAGAT SHARON AROIAN

CROSSING
THE EUPHRATES

A Story of Love and Redemption
Inspired by the
Armenian Genocide, 1915

AUSTIN MACAULEY
PUBLISHERS LTD.

A CIP catalogue record for this title is available from the British Library.

ISBN 978-1-78612-572-9 (paperback)
ISBN 978-1-78612-573-6 (hardback)

www.austinmacauley.com

First Published (2015)
Austin Macauley Publishers Ltd.
25 Canada Square
Canary Wharf
London
E14 5LQ

Printed and bound in Great Britain

DEDICATION

This book is dedicated to my husband Juergen who taught me how to see myself as a whole person. He is the template of truth, beauty, and wisdom.

To Austin Macauley Publishers. They affirmed my inner voice that wrote this book.

To Pope Francis for his courage and compassion to speak the truth regarding the Armenian people.

To Richard Diran Kloian who single handedly gathered the buried clippings of news at the time and bound them in one book creating a voice to those that were silenced for so long. To the Genocide Education Project who allowed me the honor of using Mr. Kloian's periodicals in this book.

To all Turkish teachers, scholars, and people who have stepped forward and told the truth.

To Ethel L. for believing in me. To Dr. Tom K. for helping me open my eyes to all I can do. To Beverly F. who poured healing words into me. To Bella S. for gently helping me to be free at last.

To my loved ones who have gone ahead and are watching over me.

To you Grandpa for writing the truth and allowing me the honor to care for the words.

Chapter One

HE NEVER SPOKE ABOUT it but I felt them with us all the time. My relatives, his loved ones; people crying and lost, yet deadly quiet. When I entered a room it was taken and crowded with shadows, melancholy, secrets, violence; in silken words of love I would hear them. The crowd I lived with fought me every step of the way. I wanted to get away and yet I climbed in deeper by way of traumatic nightmares, sweats, and no amount of education cured it.

I loved him, my quiet grandfather. He was gentle, strong, and lived in the present. He was settled in his routines yet I felt there was a mountain between us. He was the patriarch of our family. He never complained; he never drove a car. He never chided me except to say I had to marry an Armenian. He believed that life unfolded and in some ways there was nothing I could do about it but show up and give it my all. I couldn't shake the crowded rooms of ghosts we all lived with because no one told me they were there. *It is all in your mind; be happy, go out and play.* The ghosts came to my parents in dreams and they would quietly talk about it. Once one came to me; he came closer every time I screamed. I still remember him today. He was sad and I wish I hadn't screamed, for my father came in while I was white as a ghost and prayed over me. It worked and unfortunately the ghost never returned. I have heard this happen to those that have been slaughtered with no place to bury their pain. They come to us for solace, for help, and rarely do we understand.

My search came in fragments of truth. Sometimes death is so obliterating that the stories are only kept alive by those left to feel the pain and slowly piece together the veins of a broken body.

When I remember him it always starts the same way. I cannot get past this image that haunts me, so I write to undo the ending. I am the sky looking down on the street below: I see him dead, alongside his beloved dog who is also dead. The police are buzzing around, the firemen are holding him his broken body and I above am powerless to help him; but I breathe love into the air as I dissolve into thousands of tears that cannot return to earth.

I awaken, relieved it is a dream; but this is when I gasp for air for it happened yesterday while I slept and missed his earlier call.

NOOOO, not this ending. Seven days later while not alone a light shone above me. My friend looked up and said this was good; I felt the door of Heaven opened just a little and the light fluttered for a short while and then slowly disappeared. If it weren't for that night I would not be writing this today.

"If anything happens to me these four books are my testament to the extermination of our people. Do with it as you see fit." I fought those words as I translated the diaries; I sobbed as those who worked on it from every walk of life wept. It didn't matter their race, they still felt the overwhelming pain and victorious heart of the brave writer.

Galoust's story began as so many others just an ordinary day that was to become a day in history that no one would remember.

His father Tateos was the town peacemaker. His job was to mitigate arguments between neighboring Turks and Armenians. He was a natural at what he did. Once he was able to successfully resolve a conflict he would report it to the town council as a good official of his region, in Western Armenia. Turks and Armenians had lived side by side for centuries, bickering, feuding, fighting for land – and power was always at the forefront. Galoust loved his village and his family thrived. *Galoust* meant "light come forth". I wondered why so many of us had names that had to do with light, and fire. My own name meant "a drop of sunray." Soon I learned that Armenians once long ago were fire worshippers until our king was converted by the apostles St. Thaddeus and Bartholomew. Once the land was of one faith they were now different. They married their own kind. They stuck to their own kind, and side by side they worked with their Turkish neighbors.

This day was like all the other days in Galoust's village. The women washed the clothes in the stream. Children went to school. Nightfall came and like every other day dinner was eaten and because there were only candles for light bedtime came soon after. This was the night that Galoust always remembered for the door was knocked upon at such a late hour and his father Tateos was gone forever. As the sun began to rise so did the murmurring and quiet screams, and weeping of many. The men were taken in the night, many put in a jail with their sons. Some were given forms to sign that they would denounce their Christian faith and then be let go. No one signed, so the jails were set on fire. This was only the beginning.

Chapter Two

HOW CAN THIS BE happening? What is happening? Turkish neighbors came by to take Galoust's house. Just shopping for food, and anything they wanted. I hate this part; the ghosts sit on my fingers as I write, for I am speaking too lightly. It was worse than this. Much worse. I hear on the radio it is the hundredth anniversary of the Armenian Genocide. What Genocide? It was just some killings. No one talks of the proclamations that went up in the markets and banks. Galoust hadn't seen them because he was too young. They were being deported so settle your bills, give us any weapons, and off you go into hell. Tateos thought he had a couple more days to talk it through with the council. A surprise: it was not five days – it was now...

Walter Morgenthau, the American Ambassador to Turkey, was writing to President Wilson begging him to help the Armenians. He wrote that he was hearing of bankers and leaders taking cyanide and giving their children to others for safe keeping. Dear Walter, he knew, but you Galoust did not. The American doctor that was burned alive by the Turkish madmen because he wasn't an Arab made it to the front pages of American newspapers. The German nurses, the nuns, oh so many people were screaming for help but you Galoust did not fathom your fate this morning when your dad was gone forever.

It has been 20 years since I reopened your diary of the Genocide. I sit frozen this moment as I reread your opening page. You say the Lord's prayer. How is your faith so unstoppable? You never preached to us. How is it that you quietly add to the Lord's prayer only at the end, after Amen, "The Tri Color." "The Tri Color:" always with such subtle dignity the Armenian flag. Your diary starts with prayer rather than the genocide. How did you spend 88 years and never speak about it to me? I was at your side. I was in your lap. I loved you more than life itself. How is it that it was only at the 70th anniversary of the Armenian Genocide, when I went with you to Washington, that you spoke? Even then it was not directly to me. It was to strangers as each survivor got up and told their story. Grandpa, what is more perplexing is that I knew to never ask.

I know why Turkey can't bear to say the truth. It isn't what they did, it is how they did it, right? The Lebanese-American entertainer Danny Thomas said to me once, "Where are you from?" I was at a party, and this man just asked me this while he held a microphone. He was so full of life. I told him that I was Armenian. What I never expected was what followed. With that microphone he said that his grandfather would tell him about the train that came into a part of Lebanon. The room got quiet as he continued.

He told me that the Armenian people were starving and crushed in together, that they opened the train and they fell to the ground. The Lebanese people that were nearby were told that if they tried to feed them they would be killed. Danny Thomas was now telling the room of party guests that the Turks were throwing Armenian babies up in the air and catching them on the ends of their bayonets. Mr. Thomas said that his grandfather could never forget those stories. The room was silent. I was speechless: with that speech Danny Thomas said more than you, Grandpa, said in your whole life to me. I quietly nodded. It was like the forbidden truth was shouted from the rooftops. What happened next was the most interesting. Nothing. No one asked him a thing, no one asked me a thing. It disappeared into the ghosts that hovered that evening.

Chapter Three

SOMETIMES A SIMPLE MAN can have the mind of a great thinker. How did you recall with such clarity your birthplace, the life you had before the storm?

You were born at the turn of the century. With the past slaughters behind everyone, you came into the world when there was order. Khoumlar village in the Terjan region was a province of Karin in Western Armenia. Armenia, not Turkey. Yet you spoke fluent Turkish. I knew only about this from your writing. I found out from Turkish Armenians that words that were precious to me my whole life like "bed" and "ball" were in fact Turkish words. When I confronted my parents about that they quickly changed the words back to Armenian. Words I said my whole life were quickly forgotten and I was told I was mistaken in my recollection. My parents changed back the words but you never did. Mamakhtoun was so beautiful tucked near a river called Dougla.

I always wondered why you were so happy Grandpa when my parents bought your burial plot. It was next to a giant sundial. Time. You were so aware of time. How it drove me mad sometimes. No matter what the reason you never wanted us to waste one minute. If I were late by five minutes you would tell me. Now I discover that your town had a Ghartal Stone! Which meant you could tell time like a sundial! Sixty-three houses and thirty-three Armenian families told time by that giant rock. You write that 30 brute Turks lived there too. You don't say 63 families lived there; you separate them. You never said a harsh word about Turks to me. Yet there I read the word "brute." The stone called Ghartal, which meant "to read the rock," had been there for over a thousand years. Your town had high mountains and rocks all around. You lived near ancient ruins. They framed your village background like a new chapter in the lives of Armenians. As a child you feared that the Gartal Stone would collapse and destroy the whole village. But the amazing thing was it was the most reliable friend to you all. Watches and clocks were a rarity reserved for the rich. Noon was so important because it was then that the sun shone brightly on the forehead of the rock: the cattle were released and lunch was shared amongst the people. It seemed like a fairytale. You were too young to have to work but you would watch the workman work together, eat together, then have a light supper at 4 p.m. and then return home singing and laughing together. Even with only 33 Armenian families, your village built a beautiful church with a cupola made of granite stone. Your village was so innovative yet so remote. There was a fountain that was made with clay tubes. It would provide water for the whole village. There was always enough water for everyone. The cattle drank from stone tubs, and the villagers would wash the grain for crunched grain and millet. It was so quiet that singing broke the silence.

Local life had a set pattern as the four seasons. Work hard for seven to eight months, then in the winter rest, tell stories, while the women spun on spindles. Turkish neighbors worked on your land but stayed separate. Unspoken voices made sure there was no mixing.

I know about the Turkish man who went to the forbidden Kyorghly's Stone. He was a very special man because he shared his enlightenment. This holy section of your village was to be left undisturbed. Healing had taken place there. A girl who had a horrible falling sickness was healed there as she held a tiny branch in her hand. This Turk took some branches of the Holy Trees home to build with and was haunted with terrible dreams. He saw in his dream that he was to take the branches back to the holy place or his mouth that was now distorted would never heal. He took the branches back and was restored. He spent the rest of his life going to Armenian churches every Sunday and he was welcomed by all.

Just fifteen years before you were born your very village and beloved church was plundered by Turkish neighbors. They slaughtered 22 Armenians and the Armenian families buried the dead near the beloved fountain. Your mother would take you kids to honor your two uncles, and your grandfather every All Saints Day. The last massacre in your village was called the 1895 Looting Massacre. My great-grandmother would ask the priest to come and give special blessings to her lost brothers, and her beloved father. It was always like that... the slaughters. The Turks would come and they would go. It never started in 1914; it started centuries before, especially after Armenians as a whole converted to Christianity.

You all learned early about pilgrimages: what else could you do but walk and remember? One pilgrim there was Srpouhie Marapents: she never married but was such a believer. Early mornings, women would come from all over to have her tie the mat weed around the women and the stone called Bibbouk which was known to have spiritual powers; they would circle the stone three times and return to their homes and soon after learn that they were finally pregnant! You use to watch her and marvel.

There were other superstitions. Daoun Dara was a deep valley and belonged to your village. One side was all black stone and rock and it was shaped like a wall. You children were told that there were evil genies inside the rock. You kids were curious and when you got too close while pasturing your lambkins you would cry out to block the evil genies with their feet turned around while they sat and stared.

Winter was severe in your country: it is hard to believe that at one time it snowed for three to four months each year, and you all had to breed your cattle indoors! Your lives seemed set. Spring came in March: the shepherds drew their sheep and goats to graze. The harvesting would be finished in three to four months. Your uncle built a watering pool for the villagers and everyone would use it for all kinds of reasons. The women would do the churning of milk to butter.

It all seemed so removed from any violence, any malice; and yet it was getting closer each day.

Chapter Four

FOLKLORE WAS DEEPLY WOVEN into each day of living in tradition. It seemed that everything the wise elderly said had been true at one time. Even in these simple and beautiful days you lived in fear. Tales were always told by the elderly to keep you all close together and in some ways to protect you from what you were too young to fathom.

Before the fatal knock on your family home you all did so well with planting and harvests that your father and mother were able to hire a day laborer to help with the ploughing of new land for the following crop. The evil genies that sat in rows along the Daoun Dara in the deep valley where you all grazed your cattle and laid crops were really code for the unannounced. No one knew when the Turkish neighbors would come in and randomly attack innocent people. Simply being of another faith made the Armenian villagers targets at any given time.

In the city there were sophisticated Armenians that wore Victorian dresses, while the men wore three-piece suits with rounded collars. The poets would come to your valley for inspiration but retreat to a life that was so foreign to you in the village. No one needed watches because of the unity of working together, eating together, prayer time, and rest. The Ghartel Stone was there for everyone to use. The air was clean and the water crystal clear and delicious. There was a place called BER. This area was for all the Armenians in the village. Because the winters were so severe there was great joy in spring and BER the underground spring would surface. The women came with milk pails to milk the sheep; they later boiled the milk, curdled it and made Matzoun cheese. The milk was also churned into butter and skimmed milk soup. Many milk-foods were conserved for winter use. Armenian lavash bread was crumbled in the skimmed milk soup and was enjoyed around the fireplace.

"I remember it as if it were today." Two brothers that were farriers from a neighboring town came to our village. We only had one craftsman, named Grigor. He was a master craftsman: he could shoe oxen, buffaloes, and horses. The two brothers, from Prez, lived in Mamakhatoun City. Master Grigor from our village became so much in demand during spring. The oxen and cattle had to be re-shoed and though your uncle built Grigor's house out of brick in exchange for his service they were not on speaking terms. (Maybe that is why you never drove, Grandpa: cars driven by people were too much risk. Yet a car stole your life.) Your father had to give you a letter and you were a child but had to walk to Mamakhatoun and deliver the letter to the two brothers. You found them and came home with the good news. The next day they came as promised and shoed the cattle, and with great hospitality your family fed them and paid them for their service.

Soon after, during the busiest time of the year the buffalo's leg grew swollen, he became lame, and though you all tried to help him by letting him rest and putting his leg in the Dayin pool he continued to get sicker. I didn't know you had buffaloes Grandpa. Many modern Armenians don't know the day-to-day life of Armenia before the "genocide that never happened." I find myself comforted by the uncomplicated choices you all had to make, yet I know at the time it must have felt no different than my trying to pass a test of some kind myself. A child walking for over an hour in the wilderness to deliver a letter and doing it successfully is to me a great victory. As your family struggled and tried to yoke an ox with the buffalo to plough, once again they failed. Word got out to Master Grigor. Grigor sent word to your father Tateos that he would cure your buffalo in one week. When he came it was clear that the brothers from Prez did a terrible job and once he unshoed the prized buffalo and reshoed him properly all was well again.

"Soon after our peace was once more shattered. We were strong in our faith and when one lives in such pastures with the sky and people that work together you feel safe, you feel happy. We didn't know what it is to want. We were rich in love, and family and storytelling. It was enough each day. There was a completeness to each day like a chapter in a book. But once again a big fight broke out between the Armenians and the Turks. We were back in our field working. We had a piece of land called 'Sirouny:' we picked the word that meant 'pretty' because we hadn't ploughed it yet. We had a great tradition in our village. If a family couldn't reap their field in time fellow villagers came around to give a hand to collect the harvest together and finish the job together. It was natural for us to lend a hand just like Master Grigor did. This day was beautiful and our neighbors came together. I remember boys, girls, even newlyweds joined the volunteers while we reaped the fields of my family. There must have been around 20 people, maybe more. In giving thanks it was an equal tradition that the host-landlord feed the volunteers in order to show gratitude and remain in their esteem. One's honor and reputation were as important as one's faith. I remember the group singing together as they departed. We didn't have radios but we sang; we didn't have many books but we learned through storytelling and going to church and school.

"I have not forgotten to tell you about the big fight between the Armenians and Turks. Our pool called BER was made by a fellow Armenian we all called Dayi, which meant uncle. The Turks did not go to our area. This day deep in the valley Turks had brought eleven coaches that were transferring state grain to Mamakhatoun. It appeared that the Turks had stolen the state grain and were taking them to sell in a nearby town. One youth around 18 years old was holding hands with an Armenian girl. My uncle Armenak Mkrtichian shouted out to him to let go of an Armenian girl's hand. Two Turkish youths there ran away and a big fight broke out. The Armenian girl was scared; the Turks had come to our area to hide their deeds. During the fight two Turks were killed. There was a trial and no Armenian was convicted, I was only in early school but remember this day like it was yesterday. In the early 1900's for a while Armenians had some influence. The case was tried in 1908 and the Armenians prevailed. For once they did not lose any people."

Chapter Five

"TO BE FRANK, I can't remember the exact date of the missing little Turkish girl. She was around five years old and it was a very long and hot summer day. The little girl was playing up on the roofs and a woman who was a devil genie tricked her by acting like her mother, and she led her away from the village. The news spread to all of us and even though the Turks were not our kin we all started searching house to house looking for her. People searched the mountains and the valleys they questioned every-one. People walked as far as Kav Darasi which was two kilometers from the village. There they found the girl sitting in the ruins of an Armenian church holding an iron bar in her hands. She had been gone for three days and no harm came to her. What was amazing was the distance and the fact that wild animals roamed nearby and yet she was completely unharmed. When the news of her returning home spread to all the people they were curious as to how she survived and where was this so called Kaveghi Valley?"

People were so curious that they took her back to the ancient Armenian church and you Galoust were among them. I can only imagine how you still remembered that it was 10 a.m. when she came back to the village, and that the elders kept coaching her and saying, "Tell us who brought you here our little sweetie." All the girl said was that her mom brought her there and left her and never came back. These were times when Armenian and Turks came together to protect the children of their village.

In your village the lambs were also like children. They were valuable and very important to the wellbeing of every family who could afford them. Strange how shepherds in your region took care of cows, calves, and sheep, but not the little lambs. Each family had to do that important chore. One day it was your turn to take the lambs out to pasture and then it was your brother Ohannes' turn. He fell asleep and they all went missing. How interesting life is that they too were missing for three days and were found pasturing near the same Armenian Church where the little Turkish girl was found!

Grandpa you speak often in your diaries of evil genies which have Arabian origins. You speak of evil mermaids with behavior like the devil. It was only recently when I went to Germany and found clues to your thinking. Lo and behold while trailing the narrowest part of the River Rhine I saw the statue of a beautiful mermaid combing her hair. As beautiful as she was, combing her long hair with a golden comb, she was evil. I was stunned to learn this folklore that was so real during medieval times that sailors shuddered to go through the narrowest part of the Rhine. Horrible shipwrecks occurred in this area. It looked so wide and majestic to me that I was further surprised that a more modern calamity occurred where many workman onboard a ship died horribly as it overturned. The ship captains in medieval times claimed that as they came to the narrowest part of the Rhine a beautiful mermaid could be seen combing her long beautiful hair with a golden comb and as the sailors became mesmerized she steered them to crash into the rocks and perish. Only then could I understand this term you used to describe evil in people around you. Forgive me that I thought it strange and incorrect (as if I could live in your shoes so long ago).

In your diary you tell the story of the Turkish woman you referred to as "sister," but I must say the encounters you had with Turkish neighbors were so abrasive. "Sister" has always been such an endearing Armenian word. I hold it dear to my heart, for I was called that endearment while journeying to Armenia after you died so suddenly and tragically. I had to go to your homeland, as well as mine. To hear you call this callous woman "sister" was such a testament of how hard you tried to embrace your neighbors. You always told us know the language of your enemy. It seemed so foreign and strange, for in America I felt I never had an enemy. This woman named "Nylou" with whom you tried to communicate by calling her "Bajy"—"sister" in Turkish—was truly a bedeviled mermaid. It was spring and the sowing had ended. The cattle that had been yoked and were ploughing; while all your family and villagers tilled and sowed the land. Finally you would all get to rest for two weeks. You had a structure as to how the harvests grew that was more precise than any modern farm manual. Right after those two weeks of rest, time was critical because the snows came for months and were almost continual when they started. I learned how everyone tilled and then ploughed while sowing "the waste fields." You called them this name because you were all getting them ready for next year's spring. Even though you were a child you too went to the far end of the village to help plough the land with your older brother Hovhannes. On this day you and your brother took two mules that were yoked with two buffaloes. I was amazed to know that buffalo existed in Western Armenia. Your family also had six oxen that walked in pairs. Your uncle Manouk drove one of them and with the help of neighbors great work was done by noon! Then came your uncle's request to take the cattle and let them drink water in the fountain pool made and used by the Armenians. My heart aches as I see in my mind's eye two young children having to take these big cattle to the fountain pool while the hot day surrounded your skin. You honored your Uncle Manouk's wishes. You never knew my work with children; I never even told you that I dedicated my life to helping special children and their families. Kids that suffer and struggle. I read the responsibility you children had and I am in awe of how children can strive to do great things so young, and how we in America struggle to figure out when they are ready to feel important, not by words but by contribution and behavior. How did you find your way, being so young and small, to the "Golaghpyure" fountain pool? The cattle dove into the water—they were so hot and thirsty—but you stayed and watched.

That's when it happened. This Turkish woman, whom you said looked like a man, was bringing buffaloes that belonged to a rich Turkish man to drink from the waters of your people. This is when I see the separation. The Turks in your area stayed to themselves in their sections just like the Armenians stayed with their people. You asked her: "Nylou bajy [sister], please don't let your buffaloes into the water until ours are out. You can then bring your buffaloes in and they can relax too." I love your heart: even as a child you were so attuned to what is fair and what works best. I think you had the gift of common sense just like your father. I wish to reach through the pages to protect you from what happens next. Nylou began cursing you, the family and your religion. She was big and strong and began to beat you and Hovhannes your beloved brother. I read his name and realize Hovhaness was the name you gave my beloved uncle! You named each of your children after the siblings you lost in the human slaughter that was to come.

I feel close to your brother because I too said the name my whole life. You two children were helpless and scared while she attacked you both.

Then a will from deep inside came up. You were taught to respect your elders but this was survival and as you wrote so long ago courage overtook your fears.

"I called out to my brother Hovhannes to strike her back which we did. We fought her off by hitting her arms as they came down on our heads. We got her off of us and were able to get our cattle and go home. We didn't know what would happen when we returned to our family."

It was nearly an hour before you saw your father coming back on his horse and you told your uncle what happened as Tateos came closer and closer. Uncle Manouk comforted you by telling you not to worry and there was a good chance your father would understand. Then I see the way the daily life really was between the Turks and Armenians. That woman Nylou went back to the village and went straight to the Chief of the village who was Turkish and called a Moukhtar and cried to him that Landlord Tateos' son beat her! This is the first time I see the word "Landlord." The Village Chief did not believe her and questioned her as to why these children would beat her. Nylou then showed her arms and said she was so weak from the children beating her that she could not raise them anymore. She pretended that she couldn't raise her arms. She couldn't do this because she had been hitting these boys, not the other way around. I shout inside, "Say something Grandpa!" But, alas, the Chief now calls for your father the mediator of the village and questioned him. "Elderman Tateos, your sons have beaten Nylou Bajy."

"I was told that my father said one word, 'Amazing.' He couldn't understand how we would have done such a thing. He came home and I was scared while I watched him climb down from his horse and begin to roll his tobacco papers. My father was quiet and I knew he wanted to give us a thrashing. My uncle Manouk pleaded with him to not punish us because it wasn't our fault. My uncle had such respect for my father that he wouldn't smoke in front of him. The papers used for tobacco rolling were a form of papyrus. I stood there as my uncle longed for a tobacco smoke, and I watched my father strike his flint and light his cigarette.

"The tobacco box dropped on the ground and I did what my uncle asked I snuck and grabbed the tobacco box that also contained the papyrus. I loved my Uncle Manouk because he had four children and still was shy to smoke in front of his older brother. After my uncle took some of the tobacco and papyrus I ran and gave the tin box to my father before he left again."

Grandpa I read your words now and I have to keep rereading them because it sounds like a parable. A parable I take literally. I read it slowly and the truth of what the feelings were underneath comes through. "My father had to throw bones to the dogs' mouths in order to keep the peace." These types of clashes occurred regularly and thought to be minor. You say "With a piece of a dog's bone they'd keep silent because they were starving dogs, they lived on Armenians' bread."

I feel the hatred in the earth you all walked on. You were leaders in your village but blood in the veins of the earth was still theirs. No matter how many times you all buried your dead and tried to co-exist there was a separation that was black and white, just like the bird that landed on my window sill was a sign. As I write I want to see both sides and feel them as one. For the first and only time in my life a bird unlike any bird I have ever seen came and sat near me, with its big black head and its belly white as snow. It kept looking at me, tilting its head through the slats of my window, and I knew it was one of you keeping me on course. They keep sitting on my fingers as I write. I want to be poetic; I want stay above the slabs of dirt you walked on and not look beneath the rocks and see the bedeviled mermaids that were all around you and your loved ones. It won't happen again—I will stay in the stream that has crystal waters. With death and blood building from beneath the ground I am scared to go deeper; but I will look fully now, I promise.

Chapter Six

I TREMBLE TO WRITE this Grandpa. I have to take the sign from the black and white bird that I must. Black and white was your life as a child. I want to soften the words again. I have spent my life teaching families that physical punishment does not teach anything but bruises souls and imprints violence in return. How can such loving father figures strike you as a child, deeming the behavior a lesson in manners? Elders, teachers—and then there is your own father. You never struck us: how did you change the fate of us with such harsh beginnings? Great-grandpa struck you as a way of communicating his displeasure in something you said or did. I wish I could wipe away the brutality you endured. I always asked you about love. You were always so gentle with me; I never knew until now just how churlish it all was even in your own home.

I remember only a month before you were killed, when I hadn't died inside yet, I asked you Grandpa, "When will I have love?" You would say one sentence, "*Gagad a Ger*"—Destiny was written on my forehead. It helped because I just let go of trying to find him. No one would believe what you said was true. I just never knew your death was part of my own *Gagad a Ger*. When I died yet walked the earth in shock after you were killed by a hit and run driver I didn't care to find him.

I prayed for love to come to me from a very young age. He never came to me. I felt an intuition as we have in our family that he was out there and he was strong and your words that I had to marry an Armenian was always a pit I fell into. I grew up a foreigner in my own country, America. I felt that there was something missing when I was with Americans and I felt something was missing when I was with Armenians. It never left me. I didn't belong with the Americans even though I was born in Detroit. When I spoke Armenian I felt the sweetness of our ancestry but I didn't belong with the Armenians either. I despaired, walking on scaffolds, trying to find my balance. I was two people not one. I still am two people but I have finally found my balance. I feel American more than Armenian, but that is a lie: I am Armenian to my soul and American through my mind.

When the earthquake in Armenia destroyed 250 villages and flattened beloved cities in December of 1988 you told me on the phone that you were relieving the genocide again. It was the only time you ever spoke directly to me of this, even though it on was the phone. I cringe now as I remember, I didn't run to you, I ran to the Armenian church to help sort clothes and supplies for the victims in Armenia. I felt so guilty Grandpa but you told me to stay and help our people. All that work we did—mountains of clothes, shoes, money—and Russia refused our donations. I could have been with you. The rest is a blur. Christmas came: I was sick, and you were sad; New Year came, January 1, 1989—such an important day for you each year. You would want to toast the day and you celebrated in such a spiritual way. How did you believe so deeply with all that you had seen? I called you and told you I would come to you but that I was in bed sick and alone. You were alone and I was alone. I could feel your sadness but I couldn't move.

January 3rd you called me late and I never got the message. I am sorry Grandpa you left the sweetest message for me on the old fashioned answering machine. To this day I have the little microphone tape in my jewelry box. I will not listen to it. I can't. You never understood those silly things, you told me to call you back and I never got the chance because the next morning at 6:30 a.m. you took your two-mile morning walk with your daughter Oghik's dog. The police report burns in my mind as I see the picture of you tossed in the air (like a white bag, said a witness) and you came down, crashed into the driver's windshield and then you fell to the ground, killed instantly. There I am above the ground in the sky again looking helplessly as you lie there with your shoe near the curb and your beloved dog next to you. The sirens are shrieking because the fire department was down the street and they came and held you as I watched from the sky and your wish came true after all. You told me you wanted to leave earth on your feet. I didn't understand. You told me your legs were weakening and I would tell you to "Not worry, you are 88 and in perfect health," but you were scared Grandpa, you did not want to leave this earth helpless. I never thought of this before but your sister who saved your life during the genocide by dressing you in girl's clothes was called Oghik: the name you gave your daughter. It was her dog that you cared for before you met your fate. Your 89th birthday would have been January 10th. Instead of celebrating I was at your funeral in shock and in rage. How could you survive a genocide and World War II and come to America and build a life and be cut down by a degenerate that killed you and drove away? You would say *Gagad a Ger*. My wish came true because of you.

I boarded the first plane with a psychiatric team in March 1989 and headed to Armenia to help in any way I could. Flight attendants told me if I noticed how nicely the Russians were dressing. I only got it once I arrived and saw nurses wearing rags, in the freezing cold. The supplies were not arriving as promised; they were being diverted into parts of Russia. Unless someone stayed with the donations they disappeared.

Never did I expect that in my journey to a wasteland of loss my own *Gagad a Ger* would occur. A man of great love and light in his heart and mind was also helping the people. He came back to America and told my beloved about me. Two years Grandpa had passed, with traveling to Armenia and helping those that came to America to train, along with fighting to have the strength to finish my doctorate, when my fate that was written all the time came to me, and never left. Late one night after school, work, exhaustion, I was driving to a farewell gathering. I wanted to give small gifts to the visiting psychiatrists from Armenia to take home to their families. I saw the precious man from Los Angeles who volunteered in Armenia. He was a refined analyst who was very humble and he insisted that I meet his dearest friend. I said no, no, no, no. I felt so embarrassed, so afraid of the unknown.

Grandpa these miracles keep happening. When I was on my last return from Armenia, I met the kindest flight attendant. I never got to tell you. The whole team was leaving for America when we got word the supplies were coming everyone got on the plane but I couldn't. I stayed behind and though just week earlier with great tears I said goodbye to the nurses in the makeshift children's hospital I came back with a large cargo truck of supplies, medicine, and nourishment. They screamed "Sister, Sister, we can't believe you came back." But I looked and all the therapy rooms I set up were gone. All the work I did to help the countless children was derailed by the very nurses I adored. They had given all the therapeutic toys away because deep inside no one understood psychotherapy. Even though they begged for help because hundreds of children and parents perished in the collapsing buildings during the earthquake, playing and talking was not in their sphere of comprehension. The flight attendant on Lufthansa was so kind and told me her husband's name was Juergen. I exclaimed, "Juergen? I have never heard that name before: it is so beautiful." I truly did Grandpa, I hope you are listening. Then I forgot about it. In March of 1991 my phone rang and the deep voice on the other end of the line said, "My name is Juergen". From that moment I felt a kinship in our talks each night, and he came to meet me at my parents' home, Grandpa. Grandpa he wasn't Armenian, he was my destiny, and I have been with him ever since. Each day I awake with the same love and awe I felt over the phone that night. He is my *Gagad a Ger* and he is German with a heart that transcends the closed-mindedness of "one race or nothing at all." Albert Einstein said that we can either live life where everything is a miracle or live life where nothing is a miracle. Again, so black and white.

I believe in *Gagad a Ger* now. It is not my being passive as I mistakenly thought you meant. Instead it is me not trying to design and control my destiny.

I was afraid to write these words. The mountain stood in front of me as it had my whole life. What if danger comes as a result of letting the ghosts speak at last? I wrote a life-changing letter on May 1st. I sent it far away to ancient England. The ghosts were so happy because I was finally starting to give in to the forbidden journey of now.

Chapter Seven

I AM SAD AS I walk with you in the hills of Western Armenia and I feel no room for a child's voice. I want to stop and change the truth out of shame, but I can't. I have to say what I see: unnecessary rudeness and cruelty to you children by your own father figures which I have already mentioned. I remember how I was to render to all my aunts and uncles the same power and respect I owed to my own parents. I know it was the same for you because you passed this on to us. Talking about a subject from a child's perspective didn't exist. It didn't matter what you thought; it mattered what the grownups perceived. How stifling it must have been at the best of times! I walk with you in Armenia in my imagination and I am older than you; maybe it is my training in child development that makes me want to protect you from the grownups all around you, but you and I don't even speak the same language. You appear so foreign and estranged. I think you kids barely spoke. It was all behavior, wasn't it?

I am learning while I immerse myself in your world that your father Tateos was really a landlord in good standing. He seems very confident and very much in control. He feels like your guardian more than your parent, and I am sorry I say this, but he does. Just like I had loving guardians that could not parent me. To inspire is to parent. I see how much negative power generational omissions wield over newborn children when they enter a family system. These omissions have more influence in imbedding fear than the spoken word. I watch you walk away from me and back to your village and I chase you but you ignore me because I can see you more than your own loved ones, and that is not allowed. I watch how Turkish workers come to your house and use your father's resources by pretending they have important things to talk about. What they do instead is eat your food and take all your father's time and then they leave. You see the truth and no one listens to you. You are just a child with no pearls of wisdom. I am stunned as I realize your childhood wrote these 400 pages. I search through I feel relieved that young Galoust finally will speak and be heard by me. I only wish we talked about it all, but instead I intuited mountains of pain and harshness and violence: I thought was my imagination and now I learn I was the closest to you when I was lost in the silent ghosts that circled you all my life.

I see you going to church with your father. He holds your hand. You look like you're five or six. It is so early in the morning—not quite 8 a.m.—and now you are returning from church, nearing your home. That same Turkish man Aymed Chaoush who steals your father's time and food comes up to you both and begins to talk to your father. Father Tateos talks to this man for almost an hour while you feel faint and tired and weary, still holding your father's hand. You spat at this man's beard from the agony of standing in one place and your father was enraged at you. I am ashamed at his inability to know what is too much for a child, but I also want to protect him because I know he was reacting in the context of your culture and village. I always expect people to transcend their culture and know instinctively right from wrong when caring for children. Young Galoust wrote the words of this encounter, you knew this was wrong and yet you were not allowed to speak. So, you acted. Your father raised his hand and slapped you and the Turkish man stopped him and kindly said that maybe he, the Turk, had done something to offend you. I am so shocked that the victimizer has more sense this moment than your father who should have been the wiser. When you got home I watch the women comfort you as Tateos told them what you did. Your grandmother asks you if your father hurt you and you began to cry. I want to reach through time and hug you Grandpa but I can only hope you are with me now as I write the forbidden truth. I watch how your mother knows the way the silencing of trouble works. She gathers food for your father to take to the Turkish man. She says while I watch from my mind, "This way he will stay calm."

Grandpa I cannot believe how your village built homes. I am standing in a large field and smell the cold mud and the scents of the animals' sweat as they work, and all my relatives who later perished, working together. I am so sorry I never thought of them as people but only ghosts that filled our rooms and I am shaking with anger that all these relatives of mine don't know what is to come soon. They will all be dead and slaughtered. Little disagreements won't matter, and all the virtue my great-grand-mother had will be spilled to the ground in blood and rape. I see them around me: they are so calm and real and I cry out to them to run for their lives, that none of this harvesting will matter soon. No one sees me as I stand there; I am meeting them for the first time. My great-grandmother I see putting apples in these beautiful boxes that have painted flowers all over them. She and my great-aunts store their clothes in them and put apples and quinces to keep them fresh. They open the boxes and such a sweet fragrance fills the air; I see you sniff it in like perfume. I love them for taking time to make their lives a little more joyful. Great-grandmother went down to the bazaar very far from home and brought them for the women. I sniff the air and I can also smell the aroma. It is home to me too.

Last night I awoke with such burning in my throat. You haven't come to me in a dream for such a long while. But the others did. My beloved husband told me I was making a cringe-sounding noise like I was crying out from deep within my body. I will not stop traveling to the site of the forbidden slaughter even with the burning in my throat. Where was I last night? Why can't I remember this important dream but I remember so many silly dreams?

Maybe it wasn't a dream after all. You know I am fearless even when I feel dread and terror. I am returning, because no one can stop me now, not even me. I am walking today near the villagers constructing the new build- ing for your home. I have never witnessed such ingenuity like this. I have always been enthralled with the ancient building techniques and have read so many texts Grandpa. I have never been interested in the Armenian way of building because I too have prejudice, because of the way Turks portrayed Armenians as if they were such peasants they wouldn't even feel their own destruction. How wrong I was. Your village had so many steps foreign to me that I first thought you were all baking. I am walking through a path of dirt and it winds to a halt. I see your house: you never told me how beautiful it was. You never told me how well your father Tateos lived. You never even told me his name. Just this year I was going through the mountains of paper you left behind, always news clippings in Armenian with your little written lines underneath. An envelope fell out and there I saw it for the first time: Galoust and his family arrive to America as homeless people. Homeless... Twice you passed through losing everything: WWII made those of you who were left all homeless. You were not homeless, you were robbed—there is such a difference.

I snap back and I am here again looking as the workers prepare the cement that will protect you all from the harsh winter. The depth and width of the walls were long because it also protected you all during the hot summers. The walls were about a half a meter deep, both sides were walled up at the required height with stones, gravel and grout filled inside. Your father built a very large house for all of you. I see four columns. I enter into the kitchen (called a *tounir*): it is a lower room. The kitchen is so large that the three corners that consisted of clay granaries were called "beehives." I don't see painted walls but plain walls with nails that hold up jugs and pots my great-grandmother cooked with. I leave and let you talk now.

"In autumn, the whole food-stock and supplies were prepared and staffed. We ground the grain and made flour. We filled in those beehives with grain, barley, and whatever we had. At one corner we had shelves that were like alcoves for the beddings. In the evenings the beddings which included the mattress, blanket, pillow, and sheets were laid and the beds made. In the mornings, they were folded and shelved. Above the shelves there were vestries to keep the vestment boxes of the three brothers in-law."

(You always spoke words like a clergyman. I remember when our beloved Archbishop Sumbat Lapajian spoke at your funeral he said that every Sunday he would look out at the pew you were sitting in and if you were shaking your head he knew he was off, and when you were nodding your head all was well. You walked to that church Grandpa: it was such a long distance in America, but like ages ago when your father held your hand and walked you to church, you walked as an adult every Sunday without fail.)

"As you enter my house on the left side of the walls clay made baskets, jars, and jugs were hung. They were filled with crumbled grain, cracked wheat, various pickled cabbage, apples and other things. During wedding parties all guests were roomed at our home. They danced, had fun, enjoyed food and drinks. We had an adjacent building.

"There was a *tounir* bake-house, with an eastern stove and oven for summer use. In winter, it was safe to keep food-stock and supplies there. We also had a special room, as a sitting room for the guests. Almost every day mostly grandees, who were the elite of the Turks, would visit. Turkish dogs were the visitor. Woe is him, who had a sitting room for guests." (I had to look "dog" up. What other meaning does the word have? I found "unpleasant, contemptible or wicked." Back to the truth.) "The rooms had no windows. But sitting rooms like yours had windows. The Turkish authorities recently started to collect tax from the Armenian people for those windows." (Houses were roofed and covered like domes. They begin to construct the mounting by erecting logs from four corners, leaving space for two alcoves, one for the large room on the ground floor and the other for the kitchen.) "The windows called *panjara* [Turkish word] are built of blind, wooden shutters. A long rope was tied to it to open in daytime and close in the evening. They did not need to go to the roofs. The roofs were made from a different material instead of tiles. First, rafters were put together before the windows. Then "tumble sweet" bushes were cut and transferred on dray-carts from Boughlogh [place name]. They were laid and set on the rafter together. Hay made of mud or fry grass was laid and spread on the grass. Then black earth three to four inches was spread on. The mass was then compacted. At the end, one inch of red clay earth was laid on the black earth and levelled well. It was never locked. I remember like today, I was nine or ten years old, my family built a new room a sitting room. We needed bushes. We went to bring some on two dray-carts. They also took me with them to look after the cattle so they could work. My father put his tobacco and lighter near the cart. He came back to light a cigarette every hour and returned to his job. When he left I felt like I'd want to try to smoke. So, I did. Well, one, two breaths; I felt dizzy, my eyes blackened, I got sick. The men seeing this told my dad that his son was sick. My father told them to hurry and load the carts and go home. My grandma, God illuminate her soul, seeing me sick, told my father that he made me sick. She laid me down brought cold water and washed my head. She asked me what they had done to me to make me so ill. That is when I threw up. My mother said, 'He smoked—he is not sick.' My father wanted to strike me and punish me but my grandmother grew angry."

I never saw you smoke Grandpa. Auntie always hid her smoking from you even though she had three children. I never knew that hiding was tradition until this moment. I can't find what this bush "tumble sweet" is Grandpa but it seems to be as important as gold to you all. More trouble with the Turks: I can't watch this time, I will let you tell it as you remember.

"I want to say our future groom, my sister's fiancée, had built a room and needed some tumble sweet from some other village. In-law Khachatour, our groom's father came to ask my dad if it was possible for my father to loan them his buffaloes and oxen so that they could bring some tumble sweet from the other village. My father consented. His brother Khachik, their relative Minas and from our side Trdat Martirossian, our Godfather, who always was with us, went early in the morning. They yoked the cattle and left, so that they could reach the workplace at sunrise. On their way as they crossed past the territory of our village and entered the territory of Koughol village, servants of Koughol landlords were pasturing their cattle in the dark. Khachik told the Turkish servants to please watch their cattle so they would not strike ours. They curtly asked who were we to give them orders. They were harsh and hostile in tone and one of our members of the group stuck out at them. They went back and reported to the village landlords, not their wrongdoing blocking us to cross but our wrongdoing in defending our rights. The landlords collected many men and they came back to cause us all harm."

(Grandpa you use the word "lapidary." I am always amazed at the level of wisdom you achieved when your schooling was so few in years. It proves we are either people who want to learn or people who step aside in mediocrity. I find that "lapidary" means stonecutter, and I understand that when the Turks fought, it was to cut deep using deathly strokes.)

"A stone hit my uncle Khachik in the mouth and broke four of his teeth. They stole our cattle and took my Godfather Trdat and Martiros as a hostage. We were outnumbered and their aim was to destroy, as they struck Armenak on the head with a hatchet. Our uncle finally said to use his gun. He shot a warning shot in the air. The two Turk brothers returned to their home taking our property and relatives. Our people went to Mamakhatoun to complain. In the end, my uncle received one piece of gold for each tooth that was broken, and we got our cattle back. Our villagers won the case as a whole because the Turkish brothers had no right to block us from crossing the open road that was there for everyone. Their additional penalty was to give us two sheep."

Chapter Eight

GRANDPA I WISH THE child in you could remember more about the Armenian pilgrimages. I didn't know there was such a thing. Where did the grownups go? What did they do? I know that there is an ancient Armenian church built in honor of the Apostle St. Thaddeus who converted our Armenian king—it is now part of Iran—that the pilgrimages happen every year and that the church is open only one day a year! I wonder if this is where Great-Grandfather went when he went on his pilgrimage.

Once I was in the airport in Saudi Arabia and I saw these people going to Mecca. They wore white towel-like garments with white tassels, and bright green open shoes that looked like flip-flops. They all dressed alike; I was entranced by the simplicity. I wore a long dress with only my calves showing along with my lower arms. I was not to be looked upon. I felt shunned but didn't know why. My hair was not covered and I felt so ashamed when the women began hiding their faces from me using their headscarves.

I learned so much through my senses. I never would have thought that my own relatives used headscarves until years later. I thought Mecca must be a beautiful and holy place. What do these costumes mean? They seemed too casual for such a trip. Grandpa I never knew that your people made a journey like this. You went to church so often, morning and night. Your lives were hard and yet your relatives and Great-Grandfather Tateos thought there should be a pilgrimage as well. Because you were a child they tricked you and promised you could go in the morning. You were so clever you slept outside near the flour barn. In the early morning you awoke and they had all departed. You never told me you could ride a horse. I only saw you walk my whole life.

You jumped on the horse in your stable and ran at a chase speed for so long you endangered the horse by the time you came to Hoghek Village.

Your in-laws scolded you that the horse was ready to burst from strain but you didn't care; you were so sad that they went to pilgrimage without you.

Your family, my relatives, lived in four houses. I see their names now. I wonder which one of my ancestors came to me that night I screamed, until my father came. He had a beard and he seemed sad. I hope he is near me now as I write. I love the way the four houses shared the same roof. It reminds me of ancient times. It seems the Armenian girls did not have a voice. Their role was to remain virtuous, humble, religious, and helpful in the labor and care of the household. Love existed but was hidden by rules and traditions. One of my great cousins was beautiful and quietly loved an Armenian boy. Because the many stages of winning my great-cousin's hand was beyond this boy's reach, she was kidnapped while she walked home one day, never to be seen again. Love and marriage were light years away from each other.

Your family was still rebuilding their lives after the "Looting Massacre of 1895." Your grandfather was slaughtered along with many other relatives and children. I am so pained that it just went on and on until the last planned extermination.

Grandpa you were the happiest of us all. Every day you smiled and thanked God for the new day. I find myself doing the same. Each day I awake and say "Happy New Day;" I believe it is our turn to live and learn and grow. I never knew there were so many massacres that you all endured and yet you kept believing in God; some of my beloved great uncles became ordained priests. I freeze and remember how the Turks cut the heads off the priests and tied them to the ends of horsetails. I am so glad you are spared of hearing the senseless murders that we all hear about every day in America. All in the name of religion? I say, all in the name of greed and ignorance. How is it that nothing has really changed in the world? Instead it has worsened. Humans must have a gene that causes them to destroy and rebuild, to kill like the wild animals in the kingdom—but not to eat, instead to steal and dominate.

I see them today, Father Kerovpe married to your father's sister. Ordained, and as you remember he was handsome, kind and a true believer. I see your brothers that were devoured as you say by the Turks—Hovhannes, Haroutioun—and your sister Oghik. You never told me that my own uncles and my beloved Auntie Oghik were all named after your lost siblings. I felt the ghosts, I felt the heaviness, but I thought it was me; now I see the sweet names I have said since childhood but with the understanding that I was chanting the genocide long before this moment. Everytime I called out to my auntie Oghik I was calling out to your sister who saved your life. Uncle Hovhannes, Uncle Haroutioun: it was your secret and now I know. How is it that you were always happy, inspiring, loving, and strong and many loved ones I knew were not. They wouldn't say it but I saw shadows over them. How did you conquer so many misfortunes your whole life so that I never felt the bitterness? I was with you from my beginning. I never knew the capacity of the human spirit until now. I love that my great uncle Markos in 1912 became an ordained priest. That he was given a sacerdotal name, Khoren. I don't know why this new name is more important, but I also love that he was allowed to marry. Our church gives priests the choice to serve married or celibate.

You write of Uncle Markos' wife being so beautiful that people would stop and stare. They had four children and you weep because you cannot remember all their names. Sweet Grandfather your childhood remembering has brought to life a whole civilization that was hushed to us all while growing up. Nounoufar was their daughter's name, and I know that is my cousin's name! I know she was slaughtered like all the rest but you gave the name to my beloved cousin as restitution for the losses that never were counted by humanity.

I learnt about yet another uncle who was different than the priest and your father Tateos. Your father and the priest were goodhearted and loving to many people. This uncle was not. He was restless and bold, and did not believe in God. He disliked Lent, and would complain. He knew the Armenians were the first nation to adopt Christianity and he resented it. Our people were much more mighty and prideful before the conversion, he would mutter. Now, they were a God-fearing nation that tried to uphold the Lord's laws and ways of life. You were only ten when he made you sneak behind your beloved grandmother as she went to the storehouse. He knew meat was forbidden during Lent. You were never a good sneak. Your heart was too pure. When you followed her into the dark storehouse you pretended to be a cat as you moved slowly and noiselessly. You grabbed the "Khavourma" (buttered beef) and hid it in your breast pocket. Grandmother hushed you and when you came out of the dark cold room your father, feeling sorry for you, asked you to stand in front of the furnace to warm up. There you stood pretending to be a cat and the butter began flowing down your shirt. Father Tateos called out to you and called you Sonny while he asked what had happened and the cat thief was found out. Once again you cried and ran out while your Grandmother protected you.

Today Grandpa, before I traveled again to this page I spoke with a young girl by phone; I am a landlord now. I abhorred the idea of being a landlord. Even the word troubles me, the lord of the land people pay me to inhabit. This was my fate when my loved ones died. Now I understand why my parents were so proud to be landlords. To be a landlord was to be Armenian in this land called America so far away from their Motherland. This girl was working at a store, and I needed to order something in order to make it better for the tenants I never wanted to govern. She recognized the "-ian" at the end of my last name (we all do that). "Are you Armenian?" she asks. I say, "Yes."

To this day I say yes to that question but I am not Armenian. I am American. I was stunned in my travels abroad no one cared that I was Armenian. All they looked at was the blue passport and said your nationality is American. I still feel compelled to say I am Armenian. I did not choose to be American. My birth fell upon my parents as they too lost everything during WWII. It is surreal. They raised me to never feel American, yet to be proud of my country at the same time. So I guess I was borrowing the land so that I could be Armenian. Not anymore. This girl asks me if I am Western Armenian or Eastern Armenian. I proudly say Western Armenian. All my life people ask me "What are you?" just because I have black hair and a more "ethnic" face. I say I am Armenian. "From where?" they ask. When I say that I was born in America it never is enough. Armenians are the worst culprits. They will say, "Where did your parents come from?" I still carefully say which regions they were in before the Second World War. Then they always ask me the third question, "Do you speak Armenian?" I always answer, "Yes." Then they speak to me and I answer and it is always so funny. One will say "You are Russian-Armenian," another will say "You are Western Armenian;" it never matters that I was born in Detroit. That is unimportant now, what matters is the path to my arrival of these words. I am not a separate person, I am just a carrier of persons.

When I proudly said "I am Western Armenian" the phone went silent. I instantly knew she was Eastern Armenian. Because Easterners think they are smarter and more sophisticated then the Westerners. I am sorry Grandpa but the next time I am asked, "Where are you from?" I will proudly say "America." When an American asks me the question I go through another dance. They always say, "But where were you *originally* from?" I say, "My people come from Armenia." Now I will tell Americans that I originally came from Detroit, Michigan! I will say I am American-Armenian. Only because I still feel like two people; I still am two people. People call this bi-cultural. I call it conflicted for evermore. I feel like I left my religion, my people, since I married a non-Armenian. I don't speak my language much, yet I burn for my people, and I feel guilty that I don't speak my language every day. There I go again, I *am* speaking my language, English, every day. Even now it feels tricky inside. How did I get my doctorate?

As a child no one around me wrote English. They were ashamed that they could not read nor write. Yet my parents were heroes. English was their fourth language; they never got to go to school in this country, they worked seven days a week and sent my brother and me to Armenian school on Saturdays. All the children had to go to Armenian school. I really never learned a thing there. Except that no one would help me when this big Armenian girl would chase me through the yards. I was fast but she was big. She would bully me and some other girls. I remember her demanding I bring her things I had at home. I did it for my safety's sake. I brought her my treasured record and it was the right title but the wrong artist and she chased me everywhere that day. We were all too afraid to tell on her. One Saturday after her usual scaring us, she sat right in front of me in those school chairs made out of plastic. She got up and moved around the room, and when she tried to sit down again, I gently pulled the chair out from under her. I had never misbehaved in school before. I just did it without thinking. She fell to the floor and all the children laughed. The stern schoolmaster took me outside to hit my knuckles with a ruler. Each time he raised the ruler I pulled back my hands. I was great at patty cake, the fastest in elementary school, so he didn't have a chance. I was petrified but I couldn't stop pulling my hands back, and he finally gave up.

She died a few years later; she was murdered. I wept for her and was glad she had my record.

Grandpa this is all I know of Armenian School. Your school was so different and so much sterner, and I am sorry to say that your teachers were not stern—they were abusive. A word none of you ever understood. Children were at the mercy of having to be virtuous to grownup eyes. There was no room for the developing mind of children.

We always celebrated your birthday on January 10th. I did not know that you chose the day and month. You were born in 1901 on the day of the Holy Spirit. It was a holy day and that is why you were named Galoust. ("Let there be light," or "the light is coming.") You counted that you were born six years after the 1895 Looting Massacre. The forty days after Easter is the Ascension, then ten days later is the day of the Holy Spirit. This sacred day changes from year to year. So, you chose January 10th, 1901 as you birthday. You began going to Armenian School when you were seven. The first year, you all were taught the Armenian ABC's. Each young student had a wooden plaque that you carried to school and back home. You children did your best to learn the ABC's in the first four months of school. Because of the harvests, school was over in March of each year. One teacher would be chosen each winter for all you children. There was an Armenian landlord named Peto. His grandson Tikran was chosen to teach the year you began school. Your parents bought you a pair of red boots and you write that there was no limit to your happiness. The children surrounded you in awe and some with jealousy. It was hard for you to retain the lessons. You felt bad for that and were brutally punished. But I too felt it was hard to retain my Armenian lessons. It wasn't us, it was the teachers. You don't even blame that Armenian teacher in your diary. I am telling you he was cruel, and he lacked the education to properly teach. Later, I learned that our teachers were volunteers and not properly trained either. Mr. Tikran decided to punish you along with his only nephew using a brutal Turkish device called a *falakha-bastinado*. (My pen has begun to write Turkish with a lower case "t," let it be.) It hung on the wall and there was a loop of rope let through the holes. Those tiny feet of yours were held up for the bastinado: short rope spliced on a rope or yard for holding in its position. He laid you two little boys on the floor and hand tied the edges of the falakha and lifted it up. He used to bat the soles of your precious little feet using a stick. When you were both released you could not stand on your feet because of the pain. Yet, you had to come home and pretend all was well. If your parents should hear that you were put on the falakha you would be in more trouble because it would always be your fault.

I have to say dear Grandpa I don't know how this all works but I, too, never told my parents that the mean older girl was terrifying me every Saturday. I too learned to not speak. It saddens me that Armenians in your time under Turkish rule could be so unwittingly cruel just like their adversary.

Chapter Nine

THE WOMEN HAD SUCH conflicting roles. They quietly kept the order and rhythm of the day's tasks without any outward need for credit or control. My Great-Great-Grandmother was truly the leader of all these strong men. After my Great-Great-Grandfather was murdered by the looting Turks in 1895, she was told how he hid in the Armenian fountain's curve that was enough of an alcove to be missed during the slaughter. Close to midnight he lit a cigarette and some Turks saw the light from his match and captured him. He was so beloved by all his family and villagers and Great-Great-Grandpa Gevorg was brave. The Turks told him if he should pray to the Turks they would not kill him. He replied that he would not convert from his Christian faith for any person that if they needed to kill him to do so, and they did. This need the Turks had to convert was the excuse for all the bloodbaths. Yet, I live in the 21st Century and still I hear senseless murders, mass murders, genocides because one group is a different sect, a different faith, a different color. I am truly awestricken that our precious human race is still so primitive-minded when it comes to differences. The fear that it brings up the need to convert instead of learn shadows my spirit. The truth is quietly under the prayer rug. We are less if our faith is not the same. We are useless unless we convert. This is the truth. But what of our Christian faith? If someone entered a Christian church covered and outwardly a Muslim, would we welcome them by leaving them undisturbed or would our eyes wander over to them afraid?

When Great-Great-Grandmother Shoushanik was to quietly be the heart-beat of a male-dominated household she did it with quiet and firm grace. When I see how the young women lived in what seems like ancient times I realize I too took on these roles. But, I resented it, fought it, and climbed out of obscurity. Virtue was the reward for obedience and meekness. Father Tateos quietly asked her advice for all important decisions that impacted their lives. The young women would go to her every morning to ask what should be done today, what should be cooked today. When I was young and was taken to spend an occasion with my relatives I couldn't understand why we girls were sent to the kitchen to wash the dishes. I didn't even get to have a meal but there we were, cleaning mountains of dishes because that was our role. I wanted to have the virtue but I liked to climb trees and pretend each branch was part of my home. If a child was clever enough to climb the tree I would invite them to visit my "living room" branch. I didn't know it, but I was still being a little Armenian girl—except on my terms. I would walk to your apartment Grandpa and climb those stairs that seemed so high and run in and hug you. Just yesterday I climbed those same stairs and they seemed so small and inside were a lovely couple that rent your apartment that I was left to care for. I fought for my education. No one had to inspire me. My father recoiled at my chosen profession, but school always felt like my lifeline. No matter what degree I got it wasn't enough. I felt there was still so much more to learn. This can't be the end. I felt so smart when I was an undergraduate student. Now that I have finished three degrees I feel like I will never have enough time to learn just a small amount of all the magnificence of this life that was cast from stardust. No one got it Grandpa. When I finished my doctorate we were going to be roommates, remember? You would say, "When are you going to finish?" I am so sorry, my precious, that I didn't finish in time. It was not our *Gagad a Ger.* Even now as I write these words, I awakened early in the dawn because yesterday I had to have the virtue of tending to the apartments you loved. I walked everywhere. I sat in your old apartment with workmen saying to myself this is what it is like to be a landlord, all my ancestors were proud to be landlords, they were called Elderman, they were given respect. Even in America they use this word and my parents worked their whole life being a landlord of something. I will relinquish this virtue of maintaining your homeland in these apartments soon. Monopoly games in America are in some ways a continuation of the landlord promise and success that it will bring. But, I want to write our story and I keep being pulled away to do the very thing I am not, and I find this ironic that my American Sharon is asking me, "What are you doing?" The Armenian Shoghagat Sharon is saying "Job well done, much virtue was earned today."

My education was an aberration to you all. It was a place you came to at graduation and then wondered why I wasn't married with many children.

No one ever asked me one thing about my education. Why I chose the fields of Child Development and Marriage & Family—no one really cared. It was a mute topic and it at the same time it was all I lived for. I volunteered thousands of hours, read almost 24 hours a day, I was so thirsty to shed the inner conflict of being so whole as an Armenian, and being so whole as an American.

The only person who talked of my education was my father. His thoughts were: "I didn't come to America for you to be a witchdoctor." I remember I had spent three hours on the radio by myself taking questions. All the questions were about rearing children, family, and how to teach children faith in something greater without overwhelming them. Tired and joyfully exhausted I returned to the clinic you, my beloved Dad, helped the most to create. I saw you and said "Hello." I never knew until my mother told me that you listened for three hours! Yet, you never said a word. I felt so bad inside because I knew your silence was your disapproval of my spending some nights away from home with my future husband. I was in my 30's! Now I know how lucky I am. It is a greater act of love to help give your child the support they need to succeed when you don't believe in them than when you do.

When I was with family I never understood how the women fussed and fed the men first. To this day if someone asks me to sit at the head of a table I can't. I can't seem to shake the Armenian me. It is an American house, they don't know it, but I feel I am sitting in the man's seat. If someone puts food on my plate before the men at the table I thank them while I cringe inside. I force myself to take it. With all the strong women that were scholars that took me under their wing and taught me to know better I still can't give up the cringe because that is being an Armenian woman; it is tradition.

The Armenian women in your life Grandpa, how did they do it? No electricity, no washing machines, no refrigerators, and they kept home life moving like clockwork.

My father was one of the proudest Americans I ever knew. He felt free, just like you Grandpa. He often told me that I would never know how lucky I was. Freedom is such a subjective word. But when you don't have it, it is all you can think about. The strange thing Grandpa is I never for one moment felt freedom. I was always striving, and climbing uphill to be free. How can a person born into freedom as daily oxygen, think of freedom her whole life, and pray that school can show her the way? This is the struggle

I had until now. You all kept running for your freedom. I had to learn how to free myself. My greatest enemy was my love for all of you. What was unspoken was: never leave us, do as we tell you or you will be less in our eyes. Each Armenian event I chose not to attend I was made to feel like I betrayed my true faith. Even if I was exhausted from exams, if I didn't go to a particular event I was not a good daughter or good Armenian. School I later learned was the only thing that gave me breath away from all of you without the heavy axe. It was neutral because it was foreign to you all. So, my steam to learn was really my running for freedom in those libraries I lived in. You all had an alibi for yourselves and your friends. None of you went go to college, yet I felt the smallest and least informed in the room. I could never win an argument; no one ever cared to hear one bit of advice or thoughts I may have on any given subject. I was a girl, and I was talking from an American voice. It was all silly to you. Many of the things I lovingly warned against came to pass. You never listened. What is most amazing to me is that I spent my whole life helping others who came to me for guidance and insight. For my most adored family not one word was ever heard. Freedom of speech is the cornerstone of America which I kiss the earth to live in. But it does not mean anyone is listening.

Chapter Ten

I LIT A CANDLE yesterday. A real long candle like in church. I found myself worried about starting a fire. So I put it on an equally long candlestick holder. Then I put a plate under it and I made sure I checked on it throughout the day. Once the candle burned low to the rim of the candlestick holder I quickly blew it out. The whole room smelled even though it was odorless.

I had responsibly worried and watched over my candle vigil for my dearest of friends during his surgery that took seven hours yesterday. I had no peace of mind about my vigil until I blew out the candle and opened the windows to clear the room. Loss, impending loss, hope, denial, prayer for strength: these are things we take for granted when we live in freedom. I trained in these areas; I helped countless people deal with loss, and work through the loss, and claim their self and life again. I have had time to absorb the magnitude of my friend whom I love and feel is one of life's treasures on earth. He is a man that has always lived with integrity, self-made, there for all his friends and his family. If we had a template of his heart there would be world peace. He is dying and he is young. I had a need for a real candle, yet every candle warns us of the dangers of using one. To guard it, not to leave the candle unattended. Such interesting words of caution. We in freedom have the luxury of so many choices and ways to deal with our personal desires of honoring our loved ones.

I continue to realize the magnitude of what you endured Grandpa, and how I didn't even know you were a survivor of the genocide until I was an adult. I was a child when the first monument of the genocide was going to be built near our church in Montebello, California. I didn't understand what was happening. I vaguely remember all the priests, a few officials standing near a mass of dirt with a shovel. I have always said that the Archbishop Surpazan whom I loved since a child handed me the shovel to turn the soil. Girls were never chosen. I remember this and yet there is a part of me that questions, is it true? Is this a false memory? But, I remember it even now so there must be a need to have had it happen, so I will say it did. I remember being forced to join the Armenian youth federation; it was tradition. I sat there confused as a child. The only thing I saw was all the leaders arguing. I would wonder, "Why am I here? Nothing ever happens and nothing ever changes." Then I would go home and return the following week. I went because that is what a good Armenian child does. My parents wanted us to know our heritage. My parents wanted us to be one thing: Armenian. I never even questioned the fact that I thought differently because I was actually American. When I thought differently I was told I was not behaving as a good person; I was mistaken, what I wanted to do was wrong. Of course I knew they were right.

"They" is a word I heard more than the word "Love." I lived for "They;" I fought against "They" every day of my life. My parents lived in fear of "What would *they* say?" The shame was choking me before any action was found. My parents lived in the village where their people were judging, gossiping and competing even though they lived in the land of the free. They brought with them the heavy yoke of the oxen and placed one on me and one on my younger brother. My brother had it worse than me; he made the mistake of being born gay. I am feeling this moment like I am breaking a vow of my family name. I am not to tell, I am not to print this word "gay." It is a bringing wrath to our family as I write. But the friend I was grieving for, who later died soon after surgery, was one of my brother's dearest friends. I loved him too, I loved my brother the most. I could not protect him, I could not save him from himself. I was struggling with two selves; he was struggling with four. To the outer world he looked straight, inside he was twisted in agony. I was powerless to help him. His splitting off was made of mountainous steel. No amount of telling him to be free helped. When a son is Armenian he must be the apple of his parents' eyes. If their eyes are dimmed by silence the son is doomed. He died and I had to fight the interference and put the pictures of his friends around his casket. He never had a chance even though he was born in the land of the free. His fault was, he loved too much. My poor parents were not equipped to help him. But they loved him and stood by him his whole life just as long as he didn't talk about it. Even when Armenians asked me what he died of I was to say it was cancer and not AIDS. If these words ever see the light of day I know I will be admonished by "They." But, I think how many other boys are born gay? What will happen to them? Shouldn't they have a better life? Instead of hiding their true selves which will destroy their tomorrow? The day came where I finally had enough and so I said and say: "AIDS killed my precious brother who never had a moment's peace his whole life." He tried to be Armenian and he was good. He dated them when he was younger, was the best Armenian dancer on planet earth, and felt alone until the day he died.

As for me, no matter what I did—dance, girl scouts, plays, gymnastics—I had to do it with the yoke around my neck. As I write I check to see if it is on me I close my eyes and feel a small chain with burn marks from all the pain that was caused growing up.

"Burn marks" is what I read in your diary and it reminded me of my brother's, and mine. I know how we are still so much luckier than you were your whole life. When we want strength we light a candle, talk to a friend. Get guidance from a plethora of sources. You watched a calculated slaughter of all your loved ones. I would need boxes and boxes of candles to begin to grasp what you experienced as a youth. I accept I can never understand your pain. I accept that when the first Kurdish man snatched you from your mother you never had a moment to grasp loss because you were buried alive in it all.

I read in your diary about the conditions in Western Armenia that was under Turkish rule. You write Western Armenia but what you mean is Armenia under Turkish oppression. "Mount Ararat," which is an Armenian word, is in Turkey! If it weren't in the Bible I am sure the Turks would have changed the name just like they changed all our churches into mosques. I remember as a child my father would point to a beauty mark at the base of my shoulder that also had a smaller one right beside it. He always said it was Mount Ararat and little Ararat. I was so proud that I had this map on me. To this day I check to see if it is still there; they are barely visible so I know it is true. When I would see Mount Ararat in the Bible I would burst with joy. God knew us, we were part of a plan and we were there! When I went to our homeland I have one foot in Armenia as home and one foot in America. I saw Mount Ararat and little Ararat behind borders by the Turks. I couldn't go to my ancestor's land because I was not in Turkey. If I had to go to Turkey to visit our stolen land I choose not to. I will take comfort in knowing the truth. I will take comfort that the ghosts are still here with us who know. I will take comfort that thanks to the Holy Bible the Armenian name for the sacred mountain could not be changed.

Western Armenia in 1900 was so void of modern conveniences. There was no heating, no electricity, no bread bakeries, no washing machines, nothing that would help ease the hard work just to have the basics in your lives Grandpa. I still have a battery lit candle on near my friend's picture as I read what you all did to have light. You had to use gas lanterns and you didn't know they were really Chinese lanterns. You filled them in with petrol and lit it with a match. They hung in the middle of the room or on the walls of the sitting rooms on a chain. Sometimes if you were lucky you found a tin lantern. If you were fortunate you could buy gasoline; you would fill them and put them high on a shelf. Then you would light the lamp. It illuminated the whole house. It made a lot of smoke and smells but you all accepted that was all you had. Some families were blessed to have an oil lantern. It was flat and was lit with a cotton wick that was inserted in its center where the oil was added. When it was time for it to be lit you had to check the wick every 10 to 15 minutes and move the wick forward with a stick so that the light would continue. The stick would remain right in the center crevice. This luxury item only worked inside the house. It could not be used in the cattle stable because it was not covered and the fire might cause the stable to burn down. Just like my worrying to burn our house down. Yet, worlds apart. I never knew these things Grandpa; I wonder what you felt every time you turned on the lights in your apartment.

I found a spot in your diary that tells me about the power of the elderly. Like Native Americans the elderly were seen as wise and they were the ones who could talk about others and judge one another's behaviors. They sat in a sitting room. Men were allowed to sit with the women as long as they followed the strict rules of the elderly. The wise ones were always over 75; the rest of the younger generation kept quiet and did their chores and contributions to the household. I realize this moment why I am learning this now. I was too young to be included in the important talk that you all did around the table in my own home where I grew up. I knew to ask if you wanted anything but I also knew to glide by as if I hadn't heard a word. How does one learn and grow if we don't know more than a word or two?

"Armenian" and "genocide" were the two most powerful words that branded my insides If I hadn't been curious and searched my whole life I would never have relished the words my father said very randomly on the phone one day. As always in the past he would say one profound sentence with no explanation, with no warning and it would take years for me to understand. I knew I couldn't ask any questions I just snatched the words and tucked them under my mind mat. Later when all was quiet I would pull out the words from under my mat and read them like a fortune cookie. The last profound sentence he said was "Sharon you made it even though it was impossible." I froze on the phone; I knew he passed me a compliment. The truth of his own certainty that he thought I would never get out from the sorrow they lived in, the shroud of "what will they say?" along with his own disappointment that I became a mental health professional and then dedicated my whole life to my work. It was seen as the biggest waste of time. For me it was the breath of life helping precious children and overwhelmed parents. By uttering these words he was affirming what I felt my whole life which was one word "failure." Because I strove for what they didn't understand I was odd. I was a disappointment. They never said it out loud and that is why I heard it constantly. Marry an Armenian, join us, have children, don't leave us. I never did leave you all; I just knew there was more than tradition to quench my thirst. You all lived next to each other. Your separate dwellings were your only distance. I have to be honest that my family and the relatives migrated closer to each other and then very near as each family rose in America. I have to say that sometimes I can't shake the Armenian eyes I have. I try so hard to look out my American lens but I too am conflicted and sometimes feel the hypocrite. Only inside I say how can a relative move so far away from his people. I stop and shudder; that is my Armenian mind. I moved an hour from my mother and felt I abandoned her. I felt I left our church too far behind which was near her. But at least I did it. When the guilt starts I quiet it with my American eyes. I tell myself I am closer to work, or the ocean is good for my health. It has nothing to do with wanting to be further away. But it does...

I wish the two sets of eyes didn't make me feel like a hypocrite. But, the apex of the space in between two different lifestyles, two different truths, can sometimes snub the other. Even the battle inside shows me why there was strife. I live in these two worlds. People who are blessed and don't say things like, "You are so lucky to have another language, another culture; it must be so wonderful." That is how I know they are of one mind one soul. Americans like to say bi-cultural. That is nice, but what if the cultures clash? What if the hierarchy of success is measured by a completely different yardstick? My American eyes are writing right now. My Armenian eyes are saying: "Be careful, keep quiet. Watch what you say. What will *they* say?" My only solace is my ancestors who are not visiting me in dreams right now and they are not pressing on my fingers as I write. I will trust them more than the voices around me. Grandpa I had no idea that Turks visited your sitting rooms. That they were allowed to come in and eat and talk. This angers me even more. If they came to my Great-Grandfather's home and broke bread while my relatives cooked and gave freely. How could they have been so ruthless as they later raped and slaughtered all my Grandfather's loved ones? They are *my* loved ones too. When the Turks visited the only difference was that the girls did not come in the sitting room when the men came to visit and be fed. The men in Grandpa's family brought the water to wash their hands and then brought them food and drink. The only nice thing for the Armenian women of the house was that on these occasions the men of my Grandpa's home folded the bedding and did all the cleaning afterwards. I wonder why? But I am happy for my relatives that got to rest on this day. I learned that even military officers visited my Grandpa's home. That his father Tateos was important enough that they came to his home often. On these occasions the military officers brought their own servants who would wash and clean and serve their superiors.

Summer would start the fieldwork. It was exhausting work and Grandpa watched his "poor mother" wake before the dawn and do countless tasks alone. I am entering in the field with you Great-Grandmother. I want to learn as I watch. I try not to enter the written word because I have rushes of truth racing through my body of just how lucky we all are in modern times. We wake and complain because we are out of milk. Your virtue envelopes my heart and I am there. It is quiet and everyone is sleeping as you slowly slip your gown into the flowered cardboard box that holds your clothes. The smell of apples fill the air and you worry not to awaken anyone. You reach into the box knowing by the feel of the fabric which garment to wear. This time *I* am the ghost; I cause no discomfort but quietly wait for you to begin your day outside. The pail you are carrying is for the cows and you are filling the pail with milk. I didn't know you could mix sheep's and cow's milk but you do, and now the pail is so full and heavy. I watch you quietly bring in the milk and start to churn it. It looks hard to do. You haven't a recipe book but you know when it is ready to warm the milk. I watch you take some of the curdled milk and make *madzoun* (yogurt). You would never believe how in America everyone loves yogurt. The most popular is by a Turkish man and his company has grown to such success. I remember when I would drive you Grandpa and you would proudly tell me that only my mother was your arms. You would show me your arms and thank God for her. I read in your diaries that your mother worked too hard. So did my mother.

Your Grandmother walks into the rooms where loved ones are sleeping and calls out, "My children wake up! Hurry, the day has begun." Everyone awoke and ate breakfast which consisted of lavash, milk, yogurt and fruit.

When I see lavash in the market, I smile. It is considered to be a more sophisticated choice for the table but it is thousands of years old. I am back writing with noise outside and cars speeding by recklessly not caring about the speed limit. It was nicer to hear silence and walk in the fields with you Great-Grandmother but as a ghost I could not help you.

Summer was so important for reaping all the hard work that was done in the spring. The men would work in the fields as early as 4 a.m. and sleeping at 10 p.m. then up again for hard work. All this in between the slaughters. Once the dead were buried there was no time for grief. No such thing as Post-Traumatic Stress Disorder. But having written about this very state of mind for my dissertation research I know the routines you all did must have been the balm for the terror of never knowing the next time. The routines of family, church and work kept the pain and loss away. The holy days of honoring the dead helped dose the time of anguish and remembering. *This time it will be different.* I see the hard work, the back-breaking integrity; you all had the faith that this time it will be different. If you just keep going to church, and tolerating the intrusions of the Turkish villagers, all would be well for your children.

I still have visions of running in the fields and warning everyone. Telling them to flee now. But, I know you would all scorn me for being such a silly girl—how would I expect you to leave your homes, all four of them, your land, your church, your school, because of a feeling? No one ever leaves over a feeling, do they?

While Great-Great-Grandmother is managing the workman and the children your mother takes a nap. Soon her mother shouts, "Horop, get up! It's time. Give the breakfast to the workers so they can go." Your mother feeds them a full breakfast with butter, cream, bread, and yogurt. The workmen sit on their carts and eat and then go back to work. You were hardly a child of ten but your parents woke you up and put you on the cart to look after the yoked cattle. You too ate your meals on the cart

44

in the fields. Your dear mother then had to churn butter which was even more strenuous, and then she took care of the elderly and the children at home. She dressed them, washed their faces, and fed them by her own hands. There were no clever ways to move the elderly. If you loved your loved one you took care of them yourself. You would not permit strangers to care for your loved ones.

I shudder but I give you honor Great-Grandmother. I use to go as a youth of twelve to volunteer in the centers of the elderly. I don't know why but I wanted to and I loved helping them. They would be so happy if I read to them. I would take the bus because my parents were working at their market. I wore a very American smock-like dress and was called a candy-striper. There were long white and red stripes and I figured that we looked like candy canes so that is how we got our name. I became the Vice President of the candy stripers only because I turned down President. I had to study so I took a role that I felt I could manage. The nurses treated me so well. I felt like they cared about me because I quietly knew there was no such thing as a President of the candy-stripers; I think they wanted me to know how much they appreciated all that I did. I hand-fed the elderly and listened to their stories. But, they felt a little foreign and forbidden to me. They were all American. They all spoke English and I was only allowed to speak Armenian at home. I felt I was in another world talking with the nurses and they were teaching me so much. Then it happened one day my mother surprised me by coming to the rest home to pick me up. I heard the nurses tell me, "Your mother is here." My mother gasped when she learned I was helping a nurse with a bedpan and that ended my candy-striper days. Things like that always happened. I would discover something and would grow as I learned, then it was gone. I understand now why you did it, Mother. You had to take care of seven siblings when your mother died and you couldn't understand how your daughter sought out such a vocation on purpose. I think that experience led to my future no matter what you all did to help me choose an easier life and vocation.

Grandpa your mother would never stop just like my mother. My mother would say that she could not stop and rest and she really couldn't until she wore out her own heart.

Great-Grandmother Horop had worked harder in the first waking hours of her day then we do in our whole life. After she took care of all the loved ones she would light the *tounir* and begin to cook meals for lunch. She baked bread, and then would send lunch out to the workmen. Every day she baked new bread. I walk down the aisles in the market and there are rows of breads. Each claiming good health or breads so unhealthy that flashy names are all that is needed. You called your life "cozy" Grandpa. You said that you all lived without electricity and gas, yet you were so happy and felt so blessed sharing a meal at the family table surrounded by loved ones. (Later you found modern life had so many overwhelming choices but not the closeness and satisfaction of a good meal and complete contentment.)

Cozy is a beautiful word. You use this word several times; there is an Armenian word for this feeling. You said that you felt the same coziness as we do when we turn on our lights and have all the extras we think is so necessary for happiness. You make me understand that coziness is what you are not what you have. You called it a "convenient life."

I learn more about the daily life in Western Armenia and realize fuel is important in all cultures. Whatever the source it is vital for productivity of the group as a whole. Winter was another key time for you all. The cattle stable was cleaned, and the manure was mixed with straw then filled into baskets as a heating source. It was poured into a pressed space, piled up in a big lot and in bulk where the winter snow covered it all. It burned well in the spring which began in March. That manure was crushed and dumped. In May, it was cut with a shovel in shapes and molds laid side by side. In the summer it dried. It was then collected and piled in the hut to burn for heating, cooking, bread baking, and to burn the *tounir* for cooking. I cannot imagine the full four seasons to create a fuel source that actually worked, Grandpa. You never spoke of these brilliant survivor skills of your family. (Growing up I would ask an American friend if they would like some lavash and they would politely say no thanks!) Your mother would use this fuel to light the *tounir*: a cross-shaped iron was laid on the *tounir* and four pans were placed on it for cooking a meal, and for boiling water and milk. The food was moved when the *tounir* got well heated and reddened. Then both sides of the *tounir* were cleaned with a wet cloth. It was cleaned very well to prevent scorching the bread. Many times it took two women to do the next step which was to stick the lavash bread on the sides of the *tounir* with a fire-shovel, then take the thin flaky bread out just in time, and lay the sheets of bread down on cover sheets. Grandpa you say that the bread was slapped into your hands and you rolled cheese in the hot lavash and ate it. You say if you weren't there that your feet would be tied. That you would be "cuffed" if you were not there when it was finished. Where did you learn such visual words? How can such an act of love end with such a punitive line?

When I was young I had to iron clothes for my mother. I stood at the ironing board and I ironed. It bored me to pieces. I wished I had magic and I would make them all jump on hangers and march to the closets to where they came from. I remember a mountain of clothes. I know now it was a hill. My mother gave herself pride by my contribution. If she worked seven days a week, the least I could do was iron. Unfortunately, I seldom ironed in a satisfactory way. But, I did the best that I could. I remember my mother telling me how lucky I was that we had washing machines; they never did. In Grandpa's village there were big boilers made of copper and wooden washtubs. There was washing that was done for small families then for large ones. Laundry and bathing was done on Saturdays. Saturday mornings the young girls and the women knew what was ahead of them and got up very early. They placed the big washtubs on the *tounir*, heated the water and poured it into the big washtubs. Two women washed the laundry in a small washtub. Upon finishing the washing, the person in charge took the laundry to the yard to hang them on the ropes in the sun for two to three hours to dry. After finishing that huge laundry they would begin to prepare for the bathing. First the children are bathed; and then the elderlies, who blessed the son and daughters in-law, and grandchildren by saying, "Beloved children, let God be with you. If He held a stone in your hand, let it convert to gold." These were the kind of parables they would say to inspire the children. I remembered a saying my own mother said all my life and there I see it in your diary Grandpa. Your daughter would tell me that when your heart is pure and honest it is like a piece of gold and even if it is thrown into the mud it will always wash back to its true state. So, that is where her version came from. After the elderly were washed then it was the turn of the men. They too would bathe. Then it was father Tateos' turn. By now it would be dark. That is when the girls and women of your family would bathe then go rest and sleep at last.

I learn there was a tradition called the "Carnival." Words I have taken for granted like yogurt which is Turkish, or carnival derived from Medieval Latin, have always been English words to me. I am discovering so many customs I had never heard of. This carnival was an event for two weeks prior to Lent which lasted for seven weeks. Neighbors came door to door and together everyone cooked many foods some I have never heard of.

Pilaf, Kahshil, Herisa, Kash, Baklava, and Katayis all cooked in pans with butter, halva, and eggs. For two weeks you all awoke and did your duties and in the early evening you all feasted at your own carnival. I was surprised to learn that this word actually refers to a period of public revelry usually a week before Lent. The boys played the Leather Game. With my child developmental background I try to envision this medieval game that sounds so strange to me. Six youths at least 18 years old played. They were split into two groups of three. There was a leather shield and a sabre made of rush mat. Numbers were pulled and depending on what number you got you had to lay under the leather shield. The boys then cuffed the shield until someone ran out. If the guard caught them they were out. The boys would play this game until they were tired. These were the ancient ways and the only toys the kids had. Most of the play used a child's imagination or they sat around and listened to stories by the wise elderly men then before sleeping they sang songs.

I learned that our ancestry had many priests. Presently great uncle Markos was a loyal priest of your village. Monday morning it would begin, the washing with hot water, ash, and soap water. Everyone in the family made seven puppets out of plums that were put on soft willow branches. These puppets were stuck with a large onion and hung from the roof of the house. Every Sunday one plum was taken down until they reached the last one. This meant it was Easter. Then your family would cook the special food for Lent. They first cooked *makhogh* made of flour and prepared like soup. Kidney beans were cooked. Bakers cooked with linseed oil and various meals were cooked with vegetable oils. For the seven weeks or 48 days you were not allowed to eat butter, oil, milk, eggs or cheese. So faithful were you all. So dear to the ancient customs that fortified your convictions, and sense of safety. If the customs prevailed then the families felt close to God and their prayers were heard.

Finding love was a secret. The Armenian custom was that boys became young men and had adult responsibility beginning at age 18 through age 25. Girls became young adults by age 16 through age 20. Village boys hoped to see young Armenian girls at weddings, holiday, Easter or Ascension as they went to the pilgrimage. There were beautiful Armenian events where the young could dance while the elderly supervised nearby. The youth exchanged feelings by glances and words that had double meanings. The youth also had friends that they trusted secretly to help plan a meeting between two young Armenians. Very Shakespearian, the poetry, the glances, the forbidden meetings. During these precious moments when two young people met they made promises, they fell in love without their parents' consent. In the Armenian culture the parents of the son as well as the daughter had to agree or no marriage vows were allowed. This is why from time to time there were kidnappings. Romeo would take his Juliet. In some ways because it was beyond the control of the families it worked despite what the two young people did for love. Marriage was for honor and virtue of two families not for love. I grew up being told in jest that my parents promised me to a boy's family when I was a baby because the two families liked each other so much. They wanted to be relatives. All my life I cringed horribly when I saw this boy growing up. Even though nothing was said out loud something was said in silence. It was mockery because I wasn't interested in the least and it was done as a halfhearted gesture. But the truth is it wasn't. How silly to promise humans that haven't even discovered their own hearts on the premise of security in the future. In your days Grandpa you write that the parents or the whole family would decide it was time for the boy or girl to marry. In the evenings the parents would make statements about the person of interest. But, they would phrase it in a way that would protect their honor. They would say things like, "Mister Kirakos, it's time for your son to get married, what do you think?" The response would vary but usually they would respond by saying: "We too think he should marry, blessings to you, where can we find a good Armenian girl?" Then it would begin. Why search when your neighbor has a lovely daughter and she is pretty and good? She has good parents so you would make good in-laws. So people would spread the word without going directly to the family in waiting. Once the father of the son decides which family to approach he sets a table and invites his neighbors to dine and drink and have good conversations. Then those families go the home of the girl who is wanted for marriage and meet with the parents. They know what to do and say even though no direct conversation was ever said. The parents of the girl in question also give a feast which means they are not interested in the family the mediators offered. So word is taken back that the family of interest is searching themselves, and no match is made. There were many times that young Armenians were in love and their families would not allow the marriage. They would be forced to marry the person their family chose, have children and live unhappily for the rest of their lives. Some would not listen and run away from home.

The runaways would have each other, but to not have family was to be an outcast. In time bitterness followed them their whole lives.

There were many marriages that were positive and were wanted by both families as well as the bride and groom-to-be. The betrothal ceremony was the responsibility of the bride's family. The bride's father would take care of all the many expenses. After the betrothal party the groom is not allowed to visit his fiancée's house nor see his future bride. There were times that the relatives of the bride-to-be would secretly let the husband have meetings with his future wife. It was forbidden but it did occur. Only the women would secretly set up the meetings. Many times the boy and girl were not allowed to see each other for up to a year while the arrangements of the wedding were being made.

It was the groom's father and mother's responsibility to arrange the exact day of the wedding. Then an appointed time for the in-laws to meet would be arranged. "The groom's parents now visit the bride's parents with gifts and say that if God permits, next month or in 20 to 30 days we shall have the wedding. The groom's side begins to do the announcements. On the agreed upon Saturday morning the guests to the wedding come to the groom's father's house. Four to six groomsmen bring the groom to the godfather who ties a red tie around the groom's neck. The guests to the wedding sing and cry out, 'Here is the king! He is the King! The king is the Lord's Lamb!' The groom with the red tie around his neck stands to accept the congratulations along with the gifts from loved ones." Money was usually what was given. Grandparents, godfather, godmother and all the guests followed the same procession of well wishing. The groomsmen then escorted the groom to the godfather's house, and they stayed there until the following Wednesday. In America it would be the best man and maid of honor but in Armenia it would be the future Godparents of the couple's children. Godparents had a lifelong role in the lives of the soon-to-be newlyweds. The godfather takes care of all his guests for five days of feasting. If the bride is from the groom's village, they also begin the wedding party on Saturday until Wednesday evening. They stay at the sponsor's home which is usually someone in the wedding party.

"In our village the nuptial blessing took place on Monday at 9 or 10 o'clock in the morning. First they go to the church. The groom in front and the bride follows surrounded by the groomsmen and bridesmaids. The groom and the bride are in the middle of the procession. A young boy and a girl hold a towel so that nobody can pass between the bride and groom. Those walking around the couple played music and danced. When they come up to the church the band stops playing. All along the musicians came to the houses and followed the procession of people to the church playing beautiful music. Once the wedding party arrives at the church the band stops playing the music and the nuptial ceremony begins. People silently listen to the priest. At the end the priest sanctifies the marriage. While coming out of the church the band again begins to play. The guests of the wedding proceed to dance and sing while walking to the groom's father's house. This is when the groom's father begins his contribution to the wedding celebration. Depending on his means he will have a sheep or young calf, or a rooster, killed as an offering and it is laid at the feet of the couple. First the parents give jewelry and place it around the bride's neck. Then the guests begin to give gifts to the couple they give what they can many times a ring, food, cloth, and lamb or sheep. A trusted person collects the gifts and gives thanks. Until late on Wednesday people celebrate then begin to thank their host. The bride's brother or bride's sister are given a gift and they are sent off. The bride is escorted to her bedroom around 10 or 11 o'clock in the evening. The godmother escorts the groom to the bride's room with a basket full of fruits and pastries; she opens the door to their honeymoon and she lets the groom in. She hands over the basket and leaves and does not go in again. 'Al Shaftali, ver shaftali.' ['Take a peach, give a peach,' an idiom expressing mutual happiness, felicity. Turkish words that were said in Grandpa's village.] They stay in until Sunday. On Sunday close relatives escort the bride in the living room of the house and they feast again and this is when the wedding officially ends."

For a short while there was no priest for your village. Visiting priests would come to your village but my great-great uncle ordained with the holy name of Khoren was one of two priests being considered. Because he had a weak heart the villagers were against him. Father Khoren who was your father's brother didn't even want the position but he left his village Yerzenka and came. He had gone to Kouchouk Chamkay city for treatments for his heart and obeyed the wish of his brother. Finally, the bishop for the Armenians chose your uncle to be the village priest and after he gave his first Holy Mass your family gave a reception that lasted for 40 days.

It was summer and pilgrims from neighboring villages attended this feast that was held in the open air and all was well for the last summer of your lives.

Chapter Eleven

IN THE AUTUMN OF 1914 you were nearly 13 years old. The Turks found refuge under the death cloak of the First World War to plan their final extermination of the Armenian people. The countless massacres over the decades and centuries never really erased the Christian Armenians. No matter what slaughter occurred they would bury their dead, honor their dead every year with a special feast and ceremony and continue to believe in God's mercy and Christ's teachings.

In some areas a five-day proclamation went up that the Armenians in that area were being deported. In some areas the slaughter began randomly: there was no systematic plan but a systematic slaughter. Free rein, and if you were Turkish you could do *anything* you wanted without reproach. It was sheer madness. The Ottoman Empire was nearly at its end. The slaughters started everywhere. The front pages of American newspapers began to print of the mass slaughters. The *New York Times* Saturday November 27, 1915 had headlines that stated: "Armenians' Heroic Stand in Mountains;" "Men, Women, and Children fought with knives, Scythes, and stones, ALL FINALLY EXTERMINATED. Women who had plunged knives into Turks afterward killed themselves. Lord Bryce gets report." December 15, 1915, the *New York Times* again: "Million Armenians Killed or in Exile;" "American Committee on Relief Says Victims of Turks Are Steadily increasing. POLICY OF EXTERMINATION. More atrocities detailed in Support of Charge that Turkey is Acting Deliberately."

I never understood how the Turkish Government still, in the 21st century, says "prove it" and "it didn't happen." I think they would be brilliant if they acknowledged the thousands of documents worldwide and use it if only as a ploy to win more tourists. I never understood you, Turkey. Yes, you were demonic in your slaughters. Mohammed would have cried a river of tears if he had seen your barbaric treatment of your neighbors. But do not fear losing all that you took. We are dying off one by one;

enough time has passed so that you will be honored as good neighbors for taking responsibility for your past and even present behaviors. You will never win. There is blood that courses through your own people of the truth. Why is it that from the time I was young if I met a Turkish person the first thing they said was, "I'm sorry for what my people did?" How wonderful humans can be. You hold on tight to your shame and the whole world will continue to see you as weak. Do not fear losing visitors to Istanbul because the cruise ships will still come in multitudes as long as earth is here. I am in awe that even now you deny a simple truth. You must truly feel disgrace for each sentence and candle that continues to be lit for those you devoured with such diabolical forms of murder. In the end you only killed yourselves.

I heard 300 hundred survivors speak, my dear Turkish neighbors: they all had the same horrific nightmare with the same outcomes of being broken beyond repair. But perhaps you didn't finish the job. We're still here. You are tolerated because of where your land is. Perhaps if it were given back to those you pillaged it from we would gladly give it to America to protect this great nation. But instead America pays you a fortune each year to be America's friend.

On January 26, 1916 as the mass murders continued Lord Bryce, the former British Ambassador to the United States, appeared in the American Headlines: "BRYCE ASKS AMERICA TO SUCCOR ARMENIANS." The article went on to say: "Refugees will starve on Syrian Plains if not Quickly Fed—Inform Washington." Lord Bryce wrote a report on the Turkish Atrocities (his word) in Armenia. The slaughters went on for several years. It didn't matter what was written, it never stopped. The *New York Times* printed on October 22, 1915: "ONLY 200,000 ARMENIANS NOW LEFT IN TURKEY-MORE THAN 1,000,000 KILLED, ENSLAVED OR EXILED, SAY A TIFLIS PAPER."

The newspapers around the world continued to report on the Armenian "extermination," as it was known—not "genocide." Genocide is what you say *after* the deed. October 26, 1915: "SLAY ALL ARMENIANS IN CITY OF KERASUNT—Turks Wipe Out Entire Population in Town on the Black Sea." The newspaper began like this... "LONDON, TUESDAY OCT 28—A DISPATCH TO THE DAILY MAIL FROM ODESSA SAYS: 'THE TURKS HAVE MASSACRED THE ENTIRE ARMENIAN POPULATION OF KERASUNT.'"

November 1, 1915: "AID FOR ARMENIANS BLOCKED BY TURKEY." The article put the number of victims at 1,000,000. December 12, 1915: "WOMAN DESCRIBES ARMENIAN KILLINGS—German Missionary Says Turks Proclaimed Extermination as Their Aim—FIENDS' WORK IN HARPUT—'Let your Christ Help You!' the Cry as Torture Went on. Dr. Knapp a Victim."

As I type these headlines that I used for my thesis back in 1985 I am scared. What if you read this my Turkish neighbor and you want to kill me just because I want to honor my loved ones? When I wrote my thesis and discovered all these American headlines, English headlines, I was shocked that America has to keep their mouths shut so that you Turkey won't change your mind in choosing us to pay you for your cooperation. Some things never change. It really doesn't matter that our American presidents can't say the word "Genocide;" I find it silly at this point. As I have said before, a fortune of money is paid to Turkey every year, and I love my country because no matter what faults it has when I return from afar, I thank God to be free and an American. The Pope took care of what America cannot. That is fine. God Bless Pope Francis for his courage to just say what happened. I don't get it after spending my whole life getting postcards from presidential candidates (dating back to President Reagan) they always came to our monuments and made promises, then they never spoke of it again. The word "alleged" has always been the choice of words by American presidents, I blush for your pressure to lie. But, it is O.K. I guess if America could pay for the right to have Turkey as an ally why does Turkey still have such shame to hide the truth? That is so obvious. Why would there be an Armenian church in Singapore? Armenians stuck together and they lived together in harmony. They would never flee to all corners of the world if it weren't for self-preservation. I find it insulting to connote precious children in an analogy but when a child says they didn't do it, the grownups help them learn a life lesson. But here is what I realized: this 100th anniversary of the Armenian extermination plan was handled so pathetically by the Turks. Their plan to extinguish a race didn't work after all. So, they planned Turkish festivities on the same day so that their own people could be brought into that fanatical "poor us" versus the mean Armenians.

The flame that wrote these words was ignited while I sat minding my own business in a sky lounge in Zurich. I saw the *International New York Times* newspaper dated April 13, 2015. When traveling I like to block out the constant violence that goes on in the world. I saw these humble beautiful black faces with soulful eyes they were clearly sad. I felt I owed them the interest of reading about their plight. I thank them for what I saw next. Up in the left corner of the front page read, "Pope refers to Armenian slaughter as 'genocide'." Really? This is news? But to the rest of the world, *this was news*. Pope Francis just said the obvious and got so much heat for it. He honored the Armenian people by simply saying the truth. (This was the 100th anniversary of the Armenian Genocide, and that they were slaughtered by the Turks.) A Turkish diplomat stared out of the paper at me and said some ridiculous comment as usual like it didn't happen and prove it, he ended his flat-affect expression with the word "Baseless." I have never written on a public newspaper but I wrote over your face, MY GRANDFATHER WAS THERE.

I never knew until this chapter that I am so angry with you, my Turkish brother. I have met the kindest of Turkish people, a waiter who went to college in America: one of kindest young men I ever met. My own father told me that it was impossible to be angry or hold animosity towards such a fine person. I adored this kind student who apologized on behalf of his people the second after he learned we were Armenian. I missed him when he went back to Turkey. I knew I would never see him again. I could never write his name because he told me how the government was. Thank God I only knew his American first name. I sit in my house and fear, as I write, and hope for his safety. What a shame I have never stepped foot in Turkey. But, I would if you would bury my dead by acknowledging that they lived. You got all the money and land and power. So, all you would need to do is put up a wall that was as long as the Chinese wall and write all their names. My Great-Grandpa Tateos would be the first name I would write on the wall. Do you know that Life Insurance policies that were bought in America were not honored due to how perfectly the secret was kept. One heroic Armenian attorney from Glendale, California single-handedly got the life insurance company in question to pay on countless life policies! That victory alone brought more light than our countless marches.

There was the Pope helping again back in 1915. The front page of an American Newspaper dated December 9, 1915. "POPE MAY MAKE NEW PLEA TO KAISER—T.P. O'Conner Hears He Will Be Asked to Take Action to Save the Armenians.—British Committee Active—Resolves to Work On Despite the Terrible Events That Have Stopped its Work for Armenia." So as the long stretching massacres continued these little newspaper articles were the only truth that trickled to few that would listen and even fewer that would respond. Now with phones that take pictures shot across the world such a long extermination plan would have been difficult to continue. But in my own lifetime I have seen genocides occur right across the ocean that separates us from our neighbors. It is so strange that once an extermination process begins the true impotence of humanity shows. When I look at one American newspaper after another during these horrific few years I am reminded that a World War was going on at the time. Who could jump in for some Armenians, no matter the greatness of the ancient group? The first nation on earth to adopt Christianity and be willing to die for it. Exclusivity breeds contempt. When I read the thousands of Armenian girls raped, cut up in front of their mothers for the pleasure of watching the mothers scream, I know in some way it was the hatred underneath for never being allowed to have an Armenian girl that made them so bloated in their evil behaviors. How often the Turks laughed, "Where is your Jesus now?" Many Armenian girls were tattooed to distinguish them and sold for $5.00 to anyone who would take them. Many Armenian girls jumped to their death in rivers rather than be raped again by a Turk. Many became Arabs and only knew their difference by the cross that was blazened on their neck or numbers carved into their young necks: I have seen the pictures. The *Survey Magazine* in America, as early as October 16, 1915, began their article with the Armenian appeal to America for help. The article began in all capitals: "INHUMANITY AND RUTHLESSNESS, not of enemy invaders but of government officials, have spurred the latest appeal for American relief funds. This plea comes from American Committee on Armenian Atrocities, consisting of Samuel T. Dutton, Cleveland H. Dodge. Rabbi Stephen S. Wise..." I flip one headline after another and I am reliving it; how in the world does our own series of American presidents say such things like alleged? It is actually embarrassing in the face of so much the Americans said at the time. Even if the President could simply say "We cannot comment on this topic" or chose not to comment on this topic, this is better than making us look like fools by pretending it was just a little slaughter here and there. The first planned, premediated extermination of a race of people was truly the first genocide of the 20th century. Even Hitler quoted the Armenian people as evidence to his troops that people forget as he denounced the Polish race as subhuman and instructed his troops to murder all Polish people. Sadly, he was right about our forgetfulness. I think the thought that while we sleep multitudes of children and families are being slaughtered is so overwhelming and so obliterating for us normal humans that we split it off our consciousness collectively and think: "This is too big for me to deal with, someone greater will take care of it." It sounds so simple but it is true. What can we do? We can rescue dogs and cats from an abusive neighbor, but a whole nation of people? It is so otherworldly that an individual thinks to ignore the thoughts within seconds after they are induced by words or an image. As the individual leaves the pit, so does the collective *We*.

My ancestors are around me again. I have always been the storyteller. I digress from Grandpa because I have lived this nightmare too; was it fair that in sunny California I marched, I wrote, I suffered with all of you? I never had time to enjoy the freedoms America gives. I was different, with long hair in braids, and the boys teased me. The Latin girls couldn't figure out what I was so they use to want to beat me up in school. I never told a soul. Who was I to tell? We never spoke of such things in our home. Because anything I was suffering from was unworthy in comparison to what my parents went through in labor camps in Germany during World War II. No one had time to teach me how to be an Armenian girl in America. I was in a hellish school near my home and I was being victimized and laughed at for no reason. Every day I got up and sat in the car while you dropped me off at school. I wore a sweet dress with a matching purse and shoes. How the kids laughed at me. They threw gum in my hair and threatened me daily. Then again I came home and did my homework while feeling numb and alone. I would get up and go back the next day for more. No one knew what Armenian was in my school; they only knew I wasn't dark enough, and I wasn't white enough. Well, guess what? I didn't know what box to check and the nurse said that it was white. I wondered about how silly this all was. I was an American I was Caucasian. I was Indo/European by heritage but no one cared. I never understood this color terror of humans. My father would guide me to the fish in our shortlived aquarium days. He said, "Look how the fish of one color and type swim with their own kind." I did see that phenomena but I didn't understand it. I said our color is the giftwrapping we come in. I still believe that. Colors are beautiful: black is so strong and lovely, and I knew very young that black people were in some ways so much stronger than their white oppressors. They ran the households during enslavement they prayed the deepest, sang to the Heavens with God-reaching faith, and the white people couldn't control their greatness. No matter how much they beat them down they rose up again. It was the same for the Armenians. No matter how much the Turks beat them down, slaughtered them, robbed them they rose up again. What I don't understand is how I knew not to ask for help. The time came where I simply begged to change schools and my mother finally relented. My poor, poor mother. She didn't understand this American culture. She had worked seven days a week since she was eight years old. During the Second World War, her whole family was separated and placed in random German households as servants. As a child she worked for a brutal woman who made her work in the snow without shoes. The day came where she couldn't use the bathroom without violence. She finally ran out into the street and found the council in her district and she begged him for help. This German man put her in his jeep and collected each family member and put them back together. The farmer was admonished but not punished for her treatment of my precious mother. That is why I forgive you, mother. I forgive you for your ignorance for your fears and for your inability to teach me anything that I really needed at the time of my youth. I did get my wish and changed schools; the only thing I had was my long Armenian hair that my Grandfather would kiss in love and remembering. I lasted one day in that school. The Latin girls ganged up on me again. Strange that it never occurred to me that they were jealous. Jealous is a word for pretty girls and popular girls not for me I was just an Armenian girl lost in America. They threatened to beat me up. How funny it all was looking back and I recall the short ringleader being called Angel. I still remember the dress I proudly wore to school my first day. It was black and white stripes. The material was shiny and my hair was so long that it touched the lower hem of my dress. I didn't know there was such a term as the new kid. I wouldn't have moved schools if I had known but alas, I was the new kid. Everyone was gasping about my long hair and asking me where I was from and I would reply Detroit, Michigan. They didn't get it and either did I. It was a Friday and I was so relieved to leave the school. I always hated to hear old people say how they walked through snow to get to school. These old people were probably only 40 years old at the time. But, the day has come where I too write that I walked miles home each day after school and sat in my room relieved that all would be better now. But just like Grandpa the worst was yet to come.

Men were starting to notice me more. I remember that weekend these foreign-looking males would tell me things like "What beautiful hair you have." I would shrink and say thank you. But, something changed this particular weekend. My mother had had enough. As we sat at a soda counter having a meal, I was wondering how my mother got away from the market counter where she worked with my father seven days a week to be with me? Lucky me, my mom is with me and we are having fun. I was terrified of her Armenian anger. Life was black and white. The ghosts were always with her. She seemed so stressed all the time. She had been burned horribly when she was only two years old and sleeping. Her brother played with matches and started the house on fire; by the time they pulled her out her limbs, arm, and ear were horribly scarred for life. One precious ear looked like Mr. Spock's ear points, but her face was unscarred. I never asked about it. The truth is, I never noticed them. I learned later that her scars enveloped her. I later learned she was, in Armenian terms, "damaged goods." Only in high school when a friend asked me about her scars did I truly notice they were there. I still knew not to ask her directly. While we sat at the soda fountain a passerby said, "What beautiful hair you have." I didn't answer, and my mother glared at me with what I saw as hatred. What did I do that was so wrong? All Armenian girls had long hair and we wore it in long braids. The boys since elementary school used to sing the song from *The Addams Family*. I didn't know what that meant. This day she mumbled under her breath that one day she would cut my hair. She was sick of men looking at me. That night I sat up in bed. I strained to stay awake; I left the lights on to stay awake and I wrapped my hair in a thick band to protect it from slaughter. Alas, I awoke and there she was with scissors in her precious scared hands, madness in her eyes, and all my hair was in a pile on the floor. No one spoke of it. No one. Not my father nor brother; not until I was in my 30's did she whisper she was sorry. She didn't know what to do with me; she thought that I was too pretty and she didn't want men looking at me. How sad, I thought: I was homecoming queen of my college representing the Armenian club—all six of us—and I felt ugly my whole life. Funny how things work out.

When I returned to Junior High school on the following Monday the whole school was laughing at me for a new reason: "The new girl cut her hair off, she looks terrible." The bullying continued and got to the point that I knew I had to stand up for myself. I went up to Angel who was four feet tall and told her she was a coward. That if she wants to be so dumb as to fight, then do it one on one and to tell her tall friends to back off. I got through the week without fighting after school. I knew after the weekend

I would have to stand up to her after school. I got to school as usual and I felt something new in the air, everywhere I walked with my chopped off hair and ugliness inside the sea parted; the Latin girls backed off. They moved when I walked by. I thought I was losing my mind, how could this be? But at lunch no one threw food at me, and soon one Latin girl came up to me and said, "Are you a brown belt? Everyone says you're a brown belt." I never answered her. No one ever touched me again. It turned out that one of the gang members saw me in my Judo lesson. I went twice a week with my best friends who were Japanese. I remember the first time I ran away at age six it was to their house. I just stood in front of their house wishing I could be their daughter. It was dusk and there came my mother in the family mercury and told me to get in. She knew.

In Judo I was the 5th degree's favorite. He once almost choked me to death for a demonstration. I lamented to him after class. He admonished me and told me what an honor it was to be chosen, and that his teacher broke his leg. I went because I fit in. I went because he cared, I was ready for brown belt competition when my mother swung by to see what I was up to. My short hair helped me in that no one could grab a hold of it. I was flipping a grown man with great success when she came in and, just like the candy-striper days, it was over. She took me home and that was that. I still drive by the empty studio and remember him. Those Latin girls walked by and saw me in full uniform flipping people and using a sword and all of a sudden I was something to be feared. I never had a fight in my life, thank God.

Chapter Twelve

I BURNED MY THUMB several hours ago. My finger had dipped into a microwaved bowl of water. The pain, even with ice, is excruciating and I think of my mother: only two years old sleeping peacefully then burned viciously by the house fire. I never asked her about her burns; I knew not to. But, without modern medicine how did my grandmother console this tiny toddler? My pain is still so intense it is hard to write. That is why all is forgiven. Only as an adult when she had liver spots on the tops of her hands and asked me to help her did I learn a little more of what happened. I took her to a renowned dermatologist in Beverly Hills, California. She felt like she was visiting another world, she was so innocent and childlike. The doctor lifted those dark marks and she said that it meant the world to her. He quietly asked her about her burns. I felt the dead silence again of the question I never had the courage to ask, and she quietly agreed when he told her that the burns were caused by the intense smoke of the fire. I couldn't believe that she didn't bristle or get angry. We feared our parents but for a stranger it was fine to ask. How strange that my life's work was always about entering into individuals' greatest pain. Many times the true culprit was up to me to find and then I would gently show them how to release the split-off memory that was causing so much physical distress. To my family the greatest gift I could give was to never think for a moment that I had anything of true importance to offer. That is how the hierarchy worked. Your children made you proud but they did not teach you in any way. They did not offer insight in any way; to do so was to be disrespectful.

Grandpa, you simply mark your diary with one word "Tears." After the fateful knock on your childhood home that took your beloved father Tateos away, simultaneously the same night all leaders, poets, bankers, high ranking officials, and mediators like your father met a horrific end. These evil misdeeds were done late into the night, shrouding their malice by using the dark night for cover. Those of you out on the farmlands, and valleys had no idea about the proclamations. When I read your diaries I see that you never knew about them. Your father Tateos had hoped he would have time to discuss these matters but it was too late for all of you. Within days all the men were gone. You kids were told they were drafted but they were not as lucky as that. The Turks began to torture everyone and anyone they chose. It was truly a free-for-all. Armenians were officially seen as pests to be exterminated. Turks were told to not waste bullets on such people; the Christians were "*Gyavours*"—that is the word they shouted at you all the time even when you lived in better times. I won't look it up I don't want to dignify it with the effort needed to know.

All my male relatives were gone almost overnight; only kids and the elderly remained. Any boy of 15 or older was gone like the Rapture to hell. They took some of the Armenians and used them as labor force (sappers). They starved them, beat them, raped them and worked them. You kids tried to hide your uncle Manouk in a cave, you tried to carry sacks of grain on your backs and take them to where you thought your relatives were working. The cattle stables were empty now. Little by little the poisoned ground came up and choked the breath out of all of you. Erzroum was where you all heard many Armenian villagers were. So on foot you began your walk while the Turks pillaged anything in site. A group of Turkish soldiers stopped you all and asked what you "Gyavours and sons of gyavours" were doing. You had courage, as scared as you were, and said, "It's bread." "Where are you taking it?" "To our fathers, they are working in Erzroum and the Kaould valley near Mamkhatoun. They are building roads." There were at least a hundred Turkish soldiers surrounding you kids. They were on horseback. Many countless Turks were on your horses and butchering your sheep and cows. All of a sudden the Chief of the group yelled to stop and not touch the kids. He shouted to his men that it was none of their business as to where the kids were going and to let them go. Grandpa you were only 13 and you remembered well what happened next. You write that his soldiers took down a folding bed, they unfolded it and placed it at a distance from the soldiers. He then dismissed them. He laid down on the bed on his back and called all of you to be near him. He then asked in Armenian to tell him where you were all really going. You restated the truth and in Armenian he warned you all to not listen or talk to anybody. "When you reach your fathers tell them to secretly escape." You write he was secretly Armenian and if it were not for him you would have surely died. In your diary entry I see one word as if it is a caption and it reads "Fugitive." In this entry you write that all Armenian soldiers that were serving in the Turkish military were disarmed and driven to Malay Tabor which was the office of military service registration. The Armenian soldiers became slave labor. It was 1914 and no one was aware of the "carnage" in your area. When an Armenian man working in these horrific conditions got beaten and too exhausted they would try to desert and get home. The problem was there was no home to get to anymore. You had a large stone in your buffalo stable and it was rolled in front of a cave that could hide up to three people. The Turkish Army would come and beat and rape the Armenian women and the elderly trying to find out the hiding places. You write that the Turks beat with *"Kasa Toura"* and torture family members while having others watch. Still no one spoke. They would shout things like, "Where have you hidden your dog's mutts?" You heard the sounds and screams but no one spoke. They died by being beaten to death. Because a good Turkish soldier did not waste bullets on dogs. By autumn of 1914 over a hundred Turkish soldiers came to your precious village. They took over everyone's houses. There would be five to 15 Turks in each Armenian household. They would demand food and drink, and the children would have to butcher what livestock was left. The Armenians who survived up until now had to serve the Turks. This was a scene that occurred before they took father Tateos who was in desperate hope that your family would be saved. Over ten of the high-ranking officials chose your house. Father Tateos was the village landlord and he had gone to Mamkhatoun on business. You write how they had not touched him yet. The Turks had abandoned some of the horses because the poor animals were hungry and physically exhausted. Even though you were a child you had to go out and with the some of the others foraging for food so the horses could gain strength, and then the Turks would continue the pillaging of neighboring villages. The horses were so fatigued that they grazed lying down. It was beginning to get dark and you write about seeing a Greek man that ran the mill standing in front of you. He was like a brother to your father Tateos. He grabbed your arm and whispered to go back to your village. It turned out that the Turks sent you all out to be near the horses in order to blame you all for stealing. Nothing made sense anymore; everything became an evil game of charades. The Greek man held your hand and guided you back to your village.

The Greek man's name was Aleksiy and he was one of the few men still left; he too became scared as you both saw around 15 Turkish soldiers coming towards you. Aleksiy wanted you both to go to the stone and hide in the cave. But it was too late. The Turk said, "Instead of embracing the dog, you'd better circle around the thorn." While you two were trying to hide among the stones the dog barked and they came towards you two. The Turks shouted out that you both came to steal the state horses. They dragged you both to the rest of the men standing at a distance. The Turks began beating you both and as much as you both tried to run away it was no use. They beat Aleksiy until he lay nearly dead. Two soldiers held you by your arms. You had previously hidden your beloved watch that you wore on a chain under your layers of clothing. You feared they would grab it. You write how you were more concerned about your precious watch than your own life. "One of them held me down while the other one struck me on the chest and on my back. They loosened me a little. I freed my arms and ran away. They fired after me. It was dark already. I crawled in the fields and went into the valley. They could not catch me. I went home. The priest was sitting near the *tounir* [furnace] in the sitting room, the Turkish commanders sat there also. The Armenian priest did not want to see their dogs' faces. As I explained what had happened, he whether he wanted to or not went and explained the event to the Turks. Those high-ranking Turkish officials stood up and they took the priest and me with them. We found the Greek lying on the ground barely alive. Seeing me, one of them said, "Here he is, this is the boy who ran away." They jumped to catch and beat me again but the superior respecting the priest's mediation did not let them beat me again. Instead he said, "Priest Effendi [Mr. Priest] It's for your sake I didn't let them beat the lad."

You were so brave Galoust my precious Grandfather and with help from some other kids you got a cart and went out to Aleksiy the Greek and put him in the cart and brought him home to care for. You blame yourself in your diary but it was not your fault. You write how this poor man suffered because of you. He suffered because of his integrity to help a child in distress. He suffered because of the barbaric Turkish soldiers not because of you. In the morning the Turks took him to Mamakhatoun claiming he was a horse robber. Later that day your father returned from Mamkhatoun. You ran to him holding the horse bridle so he could get down. Your father Tateos had bitterness in his eyes and slapped you. He began to strike you—the ghosts press on my fingers again. Alright, the truth is he began to beat you and the people standing nearby stopped him. You never wrote in your diary how you felt when he struck you. You only say he didn't beat you much. Dear God, how was it that you never struck us? You were very principled and would demand appropriate behaviors from us but you never laid a hand on us. I marvel as I sigh. Your father had bribed Turks in Mamakhatoun and the officials living in your house and saved the Greek from the beasts' hands if only for a while.

That same night at 1 a.m. came a knock on the door. Your father Tateos asked who it was and an answer came "Uncle Tateos, it is me from Aprank village. Please open the door and let us in." Your father asked how many people and he responded that there were two of them. With that your father let his nephew in and there were eleven more exhausted fugitives from the Turks. You write how your father told Nshan that he was surprised by how many people there were, and with that Nshan said, "Uncle if you knew how many of us there were you wouldn't have opened the door."

All of them had been running and starving for days. Now, I know why you did it Grandpa. There were times in my life where a secret thought was whispered by my mother. I knew I had to file it away quickly. Her pained whisper would be how you wore out her mother during World War II. That with 10 mouths to feed you would still bring home a hungry, lost person and ask her to find food for him. It was what you saw. You survived an unspeakable time, and did what your father did and help others in need. My poor Great-Grandmother in the middle of the night she was asked to get up and cook for these men. Tateos new if the word spread that they were harboring these men they would be killed. The Turkish officials slept in another dwelling and the family secretly fed them. There were no stoves. Your mother had to churn the *tounir* and cooked a meal as fast as possible. They warmed up, ate and drank but ten of them left early dawn, and your two cousins stayed. They were hidden in the buffalo stable cave. "We kept them in the cave during the day and they came out and ate during the night." Within a week they had to leave and head back to their village. Because Tateos was the village mediator and bailiff he had to be extra careful to not get caught protecting his own people.

"It was March 1915 now; the snow had just thawed and the ground was still wet. Everybody had a bad feeling. Something evil was expected. In the evenings, instead of sleeping to relax, they all wondered, 'My God, what will happen tonight?'

"One night approximately one o'clock a.m. There was a wild knocking on our window. We all awoke trembling. My dad calmed us down saying, 'Don't be afraid, nothing is going to happen.' He answered the knock by saying, 'Who are you, what do you want?' A Turkish official announced that he was the village burgomaster his name was Hassan. He spoke to my father in Turkish, 'Tateos bailiff get up and come, we have arrested a state enemy.' My dad went with the official Hussan and returned an hour later."

I don't understand Grandpa: why didn't Great-grandpa find a way to escape with all of you? Was it denial? Was it false hope that the carnage would not happen to you all if you obeyed the Turks' wishes? My great-great-grandmother asked why they sent for him in the middle of the night and was informed along with everyone in the household that an Armenian man had been imprisoned in a nearby village. The *moukhtar* (Turkish chief of the village) had this poor man tied by his hands and held in a room that was used to store shoes and slippers. They made him sit on his knees. What is so strange to me Great-Grandpa was your power and confidence.

There were four Turks hiding in the Armenian fountain and you Great-Grandpa called for men to arrest the four Turks and bring them to you so you might prove the Armenian man innocent of any crime. The Turks learned of the ensuing investigation and ran away. The Armenian youths he asked to help with the search came back empty-handed and reported that they escaped. I do love you Great-grandpa even though you were too heavy-handed sometimes with your son. You truly were a peace-maker. You were risking your own life trying to shed light on this poor Armenian man's fate. No one could sleep and in the middle of the night you told everyone the story of this poor man. He had run away from Turkish oppression and had found your village fountain. As he drank water and gazed at the Armenian church these Turks came up and told him to feed them. This exhausted Armenian man wandered past the houses right near the church and went to the edge of the village and knocked on the door of a what grandpa called a beast Turk. This Turk spoke fluent Armenian and began to question the man. His crime was that he was hungry and asked for bread, and confessed to running away from the Turks that were killing Armenians nearby. With that he opened the door and arrested him. Great-grandfather Tateos took food and went back to the Turkish Chief's residence since they moved him there next. After feeding the prisoner he asked you for a favor. He asked that you loosen his handcuffs tomorrow while he is taken back to Mamkhatoun. You make a secret promise to him.

You warned him that you will be harsh with him in words in front of the Turkish officials, but you will honor his wish. One Armenian and one Turk will take him to the village. The Turk will be the one to loosen the handcuffs not the Armenian. But how? Grandpa writes how he will always pray for you Great-grandfather. Grandpa says that your brave spirit will never be forgotten. He writes that he loved you so much. I see why. For this one person you risked everything. The next morning you yelled at him just like you told him. You had chosen an Armenian man that you respected that was elderly but strong. His name was Ohannes and he was one of the bravest men in the village. You told him your plan. You told him that he must get the Turk to loosen the handcuffs for his own safety. That there would be a mountain on the way to Lousaghpyure village and that would be the best time to let him run for his life. That Hassan the burgomaster himself will be the appointed Turk to travel with him to Mamakhatoun. The journey began while little Galoust listened to the plan. When the three arrived to the top of the mountain the lad began begging for a rest and to please loosen his handcuffs. The Turk told Ohannes to loosen that faithless gyavour's belt, and the Armenian said, "No." Ohannes told the Turk that it would be best if he did it himself so that no one would later say an Armenian loosened the ties. Finally, the Turk went to loosen the lad's tied hands and Grandpa you write the most beautiful words *"Achke sirem"* ("May I love and behold your merciful eyes") because what happens next is what happens in the movies. The boy hit the Turk and pretended to hit Ohannes and ran for his life. Later Great-grandfather received a letter that the lad made it home safely. He thanked Tateos for his courage and valor.

At this time, the area where you all lived still did not know that the extermination was speeding in their direction. You all thought these little victories were restoring order and safety again. The Turkish neighbors heard about the story about the boy who got away and would come and question you all. You all pretended not to know what they were talking about. The Turkish neighbors began to accuse your father of protecting fugitives and state enemies. They bellowed all day that he was the premier of the village but he was not serving properly by hiding people in his house. A group went and informed the Turkish state officials that the village bailiff hid fugitives in his house. Then the fateful knock came to the door of your beloved father. Turkish officials pounded the door and demanded to be fed. After they drank and filled their stomachs they turned on the faithful Tateos and said he will be taken to Mamkhatoun. He would be questioned. Everyone began crying and father Tateos quietly comforted you grandpa and he comforted all his loved ones before he was taken away. You were only twelve years old when all this happened. The Turks made you along with the other children push carts of supplies to the Turks nearby. Your mother and grandmother shouted at the Turks that you were all children. But the Turks didn't care and they forced you Grandpa to go with the others. In vain your grandmother tried to bribe the Turks to let you go. At dusk you were on your way back home with the other exhausted children when you saw a group of Armenians being driven across the fields. You recognized your father! There were at least 50 to 60 Armenian men of all ages being forcibly driven to Ezroum. The Turks used the same lies they were using in other parts of Turkey telling them they were being drafted. You tried to hug your dear father and you write: "The Godless, cruel, wild Turk gendarme hit my dad on his head with the whip in his hand saying, 'Get out of here *gyavour oghli gyavour!*' They called us Christians gyavour, and faithless. That beast caught hold of my arm and threw me aside. My dad was in agony from the pain, tears flew down his eyes, sighing for the light of his eyes his son Galoust. My sweet dad as if his sufferings were not enough, he got beaten because of me by the dog gendarme. When I reached home my grandma and my mom had wept for me."

You told your mother that you saw your father at Kav Darasi. I am with you grandpa and your pain I can hardly breathe but I listen to the voice inside me guiding my pen.

Chapter Thirteen

"I WANTED TO EMBRACE my dad for our last farewell, they did not let me." It is Father's day today; you are all around me today. I circled all day not wanting to listen to the voice inside. It is so painful, I feel you all and mostly you Great-grandfather. My Dad was too good for this world, too pure, too sensitive, too proud. When customers at his market stole from him he would confront them and once they confessed he would open the soda fridge and tell them to have a soda to go with what they stole. Once they took the drink he made one request, "If you are hungry come and ask me and I will give you food, but please don't steal from me again." Years would go by and those same questionable people would come into my Dad's and Mom's market and say how much my Dad helped them feel good about themselves. They would become his customers. You were an artist who couldn't follow your passion. You had to take care of us, and you were so unhappy underneath. You tried never to show it. You would gently tell me all my life, "We are D.P.'s Sharon, we are displaced people." Your other comment that haunts me to this day is: "Don't forget you are a guest in this world." I believed it with such faith that I still don't feel I own a thing, or belong. What were you teaching me dad when you would say that all us kids didn't know how lucky we were? It is hard to be raised by displaced people and not know it fully until adulthood. You cried in the hospital bed while you were dying. For the first time in my life I helplessly watched the child in you cry because the Bolsheviks stole your red bike, your horses, home. They sent your mother to Siberia, and we didn't under-stand what a miracle it was that you found her after 30 years and brought her to remarry your father in America. I was too young to fathom the abandonment you experienced once again when she left with your very disturbed father and didn't call or write. It made you relive all the loss and hell of being pushed out into the cold all over again. Grandpa became your surrogate father. You never talked about it but we felt the agony spinning

69

around you and thought it was us. We thought it was us that caused you your agony Dad. Perhaps it was.

How hard we try to make our parents proud. I tried making all of you proud because all of you had the same authority over us kids. Whatever I did, whatever I accomplished, had a short shelf life. I would have to start all over again depending on your mood, your own sorrow, your own emptiness. Grandpa didn't require starting over. He accepted me as I was. He never judged me; it was quite amazing. Now, to know how the Turks didn't let him even hug his father goodbye and I gaze at his picture with my arms around his shoulders and his smile looking out and I feel better. Somehow I knew to hug him. How I wish I could hug Great-grandpa right now but I feel him pressing on my right shoulder as if to say "Keep writing, keep telling the story of what really happened." So I will.

One month of tears and silence then word came that Great-grandpa had become seriously ill and that he was taken to a hospital called Yonjalik. Hovsep who was from your village came and told you all secretly and ended with "I know no more about him." Thinking that your father was surely dead your beloved nurturing mother Horop along with your grandmother began to weep uncontrollably. Though their lives would be at risk your grandmother told your mother to pack and try to find him and support him in Erzroum. This time you got to go with her and it took three days of perilous travel to reach Erzroum. The sun was setting and the two of you were complete strangers to the town. You got to spend your first night in a town inn with your mother.

When morning came you both had breakfast and began your search. "My poor mom held me by my hand and we were wandering from street to street, like sheep that have lost their lambs. We were hopelessly lost and it was difficult for my mother to find the hospital that her husband was in. We would find a hospital and he was not there. Females were not allowed inside the hospitals so she would wait outside and I entered in and searched for him, came out and said, 'My Dad is not in this hospital.'"

I remember that as a child I watched a war movie with Shirley Temple as the star. It left such an indelible mark inside my heart. I cried and cried while she went searching for her father in various hospitals, everyone shaking their heads and quietly looking at each other with the knowing that he was dead. When all was lost she entered a room with a man who had suffered a horrible head trauma and couldn't even remember his name. I jumped up and down, so relieved: "It's him!" I cried. Don't give up, it is your father! Never did I think that Grandpa you had the same experience. You never ever told us. You never hung your head and remembered with us. You were always trying to motivate all of us to excel. How unselfish you were Grandpa: you are the light of my heart, and my father is the orb that I strive to hold. He was purity and you were strength. My Dad was not perfect and had many shortcomings but he had a pure heart; everyone could see it shine through his sorrow.

People in the street knew your mother was an Armenian's wife. She covered from above her nose down. The passers would say things like "Armenian patients were taken to Yonjoloukh." They would bother your mother with questions like why was she standing there and who was she waiting for. These Turks bothered her while you had to go into yet another hospital in Turkish territory. "I entered the Turkish hospital and downstairs was where they kept the Armenians. People that were dead were next to people that were still fighting for their lives. The Turkish doctor was walking along. I called out my Dad's name and walked all along the hospital. There was no hope to find him. The Turk patients looked at me with hatred. The doctor called me and scolded, 'Why are you yelling, *gyavour oghli?*' He then threw me out."

Each time I write the word *gyavour* I feel sick inside, I don't know what I would do if a Turkish person ever called me that. So far I have had only positive experiences. But, I am truly shocked at the absolute ignorance in humanity. I am writing about hatred and prejudice and if my pen wrote 2015 it would be no different than 1915. How is it that in the 21st century I watch and read of the torturing of innocent people by beheading: you are the wrong religion—no, *you* are the wrong religion. Everyone sure that their God is better. That He talks to their tribe and not to your tribe or church or mosque. People enter to renew themselves to better their character to give thanks, pray, to grow, and yet everyone fights because someone slandered their God. When I was young I thought myself so unknowledgeable that surely there are reasons so beyond my small mind that I must study and learn and understand. Thirty years I loved dear friends of a very different faith. We grew up together I visited there country where few Christians were ever allowed. Yet, I felt a barrier between us as long and as high as the Chinese Wall. Unless I adopted their religion I would always be less which I felt, and lower which I felt daily when with them. I loved them like family. If love and decades of devotion could not penetrate that barrier then neighbors who suffer from greed and want what their brethren have would be so much easier to justify killing for. Make no mistake, anyone "fighting for God" is fighting for themselves and using false virtue as a shield to gain power and means.

Now, as an adult I am truly at a loss that grown adults can see themselves as superior to their fellow man because of what they believe makes them holy, better, spiritual. The contradiction is truly pitiful.

On this Father's day I am searching for hope but I see that after all the walking and searching and praying and hoping you were both still so lost in this Turkish town. Someone shouted to go to the office secretary. You and your mother still did not know of the mass killings. You were all in these very rural areas, the Turks knew and the hatred seemed so much more pronounced as you both walked. I marvel at how brave you were for your mother. You had to walk strong like a young man because women were not allowed in most places. Even at the secretary's office your mother had to stand outside. The cruel secretary shouted and cursed at you; he then took a large book and continued to curse you and tell you that your father was not registered in the king's registry and that you were a dammed gyavour and to get out of his sight! He then grabbed your arms and threw you out. Your mother was crying and hoping you had word. Though you were crying, tired, hungry, and lost, you both began your long road home which would take three long days. You use the word grieving and I look at that word. I read countless books on grieving; I helped so many, but, never my own. Never could one word I say be seen as useful. I knew that being their child made me useless. How odd. If you are the child of an Armenian parent who has suffered greatly the show of respect is to not notice. If I am their child I am insulting them by offering any words that could possibly help the healing process. This is the first time I am writing the truth of my family life of perpetual inconsequence. No one ever healed; they just carried on. The custom of ritualistic flowers on the graves along with more incense and donations to the church, but no release from the Post-Traumatic Stress. It didn't exist for any of you, and yet you looked out into the world through the ashes of your past. You would never know what it was like for me because to hug a shaking voltage of pain that says "I love you" is truly the most traumatic lonely experience in the world.

In your world Grandpa the end came slowly; the life of the Armenian spirit slowly drained out of your land and hearts. Within two weeks the Turks found your uncle who had been hiding on your land. They arrested him and took him away. Your Grandmother wept for her sons. She was

85 and all that was tender in her life was again being murdered and destroyed. The Turks murdered her husband and now all her adult sons were gone. You called these Turks outlaws because now mayhem occurred and there was no order or consequence. These Turks murdered the priest Yeprem from the Norandents family right in his house, so your family moved your precious uncle Father Khoren to Vztents house to hide him. He couldn't perfom the funerals but in the dark would perform the interment order. So, his prayers in the night after your dead were buried was his contribution.

It was May 1915. The whole year was a slow killing wound. All the men were gone and though this particular day was bright and beautiful, by late morning more Turkish outlaws entered your village. Because there were only kids and the elderly you were defenseless. These outlaws forced you kids along with the elderly to destroy your village's important hayloft. It belonged to the Vztents family and it was known as the Kirakos Hayloft. These Turks wanted the logs so that they could then force the Armenians left in the village to build a bridge across the Tougla river near Mamakhatoun. They wanted the Turkish soldiers to have easy access into the roads nearby. All the workmen were Armenians crowded together in Ameliye Tabour (workforce, sappers). You the children and the sick elderly having little to no tools were forced to tear down a treasured, life-sustaining hayloft. Only one adult was with you children, and he was an older man in his 70's named Ohannes from the Sero family. You remember that you kids worked without a break from 10 a.m. until late into the afternoon. The children asked to leave and eat and drink water but it wasn't allowed. There is a mechanism called denial when something is about to happen that is diabolical or beyond human comprehension. One thinks this can't be the end.

You children still didn't know what was truly happening to your lives. These outlaws were going house to house looting and stealing children to be slaves and you write that they had seized your village for nearly five hours. As darkness came there were no Turks near you kids as you continued to destroy the Kirakos Hayloft. The same outlaws that would not let you leave were now looting Armenian homes so you children began to run away, but where to? You write how these Turks were behaving like dogs looking for bones. You saw two Turks walking to the Kirakos house where your uncle the priest was hidden along with Karapet from Peto's landlord's family. You watched as they dragged out your uncle Father Khoren. As you stood paralyzed in terror you witnessed Karapet run for his life into the cemetary. They chased him, and dragged him like an animal. You children ran for cover and separated. You ran to the cattle stables. Not your own but Vztents Grigor's farrier stable. You looked around and nobody was there. All the family members had run away. Their cattle still remained. You hid in furnace chimney.

"I climbed high in the chimney. There was much disturbance; violence in the village, clashes, and screaming was heard everywhere. What could I do? I waited there until dark came. I realized that waiting was useless. I had to come out of my hiding place and go home somehow. If I stayed there, the outlaws might come and kill me. I had to go home from dark corners. I came out from my hiding place and went further into the stables. The starving cattle were staring at me thinking I would give them some forage. Those lying on the ground got on their feet, and began to bellow as if crying. Tears began to flow from my eyes, too. What could I do? Oh Dear Lord... I slowly opened the door and came out. I heard folk's voices. I went towards Saint Nshan, The Savior Church. I found all the people gathered together at the church door, screaming and praying."

There was a young man named Sarkis from the Norbad family. He was once lucky enough to be educated and graduate from Sanossian School in Karin. He was also a newlywed. Sarkis had been forced into the slave army to build and die, but he got away. He had been in hiding, and knew his days were numbered so he came out of hiding. He did this so he could glance at his beloved's eyes once more. The Turks were destroying houses as they pillaged, raped and murdered. Walls would tumble down while they looked for hiding spots. Sarkis saw you and asked, "What shall we do Galoust?" He was a relative because your sister Oghik was his cousin's wife. You looked up and said what any child would say, "I don't know." You asked Sarkis to run away with you. He wouldn't. You were a child and you could feel the end was near. You told him so but he chose to walk with his people and weep. It was almost ten at night. Now you saw Vartan; he was one year older than you. He must have been thirteen years old. You asked him to run away with you but he too said, "No." He warned you that the village was surrounded and that there was no way out. The denial again. Vartan's argument was that if he left with you he would be killed. But, all he really meant was killed sooner. We cling to life it is our nature.

Once you told him that you were all dead already he agreed and began to run into the cemetery with you. The outlaws saw you both and began shooting. "We went into the abyss and disappeared into the darkness. But alas, I lost Vartan, my friend. He went to the right side and I to the left. I chose left because it was the direction to my home. I wanted to reach home somehow. Perhaps I could learn about my family."

You write that you thought of Vartan. You stood in the dark frozen for what seemed a long time then you began to run towards home. You thought to yourself: "Whatever happens I'll go." "I must go home."

Your house was at the lower part of the village near the abyss. You write of the abyss and I think it is the deeper part near Turkey. Your father bought the Turk's fields near your property for 20 gold pieces. He was allowed to purchase Turkish fields for the right price. Tateos did this so that all of you could feel a little more comfortable with the Turks further away. The barley had grown tall this year and the crops were a place you children could hide in. You saw Nounoufar, your cousin and the daughter of Father Khoren. She was seventeen and brave just like you. She was hiding some household belongings in the crop fields and you quietly called out "Sister, Sister."

She recognized you and began to cry; you both hugged and she called to your mother nearby that you had made it back. Your mother hugged you and wept. I weep as you write that your sweet mother was like a sheep that had lost her lamb. Great-grandmother Horop then took you by the hand and you both passed by those that were crying helplessly on their rooftops waiting for more carnage. You both stopped when you witnessed a Turkish man dragging your Uncle the priest to the area where your family hid Armenians. The Turk took him straight into the *tounir* room. Your uncle called out to your mother who was his sister-in-law, "Horopsima come in and bring some money." Your mother was the keeper of the money for all four households. She was the eldest daughter-in-law and that was how the custom worked. Your mother entered the shed where the key was hidden. The box was in a secret place and as her hand trembled the keys clanked loudly and the Turk could hear every sound. Your mother brought the 10 gold pieces in a small purse and gave it to your uncle the priest. The Turk counted the gold pieces and tied the purse and threw it back at your uncle. For some reason this Turk cared to say that he didn't take one more gold piece than agreed upon for saving Father Khoren's life. He falsely promised to come in the morning and help them run away from the Turkish soldiers that were slaughtering Armenians by the thousands. Grandfather you remember this moment well. That this Turk spoke Turkish the whole time and he said that he would bring you all some beddings, and household items for your survival and voyage. He had the tenacity to tell you all to not fear. Fear was the only emotion everyone was feeling. He never returned and though it was well into the night, you my precious Grandfather were starving, there was little food left. Your mother found some scraps and you all came down from your rooftops and for only a sleep's rest did you think you were safe again. In the early morning as those that survived awakened and began their daily chores in order to feel some sort of sanity the Turks returned. They shouted to all of the people left in your village that you had one hour to prepare for exile. That you could carry your belongings but that you all must get out of your houses.

Evil, evil, evil, is all that passes through me right now. How chilling your grip is on the truth. You butchered and killed and laughed while you did it: why such hatred, my Turkish neighbor? Was it Christ that you laughed at or your smallness that finally was murdered for a brief time. You knew of the virtue of Armenians, how they praised God, and Christ. How they wouldn't marry your children because of the massacres and because of your brutality. Still to this day you choose the 100th anniversary of the extermination (that you still say never occurred) to create a false celebration for your people. Your scholars that have had to flee Turkey to survive that have written about the Armenian extermination are trying to help you, not hurt you. We do not succeed with your apology. How can you apologize for such barbaric behavior? You can't, and you my Turkish neighbor have helped the Armenians be heard throughout the world because of your false pride. If you had absorbed your hellish murders as the insanity of the Ottoman Empire we would be lost now. Your refusal to bury our dead has been the very beacon of the world knowing the truth. Politics is not humanity. Politics is what you need to help humanity. It is a deformed passageway that men and women move through fighting for people's rights as they dominate and have others submit to new rules.

Because of the rural living in your village the Armenians were not given a five-day proclamation but a slow picking off of humanity month by month. They got one hour to pack and leave for the death march the Turks called exile. In 1915 the *New York Times* stated, "TURKS HAVE KILLED 500,000. Evidence Taken from State Department Shows Quarter of a Million Women Violated." My Turkish neighbor, why didn't you protest for the three years American papers wrote of your atrocities? I heard women for the first and only time who stood up at the 70th Anniversary of the Armenian Genocide describe how the Turks slaughtered and raped and cut open pregnant women and chopped their babies in half while making the expectant mother watch. Why the horror? In all my life I only knew of one Turkish man who enjoyed watching people cringe; he laughed when people were humiliated. He was sick but a whole race with the same insanity? If Armenians were Muslim would you have treated them better? How odd religion is. To be a neighbor of 10,000 years and no empathy, no love for thy neighbor because he prays to a God that you disapprove of. Then on December 13, 1915 the *Independent* newspaper wrote the "Story of the Week." They showed the Armenians in a picture on foot walking across Egypt trying to escape the atrocities. The article quote Lord Bryce again saying that he was "heading the reports showing the extent of the massacre and the cruelties practiced are greater than at first supposed. Since last May 800,000 Armenians..."

Grandpa I must let you speak now. "It was the morning of mid-May in 1915; and it was a beautiful, sunny, and bright day. People were tortured last night like Christ. They were in mourning as if black clouds had knelt on the village. We were still asleep in bed, we were all exhausted from the night of hell when we suddenly heard the roaring of torture and crying. My beloved mother had tears flowing down her cheeks while she called out to us as her innocent babies. 'Get up! Enough sleeping! See what's going on in the village. We have to abandon the house. They are expelling us from our houses!' My cousin Nounoufar had a hammer and was smashing all the containers of our winter food stock supplies; jars filled with cabbage, apples, pickles, baskets with food that hung on the walls all the crumbled grains, and milks."

Somehow I feel like I know Nounoufar so well. Your grandmother was admonishing her that you would all starve and she shouted back, "You good-natured, simple minded unlucky grandmother you are 85 years old. You have survived these obscure days where the headless murderers and wild beasts come destroy everything in sight. You believe their lies that we will come back in three days!! Dearest Grandmother forget it all. The Turks deceive people like you to confiscate our belongings. Be aware that our Armenian nation is totally destroyed. They want to take us out of the village to slaughter us at the bank of the river!"

You heard all of this Grandfather and wrote it down for those of us that will listen. You decades later named my first cousin Nounafar but she was an infant; how did you know that she out of everyone had the heart and spirit of your cousin? The Nounafar I know is as brave and outspoken with the truth just as my ancestor Nounafar was. Thank you for letting me say her name all my life now that I am just now learning of the twin spirit of these two wonderful people. After all that, your cousin Nounafar said her grandmother still did not believe her. Outside the Turks were telling the Armenians that it is the King's order and that they had to carry out his command. I never realized you lived in a country where there was a king—a weak pitiful king who was losing the Ottoman Empire with each passing day. You overheard the lies that you all had to go to the bank of the river and that after three days you would return to your houses. While you all had to stand outside waiting for the death march you noticed that strange Turkish woman called Nylou who looked like a man. She had caused you all such problems long ago at the Armenian water pool. There she was again stealing your familie's agricultural instruments. You ran up to her and still had the kindness to call her sister Nylou. You children were taught to respect your elders no matter who they were. You asked why she was taking your instruments for ploughing the fields. Even you Grandpa were in such denial. You were trying to reason with this evil woman by telling her your family needed your equipment back in order to harvest your land. She shouted back at you to get away and out of her sight. "Don't you know that they are already deporting you! Do you hope that you'll return back to your houses? If you talk too much I'll slay you this moment!"

In that young mind of yours you thought that she wasn't worth dying for. You told yourself that those items could be bought again. You were sad knowing that she had wanted those items that Manouk had made for ten years and now she got them. You wrote how she looked at you with blood in her eyes. I say a prayer as I write: *Oh, Lord I am an American and I live in a free nation that cannot still use the word genocide.* I think that is why I am afraid that the Turks will hear of my writings and come and destroy me and I am shuddering as I write because for the first time I truly understand why I have been afraid all this time. It is America's fear to say the word that makes me feel unsafe, not you Turkey. What hold do you have on my precious country that each president has feared saying the simple truth? It is in all of America's documents. It doesn't make sense.

Pope Francis said the simple truth that is in mountains of documents along with pictures and even he gets troubled by the ugly politics below the truth that is poisonous and vulgar but at the end of the day it is still the bargaining chip to hold onto.

Grandfather what you saw next was the Turkish outlaws Turkey hired because Armenians weren't even worth Turkish soldiers. Turkey, you emptied your prisons and sent the criminals to do many of your horrific deeds. You fed them my loved ones. You crucified my own life in sunny California because you calcified my youth with shrouds of ghosts that lingered and wept in my dreams. You even stole my happiness because I couldn't be free as long as I carried my dead relatives in my subconscious. It was everywhere: what I thought was patriotism for my people was really trauma that I slept in, trauma when I ate food. Everywhere I walked with my loved ones I felt oppression and I couldn't breathe and I thought it was me. It was your cruel and bloodthirsty Turks that came to my loved ones village. You robbed us all but I prevailed and so did you Grandpa. We both loved reading and writing and learning, many did not.

It saved me and now it is saving us.

Protect me America! I have been your proud benefactor all my life. Let this truth be said without the violence just this once.

Grandpa you had to witness the Turkish outlaws forcing the Armenians to leave their village. The upper neighborhood was where all the disturbance was. Screaming, cries, and clashes of arms were heard. They killed and beat the people. Then they pulled out little Armenian girls and women and raped them like savage beasts. The fiends were like a blanket of pestilence. The Turkish plague took hold of any and all Armenians.

You my dearest Grandfather entered your orchard that still had beehives full of honey. A Turkish neighbor named Ahmad who was Injay Mamo's son was a couple of years older than you and he was standing there on your property on your doormat pointing a gun at you. He wanted to kill you. Ahmad Chaoush, one of your other Turkish neighbors, came to steal your home's belongings. It just occurred to me that I am writing the murderers' names: for the first time they are being brought into the light of day, and perhaps one of their descendants recognizes their relative who took part of the neighborhood butcherings. Perhaps the home you now live in was once our hearts.

"Ahmad Chaoush didn't let the Turk kill me for the sake of our belongings, as if doing us a favor. He held my hand and escorted me in. He said to my mom, 'Injay Mamo's son was going to shoot your son. As a neighbor for these many years, I didn't let him.' Ahmad told your mother that he had eaten much of the bread of Tateos your father. He wanted my Great-grandmother to give him all the valuables and he would guard them for the family. He asked to see the secret hiding places and that he would keep the door locked and when the family returned in three days they could have it back. Great-grandmother promised to repay him for his good deed. There were no males left in your house and Uncle Khoren was still hiding. Grandpa I know you knew it was all in vain but your mother did what she thought was best in this most monstrous of situations. She continued to hope that you would all survive. The strange thing is with each tiny gesture that was made during this Turkish apocryphal story telling time a miracle did happen. Somehow you lived to write the truth. I only wish that you had instructed me to translate your diaries while you were still living but even with that it was death that bonded us even closer by my struggling for years to complete the translations. I sit in awe that you are with me in spirit for the 100th anniversary of the Armenian Extermination. Genocide really sounds merciful just too light of a word. As if it all happened in one horrible blow. It was much worse being searched out one by one and slaughtered for being better organized as a group, better loved as a people, better in all ways which only provoked the slovenly Turks to psychotic levels of envy, especially the pitiful King who could have gained such standing by uniting the Armenians with Turkey instead of destroying them.

Chapter Fourteen

WHEN I WAS YOUNG I loved to sink into the water until I could sit at the bottom of the deep end of the pool. I felt so free from everyone I pretended to have a tea party, I listened to my self holding my breath and counting so that I let go of the air very slowly. People on top were amazed at how long I would be underwater. Then up I would come with a slight desperateness as I struggled to reach the top of the water. My breath was very controlled and yet I felt just afraid enough to swim faster to reach life. It isn't something you talk about but it all came to me right now. It is so personal and sounds very unlike the magic of how it feels. But I think even then I knew Grandpa about the death all around me. I kept dying a little then fighting back each time. I loved to hide and not be found. I ran faster than everyone I knew, I climbed higher than all the boys, but I didn't know why I did it until now. I always could intuit. I wish I couldn't. But I could see and feel thoughts that weren't being said. That is why I would say, "Say what you mean and not what you're saying." No one did what I asked. I think later it helped me greatly in the work I chose to do. I loved the sacredness of psychotherapy I loved intuiting the undercurrent that was not being said. I loved diving into the deep part of the unconscious and bringing it up at the right time to show the person I was helping to be whole. I lived in the deep part of the water at home and with you. Yet I was diving into perpetual quicksands never coming up with any clues when I was with you all.

Children are the purest route to the problems that no one will talk about. They are still stardust taking shape to be a bright light or a stone. That is why only now Grandpa do I understand why I never came up with a clue for those I loved. Quicksand was the safest place to rest your heads. You never had any more surprises but I never got to be close to you. Only God knows how much I tried. So, I know how you held your breath after your mother gave the ten gold pieces to that evil Turkish neighbor. He knew you were all to die, he was too lazy to search for the hiding spots himself so he lied one more time to your mother who had been torn from everyone she loved. Horop only had you and a few others to have hope for one last time.

Your land was large and in the back stables your family had lots of animals. I cannot believe with all your candor that in your diaries you ask to be excused for having to write the word donkey as one of the animals. Your benevolent heart shines through each word you write. The menagerie was so amazing to learn about. In second grade while still only speaking Armenian at home I won the spelling bee. I never told you about it but the word I spelled was menagerie. Now I write the word again and learn what a rich menagerie my ancestors had. Buffaloes, oxen, cows, sheep, goats, and lambs. Your family had donkeys and one beautiful horse. It was thought to be Arabian. My own father had a beautiful white Arabian horse named Silva. She would respond to all my Dad's commands. She would lie down, and bow. He too was robbed of his beloved horse by the Russian Bolsheviks during the Second World War. Cruelty and stealing are the cornerstones of war.

You write that Ahmad Chaoush was a blood-sucking man and he kept calling your mother sister while he pillaged your home. He knew all about the cattle and animals and wanted to see them. But, first he kept wanting the household assets. Your father had built secret wells under the hayloft in the stables. There your family filled the wells with grain, weapons, and copper pans. Your mother relented and showed him all the secret spots. While Ahmad rubbed his beard he asked to be shown the cattle and other animals. He was told they were out pasturing in the fields and later in the day the shepherd would return them to the stable. She also told him that the animals were so obedient they would come home themselves at dusk and would he please let them in. Ahmad, sneering all the time, promised to help and because your family had been so good to him over the years he continued to promise that he would return everything once the exile was over. So in a way he was covered; he knew none of you would return ever again. Then Ahmad hurried your mother so that the outlaws would not harm her or the rest of you. Your mother begged Ahmad to let her take one donkey for her mother-in-law that was 85 and had great difficulty walking. She even told Ahmad that she would bury her when she passed away but to give her this one wish. This degenerate gave her permission to take her own animal. He warned her that the outlaws may not let her. She asked you to go and get the best donkey and hurry back to the house. You did as asked and you both loaded the sides of the donkey with some provisions, and sat your grandmother on top. I think of Jesus sitting on the back of a donkey with his reverence undiminished and so was my great-great-grandmother. You brought out your uncle the priest and made him change out of his vestments into regular clothes and you write, "We bade farewell to our thousands of years' patriarchal home. It was very hard to abandon our house. What else could we do? Some embraced the columns, some cried, screamed and groaned. How much could you tolerate? The Turkish outlaws beat the people on their heads. I could hear the blows, blows, blows, along with their whips."

Tell us Grandpa, let your sight be ours even though the pain of looking out is so great right now. You lived it; we should at least revisit it. After all it didn't really happen, say the Turks.

"While I held the loaded donkey's bridle, my Grandma seated on its back. She was motionless and confused; and did not know what to do or what direction to go. Suddenly, I saw people from four villages: Ghorghoulou, Srghayanou, Aprankou, and Tchekkhenetsou. They came and crowded our village. They were passing right in front of our door. I asked them, 'What's this? Where are you going?' 'Sonny, no one knows where we are going. The outlaws came to our place this morning and said we had to leave the village for three days. [I always wonder if the Turks chose three days for the villagers as a cruel joke. Christ rose after three days. Armenians practiced many of Christ's teachings. In a strange way a word can have power of reasoning even in a monstrous situation.] They dislodged us and drove us here.' One of them said to my mom, 'My sister, why are you weeping? Crying doesn't help. This is the last day of the Armenian nation. They can do whatever they want to'"—and so they did.

Now people of a total of five villages were pushed forward onto the Turks' evil path towards the river two kilometers from his village. The river was called Tougla. It flowed by the edges of Mamakhatoun then headed towards your ancestral home. It then curved the Black River that the Turks called Chara Chay flowing to Erzroum which was Armenian in name. Both the rivers' mouths, as you write, joined near the Kouter Bridge. Their black water washed the edges of Prize, Hoghekoun beneath the bridge of Kouter. The rivers then joined and continued to flow to Kyamakh.

Grandfather you were a brilliant child that no one knew about. Your ability for detail, and sequence linking is one of a scholar. You are great to me. In the early spring of each year after the snow thawed the river rose. It would get so high that it would be hard to cross the bridge. But now at the end of May in 1915 the water levels were lower. It was possible to cross the river now. You were one of the most spiritual men I ever knew. Yet, you never explained how you kept believing after what you saw. You write that it was dusk, the sun was still out and you could hear the people crying, and screaming. "That they were all confused; and who cared? God did not see the people's tears." People from Gyourjoulou and Sargharou had never seen such an inundation of people. But people of your village had seen such madness before. "The Turks began to force the people into the water by beating them. Boy, girls, brides, and mothers now embraced each other and cried, and begged. Nobody listened. Whoever could cross, came out to the other bank. Those who couldn't were drowned by suffocation. Their corpses rose to the surface of the river and floated. The barbaric Turks rushed into the bewildered folks and began to rob them. They forced them to be naked and began beating them on their heads with sticks and axes. They stripped them of all they had." I am hunched over holding my belly Grandpa; I feel them all inside. It is such a familiar ache in my belly but now I know why, now I see the hell you saw and I know what that faraway look in your eyes meant. I am with you right now but I pray for strength to keep going across the river with you. Shame on those weak human beings in Turkey who care more about their cruise line visitors than humanity. It sometimes seems as if they haven't changed one bit. They just hide it better.

"They took the nice looking Armenian girls and the women and laid them under stones and did whatever they wanted." Grandpa you still can't say the words raped and because you were so tender that you apologized in your diary for describing an animal by the word donkey. They also cut off their breasts for entertainment and would send them to their sick cohorts. "They took our donkey and threw my grandma down. My mother, a tall, strong, well-built woman embraced my grandma and took her to the opposite bank of the river. A priest was still alive and snuck across the river and my mother put more clothes on him so the Turks would not recognize that he was a priest. My mother than crossed the river once more to help us cross over to her side. She arranged us like a cord. Wives of uncles Zarneshan in the middle, Khanoum at the end. She told us, 'Hold each other by the hands, and call God for help.'"

How I wish I knew you Great-grandmother. I am with you and up in the sky watching again. You are comforting Grandpa's crying by telling everyone around you that they should not be scared, that nothing could hurt them in the water. Grandpa is holding you around your neck and you keep getting pulled under the water but you manage to help everyone get across like they were your ducks that were being guided to safety. I see a man named Martik; you write about him, Grandpa, because he has gone mad from all the murder and screams. He is drowning the Armenian women and the Turks are standing on the riverbank laughing at this insanity unfolding. He is killing his own people. Martik had gone to America for a vacation and now he was in the center of total destruction. Upon leaving you were robbed and now you were being murdered; of course you went mad. How could any mind process going to America for a vacation and returning home to a living hell? But slaughtering your own people must have been your only sick hope as you bled with their corpses and died. I hear cries and see nothing but death in the air as I watch my people shaking from the cold and being naked. Naked the one thing they could have kept was their virtue and that too was taken. The few girls with clothes on are being raped now. The Turks are raiding your souls and shouting, "You Armenians where is your Christ now, is He sleeping?"

Grandpa I didn't know you had to watch the girls and women being raped, and murdered. I know now why you wrote last in your diaries, "Goodbye dears, sweet light of my eyes, Goodbye oppressing world, live peacefully and happy, may your light remain ever living. Your loving parent Galoust." The savage Turks were shouting as they raped the girls that they should call their Christ to come save them. Darkness came and you write, "Raping continued until dark came. God's anger began. Clouds roared. Thunder and lightning beat us, rain poured on us. We sat in the mud until the morning dawned. God pitied us. The sky cleared up. The sun rose and God's heat began to warm us up. There were people who had jewelry with them. They buried them in the sand during the looting. My mom had some gold coins. We buried them in the earth and sat on it. In the morning they told us to pack and leave we could not unearth our gold coins. We couldn't even remember the hidden place anymore. Many others also couldn't locate their hidden wealth. The barbarians again came and began to undress the people, making them naked."

I am writing and no longer above the horror watching from the sky. I can only hover for a few minutes and then pain brings me back. I think it is my soul's way of seeing it as it really was, and my wanting to be near you all.

The Turk neighbor Ahmad Chaoush who stole all your familie's possessions had found your uncle the priest that had been in hiding behind the stone in the stable. His evil was by far the worst of all of these fiends and demonic plague worshippers. He actually came to where you all were being tortured and threw your dear uncle in front of you and shouted to your loved ones "Here, I got the *gyavour oghli gyavour*—the priest. He took his gun saying, "now I'll show you how to escape." He shot and killed him. Your 85 year old grandmother fell onto her last child's corpse. I hope someone Turkish that cares to know the truth and be merciful reads the words I write of just what these savage ancestors said, and knows what they mean. Again, I won't dignify it with a search. I know hatred by its actions more than by its words.

It was still morning and the Turks began to order you all to continue to move towards the Kouter's bridge. They now warned that the women and girls would be separated from the men. Your sister Oghik dressed you in some female vestments. It was well known that the boys were being driven to the slaughterhouse to become meat stock for the animals. The insanity continued and by noon a cart loaded with bread arrived from Mamakhatoun. Those that could walk were told they could take one piece of bread for the journey. They were in chains and movable fences to keep them together. These sick maladapted Turks actually said that they were a humane government and if anyone tried to run they would be shot on the spot. No one wanted to come near the bread even though they were starving. The Turks were randomly letting some people walk forward without the chains. They knew the people couldn't get away. One Turk took my great aunt Oghik's head covering off and said, "Go." Oghik held your hand and dragged you step by step by her side. She was one of the few still partially dressed and covered. The Armenian women covered their hair and face when in Turkey out of fear and custom. He uncloaked her cover and revealed her hair. You write that if it were not for her you would not have survived to write your diaries. By being able to write the truth you say, "I am my sweet, dear sister's savior." I still find it so unnerving that my aunt you named for your sister was the house you went to the day you were brutally killed by the hit and run driver. Why?

As you all walked you were told like a scene from the Bible that if any of you looked back you would be shot. You could not look back at your loved ones while you were herded forward. As you and your sister marched on you were spotted before you reached the Gouter bridge as a boy. Your sister had a necklace on her at that time, she had hidden it under her clothes. She took it off and gave it to the Turk and she begged him to leave you alone and she grabbed you and kept marching on until night when your remaining people arrived. All along the march people were shot if they stopped or sat down from fatigue. The village they brought you to was called Khorkhin village. I am sitting and still in shock from what I am feeling but I recognize this as an Armenian word. "Khorkhin"—I never heard of it but it feels Armenian. I later read that it was a depopulated village of Armenian homes, haylofts, and stables, that you were all starving and exhausted. The local people had been deported to Yerzenka. Armenians were lying on the ground calling out to God, the children were crying, so hungry and confused. They kept saying they were hungry.

I remember the pathetic attempt the Turks have made during my life to dare to say things like Armenians killed too. There were a few Turks that died, what a joke. I remember well when I was 13 years old. We were at the Armenian monument honoring our dead as we did every April 24th. No reporters in Montebello, no one locally cared; there were about a hundred Armenians walking to reach the monument. I saw my father turn crimson red with rage. It scared me; my mother was pulling him away from something that was happening nearby. I was so scared, he motioned to me with his eyes to something, and I did. I walked over to the crowd of Armenians standing around this Anglo man holding a sign which read, "Armenians killed too". I was crimson now but I really didn't know why or what to do. Grownups were all around me. I pushed through and went right up to this man and said, "Who is paying you to hold this sign?! You know nothing of what you say. You are too calm and relaxed. Who paid you?!" I was shouting at him and I will never forget his eyes looking at me calmly and throwing down the sign and walking away. I ran to my father and told him what I did and felt so proud that I could help. I felt I knew so much; I knew nothing, but felt everything.

You sat Grandpa on the ground with the starving children and watched people die in the streets. They laid down and died from exhaustion and hunger but mostly from broken hearts. You write that you saw mothers throwing their children into the black murky waters. You write how the children became the food for the fish. That the nightmare you were in was with real people.

My arms feel as heavy as lead. I drove today and felt bad that I left you all in the mud in the horror while I got rest last night. Grandpa you lived it and yet it is so hard to fathom this kind of diabolical madness. As I drove today I had a revelation. It was so clear and I felt free to pursue the obvious. I couldn't return to the mud and horror without something. I didn't know what it was then it hit me. You all have no graves you have nothing but Grandpa's diaries. I feel so close to you Great-grandmother and my dear Great-grandfather. I had to start a touch point on earth. You all perished for your unwavering faith. You refused to convert no matter the cost. I can't bury you, I have been carrying you all my whole life and this moment of insight just came and won't let go. I will donate to the church and when I give a certain level of a donation I can get a plaque and have it hung on the wall in the church alongside all the loved ones that others have written for. Their loved ones passed in this generation but who is to say I can't put one for you both. I can put you back together again side by side! I just sent off my request and my offering. You can both be in the Holy Church that is replicated from the sacred Apostolic Church in Echmiadzin. "In this tiny spot your names will be lit on earth. Beloved Tateos and his heroic wife Horopsima the parents of Galoust, Oghik and his other siblings. They are now Saints in Heaven 1915–2015."

The Armenian Pope declared on April 24, 2015 that those million and a half slaughtered Armenians are now proclaimed saints in Heaven. The number always is a round number. What if there were two million or two million and four people? Everyone counted. So, the brilliant Pope found a way to bury our dead. I will find the way to illuminate the dark path that politics have buried for so long. When I was thinking of your sister's brave and heroic gestures to save your life I realized with the oddest feeling of shame that she survived to help you because she wasn't one of the pretty ones. The evil Turks raped and buthered the youngest and prettiest. So much even in your time was about beauty. Yet my great aunt was angelic in her beauty and so important for she lives now through my writing because her beauty was one that lasted until now. My hand is frozen now my eyes are looking away I don't want to see this next part but I must look and feel and weep and find a way to lay you all down in your final resting place which is on these pages.

As your bodies warmed in the sun after the horror of the day before you could see bearded men creeping in among you. You saw a range of men from adolescence to elderly. They were searching for whatever they could find. They began to drag away the pretty girls and young brides. You could hear the girls screaming and begging to God. While they cried to the Heavens the Turks laid them down and did their monstrosities. There was no help to be found. You write that the raped girls and women could not raise their heads and would not look at their loved ones nearby because of their disgrace. Those Turks knew about Armenian traditions and the sacred virtue of their women. That is why their lowly barbaric vengeance was so final in its killing the spirit of my people. Grandpa you write how you heard these girls beg God to take their souls so that they could be saved from this disgrace.

Night fell again and you all laid in hell praying for deliverance. There was an Armenian woman amongst you all that people called "*Gzoghlan*" (bisexual). How such a word circulated in your time amazes me. Women had to be chase and I didn't even think you knew of such things. But this woman was older than all of you and you all knew she was from Sarghayan village. She was talking to some boys around your age and you wandered away from your own mother and went near the circle in discussion. There were about six young boys she was trying to convince to run away with her back to her village. She told them she would be able to place them with Turks and they would become laborers. She went on to say that they would work and live. If they did not go with her they would simply become martyrs, and victims. You were convinced by her words and you write that you separated from you mother, sister, and all your relatives. Once you parted you realized that this was foolish and wanted to head back to the death march. You knew that there was no home to go back to. You write how you began running and running to find them. Your family had gone as far as 10 kilometers.

"I didn't know how to run to reach my family. I began crying. Suddenly, I looked around my sides and what did I see? The most unspeakable, vicious, disgraceful scene I've ever seen in life. Every Turk and Kurd had forced and laid down young girls. Women were along the sides of the road where they were violated and raped. Those that resisted, were beaten, punched to death, and thrown aside along the road. I saw a girl naked, lying on her back. She was screaming, begging, 'Help me for God's sake!'

Who could come near? They would kill the rescuer right on the spot. I ran. Sometimes, I met acquaintances and asked them if they had seen my mother. The answer was 'No.' I now only ran without looking around until I found my mom, sister, and brothers. Breathless, I could hardly breathe. My mom, seeing me like a sheep who had lost and found her lamb, embraced me crying, 'Where were you? Where have you been? Why did you separate from us?' I explained to her everything that had taken place. I also thanked God for helping me find my family. We went on our black way. It was four or five o'clock in the evening and the sun hadn't set yet and we had already reached Jibijan Peak. At this point, mountaineer Kurds, young and old, came and mingled among us. They began looting and vandalizing the crowd. A Kurdish lad came up to me and said, 'Take off your shoes.' I didn't want to surrender. He knocked me down and took off my shoes and left. I remained barefoot.

"We descended a little into the abyss. It became dark. There was an inn there. We spent the night under its walls in the open forest. We laid there, thirsty, starved, and exhausted. My mom still had a little gruel. She found water and mixed and kneaded. She gave everybody some. We ate, and fell asleep. In the morning the Turks woke us up saying, 'Get up and move!' That night they didn't harm us and we were quiet. My mom gave us some gruel again. We ate and started on our way until evening came. Although we were exhausted and dead tired, we somehow reached the outside of the inn Khal Agha [Turkish words]. Even though the people had been driven such a long way, people continued to walk. They continued moving forward even though they had lost so many loved ones their children their parents. Those that couldn't walk anymore were shot and killed by the Turk gendarmes. Those beasts didn't even let you turn to take a glance at your beloved ones to see what had happened to them."

By the time you reached Hassan Khan the sun was setting; everybody who had survived gathered together. They didn't know it but they were trying to sort through the hell they were in by telling each other the fate of a loved one.

You heard them speak about acts that no one could find words for. How the Turks dragged a young wife and how a father was shot in the head because a Turk told him to walk one of their dogs and he was so exhausted that he couldn't. They talked of their sufferings and hunger.

I know now why you didn't let me find your diaries until you died. You wanted to protect me. You wanted to protect yourself. You knew how I wanted to know and wipe the pain from your heart. But you didn't want to remember anymore. Not until now do I weep remembering something you said to me just a week before you were killed. You whispered under your breath that you were remembering and reliving the genocide, you told me this on the phone and I just froze on the other end of the line. The American news kept showing the destruction in Armenia due to the massive earthquake in 1988, and the people were wailing and crying because most of their youth perished in the schools and colleges. I am so sorry that I never got to talk with you and hear the pain you guarded so well. Only in Washington did I quietly listen just enough to know you were there, you were a survivor. You never told the depth of hell you really survived. I spent 30 years listening to people's problems and their pain. Helping children that were autistic or just beautifully unique and brilliant but people didn't understand them. Autism was a dirty word when I started. Now the world knows its name. I don't regret one minute of the time I spent with strangers helping them fight for their life, strive for happiness, but I couldn't be let into any of your lives. I keep coming back to it because I am still so sad I couldn't help. Not yours, not my family, not anyone that I treasured. I dealt with the tidal wave of pain that I perceived from a young age along with the ghosts that visited and filled the rooms I was in. I kept learning and moving away from the tidal wave of pain in the stories of others. I was always working through invisible torment and as I write I realize I still am working it out.

I love life, I love humanity, I love those who want to learn and think of others, and yet I spent my life helping children rewire their pathways to look up and to look into my eyes and choose people. Now, everywhere I look people and children are looking down. They stare at their little phones that make lovely sounds in anticipation of something special.

The anticipation is the addicting hook. They are searching for messages and are distracted. If someone has to call someone else it took too long. I watch children in diapers playing on video games in restaurants and I think poor humanity. We are bored of our surroundings and yet all around the world humans are fighting for the freedom to just be in their surroundings.

Chapter Fifteen

SIGNS: THERE HAVE ALWAYS been signs in my life. Last night I was reeling from the utter powerlessness I felt in not being able to help those precious Armenian girls and women. I forced myself to watch some comedy. In the long run it didn't work: I was still shaken awake by all of you while I tried to sleep. It is O.K.; it has been a while since the night jolt awakenings. It literally feels like someone is shaking me awake but no one is there. I chose to watch an old episode of the comedy *30 Rock* hoping for some recall that would divert me back to my home. I have no right to complain and I am not, but it does feel like I am getting bolted to the paper by the pain I am watching. A very funny scene came on and I laughed, then I heard a sign. The actress says that the color of her hair is the same as her grandfather's shoes. I froze again. I had just written about that Kurdish (sometimes I have to use a lower case "t" or "k") teen that knocked down my poor grandfather who was still fighting for his rights by refusing to hand over his shoes. He gets knocked down and robbed yet again. My hair is the color of my grandfather's shoes. So is my heart, my spirit, my mind, my love.

When the 100th anniversary of the Armenian extermination came up this April 24, 2015, I felt so anticlimactic about it. A number makes it better? It has haunted me as well as thousands of others, every day of our lives. Not because we are dramatic; it is an unresolved homicide, a cold case for millions of people. It is loud: it has spread across the world and today doesn't change a thing. There needs to be walls that we can go to and write the names of our dead on. We can pay for it, and the last place I would want that wall is in Turkey. But maybe that is how reparation happens. The wall would be so long and wide if it were all in one place. I know Turkey is waiting for the rest of us to die off so all the names can be quieted and forgotten. It is working to some degree. Because a march and outcries are really just rituals on a larger scale, they comfort the living.

But there is still an abyss that separates us from the thousands of girls who laid there hoping for death on the sides of the roads. They were litter thrown out by true evil. Religion can be such a refuge for liars: Turkey which chooses to suppress their people by using prayer as an artifice for virtue and superiority.

I feel different today. I wrote in my appointment book "Great-grandfather Tateos and Great-grandmother Horopsima." You exist in my book and you will be real on the wall in our Holy Church with other Armenians. You are no longer obliterated.

I cannot believe how these evil men kept coming back each day and raping the pretty girls that survived. You write how they came back yet again to rape. You write how you spent the night near the inn and that in the morning a gang of Turks and Kurds came and they separated the children ages five through 15. They took away your brother Hovhannes. He was younger than you. Your sister had not dressed him in girl's clothes. One of the Turks had an impulse to feed little scraps of bread to the Armenian hostages he favored. It was as if they became his beaten and tortured pigeons. He almost gave you a scrap of bread Grandpa and another Turk stopped him and said, "You're pitying the gyavours. So, you are a gyavour get out of here!"

I realize this is it. That is why I will never step foot in Turkey. Where is your pity? The word is disgusting but needs to be said. Where is your embarrassment? Your empathy? You're taking responsibility and praying for all the thousands of Turks that participated in such barbarous crimes. You show how you still are a hating nation underneath your façade. Some people have all the luck even though they murder their own in the 21st century. Right now there are hundreds of Assyrian girls up in your mountains. If families don't have 20,000 Euros for their freedom they stay, they die, and they are raped. You can say it is a different group, not the Turks, but it is kept out of the newspapers, spoken only in Assyrian churches, and it is happening in your mountains. Is your strategic position in the world so amazing that you can be pardoned for centuries?

Mount Ararat is Armenian. You can't change the name because the Bible got it right the first time. This needs to be said just one more time.

"When we came down the hills we saw a terrible and vicious scene in the fields; corpses were scattered like melons and all of them were blackened.

The sun had made all the bodies sticky and decayed. The corpses' fat melted and flowed down to the ground, making rivulets.

"We had to walk across those corpses. We could see nothing; we blinded our eyes. In the evening we came to Yerzenka [a mountainous area]. We spent the night outside, under the walls of the city. Approximately half of the people remained there. My mom, my sister, and Voskian, the miller Kinos' wife from our village, who said, 'They took away my daughter.' Two sister in-laws embraced each other and wept bitterly. Salty bitter tears flew down their faces. They embraced my mom. My sister and I, both, cried and begged to God.

"Again the Turks, Kurds, mingled among us. A Turk hit my mom on her head saying, 'Why are you crying and weeping? Why are you so overly excited? Nothing has happened. Why don't you call your Christ to come rescue you from our hand? You will all die. We shall slaughter, we shall eradicate you all, no Armenian will survive. Do you understand?!'"

Horop we are with you. Anyone who is reading this is with you now. The whole world sees the secret filth that the Turks scattered like chards of glass in people's souls. I will go to church and put flowers on the floor beneath your name. I will never forget you. We will never forget how you carried gruel and fed your loved ones while they were being slaughtered. You are what a true Armenian woman is, and not what I see in the 21st century. There are a few who relish in being vulgar, and shock attracts humans. They are not intelligent but they can be the best vulgar people carrying the Armenian name. People like you, fade and disappear because character is what lasts not senseless stupidity.

"In the morning, at sunrise, they drove away the people again. Many people left their toddler babies and elderly under the walls; and many old, sick people remained there. They drove us to the center of the city. They ordered us to sit... rest. Turks came near to us, but they did not mingle among us. Turk, Kurd, lads, bribed the guards to come to chase the girls and women that were left.

"I remember it as if it were like today. A well-dressed Turk talked to the guard and mingled among us. Aperketsi Abbot's daughter in-law was sitting near us. We knew her.

"A rather nice looking woman she was. The Turk came up to her and held her by the hand; but, she resisted. The Turk talked to her and forcibly took her away saying, 'Why don't you come with me? A little farther and they will drive you into the water.'"

I'm remembering another friend. I loved her dearly; I grew up with her during my college days. She was a very religious Muslim and I of course a religious Armenian. Our difference in faith never was a problem. How can one judge a person who functions purely in their day-to-day lives with virtue and prays five times a day? It is the opposite of violence and hatred. I admired her. I still do. The only difference was that I had a very distinct feeling that I was "less than," no matter what I did in the friendship. Same experience with this friend too: I knew if I had converted to being a Muslim we would be sisters. She called me sister but deep down I knew I wasn't. I really lived among her people for decades. I covered in their country, I felt safe, I loved the stopping of commerce and people falling to their knees and praying to God. It was the most important thing of all. However, there was no tolerance for Christianity even in this beautiful country. Nowhere could you put a cross or go to church. It was stifling. Only once did I hear her say that her grandmother had a tattoo of a cross on her and she asked once if she were Christian and she was struck across the face by that same grandmother.

Looking back I now know why I spent all this time being treated nicely but "less than." Only later did I learn about the auctions. I saw the pictures of Armenian girls sold all over the middle east for $5.00 in American money. They had tattoos across the face and neck. This way it would never be hidden that they were Christian. Yes, many Armenian girls were beautiful and they still are. I saw these pictures during my research for my thesis which was on the Armenian Genocide.

I also did a study which had 145 questions and was administered to Middle Eastern Armenian women, Russian Armenian women and American Armenian women. The ages varied, and the names remained anonymous, though I recognized my mother's handwriting. How I thought of those questions I will never know. It came from my ancestors and my DNA. The main thing I learned was that all three types of backgrounds suffered the same malady, myself included. They could still hear the echoes of Ghosts from the Armenian extermination.

I am back with you Grandpa I had to go for just a while. I am sitting next to you and I am a ghost right now. I see your mother pull some scraps of lavash from her apron. How did she do this? I love her more each day.

She is passing them quietly to you like they were old relics, you write. You ask her to have some. She begins weeping and quietly says, "That is for you." About an hour later they began to drive you all towards Kamakh.

I call out to the Turk who is perhaps reading this and sneering or reading this and remembering the towns he or she learned about in school. I know you know this happened but all your history books are void of the first massive murderous campaign your country embarked on in the 20th century. When I wrote my thesis on the Armenian genocide I only used non-Armenians as historical support. So if I am lucky and one of you Turkish citizens are reading this right now, go and look up what Hitler told his troops before he annihilated Poland. He wanted to comfort his troops that were scared of the level of destruction they were about to do. So, to motivate them to kill and destroy a nation he said, "I have issued the command—and I'll have anybody who utters but one word of criticism executed by a firing squad—that our war aim does not consist in reaching certain lines, but in the physical destruction of the enemy. Accordingly, I have placed my death-head formations in readiness—for the present only in the east—with orders to them to send to death mercilessly and without compassion, men, women, and children of Polish derivation and language. Only thus shall we gain the living space [*Lebensraum*] which we need. Who, after all, speaks today of the annihilation of the Armenians?" (Adolf Hitler, August 22, 1939.)

But oh do I love what the American-Armenian author William Saroyan said, "Go ahead, destroy Armenia. See if you can do it… I should like to see any power of the world destroy this race, this small tribe of unimportant people, whose wars have all been fought and lost, whose structures have crumbled, literature is unread, music is unheard, and prayers are no more answered. Go ahead, destroy Armenia. See if you can do it. Send them into the desert without bread and water. Burn their homes and churches. Then see if they will not laugh, sing, and pray again. For when two of them meet anywhere in the world, see if they will not create a New Armenia."

As I sit sifting through mountains of research and finding my loose documents I got in Washington so long ago I sigh and think I have been a broken Armenian born in Detroit. I who was given freedom at birth have spent my whole life trying to piece together proof and hope that I could tell the story and help my loved ones who perished. I found the proclamation that went up before the extermination. During my research I was able to locate copies of telegrams sent by Turkish officials asking how the extermination was going? Literally ending the telegram with question marks. I have to think: good, kid, I had the smoking gun. But I also think: who cares. Does anyone really care? Or will they say another fanatic just obsessed with the past? So, if this page is lucky enough to be in the hands of a Turkish person in Turkey who was part of that very silly day in Turkey on April 24, 2015 and took the part of Turks who died too (which isn't the topic folks), read on.

"Telegram of English Translation regarding progress of the Armenian massacre.
    Ministry of Internal Affairs
    Superintendent of the Imperial Possessions No. 33
    Director of Office, date of dispatch
    April 21 (1915), hour: 3, minute: 43
    Director of Information: Mehmen Fakhri
    Place of dispatch: Erzerum No, 2597,
    Number of words: 20, charge: 36.
    To his Excellency Sabit Bey, Governor General of El-Azia No. 5, to be delivered to Nazim Bey
    Are the Armenians deported from there wiped out?
    Are the dangerous persons massacred
    Or only expelled from the town and deported?
    Let me know it clearly, my brother.
    April 21, 1915
    April 21, 1915 at Erzerum
    The President for the Special Organization:
    Behaeddin Shakir."

Just in case you would like to research it yourself this was a photostatic telegram in the file of the martial court; signed by Dr. Dehaeddin Shakir Bey, President of the Special Organization. The telegram is addressed, through the Agency of Tahsin Bey, Vali of Erzerum, to Sabit Bey, Vali of Harpout, to be delivered to Nazem of Resne, Executive Delegate of the Union and Progress Party in Mamouret-Ul-Aziz.

    If I am lucky enough to have a Turkish reader I want you to know that I know you weren't there. That you are part of my own humanity. But, if the tables were turned I would be mortified that my ancestry could do such a thing. I would be donating and helping you in every way that I could because I would want the world to know that the one thing that distinguishes us from other animals is our ability for reconciliation. How silly that as I write I am still wanting to prove that it happened because all my life that is what I was taught to do. Stand up for my people. But, I am American and proud of it. I am not proud that my country has to bow to some ugly force. That is truly Un-American. How is it that I saw postcards that the Bush administration sent just like the Reagan administration saying, "Vote for me and I will help the Armenian cause." The second they get elected it disappears again.

When I attended the 70th anniversary of the Armenian Genocide which was the only time in history that the survivors flew in from all over the globe; around the corner was the *Washington Post* newspaper. We were in the heart of Washington D.C. and guess what? It is 1985, and the event didn't make it to the last page of the paper. When I was in Washington I met individuals that assisted me in locating copies of letters dated August 12, 1915. I was able to locate a letter sent by the Honorable Henry Morgenthau, American Ambassador in Constantinople. At the top of the once classified document it read: "Classification cancelled authority letter of 1-8-58 from W. H. Anderson State Depart." (See page 134 for a facsimile of the letter and page 135 for the transcript.)

In this letter Walter Morgenthau actually sent the American State department a copy of the proclamation that went up everywhere in Turkey and neighboring areas. He stated that it was put up in public areas notifying Armenians that they had five days to turn over all their property to the Turkish government. It is worth reading at least once in our lives. In the Smithsonian 100th anniversary photo exhibit one of Walter Morgenthau's photos glare out as they depict rows and rows of dead bodies.

"Honorable Henry Morgenthau
   American Ambassador,
   Constantinople
   Sir:
   I have the honor to enclose herewith for the information of the Embassy a copy of the proclamation which has been posted up in public places by the local authorities notifying the Armenians that within five days from its date, namely, on July 1st, the entire Armenian population of Trebisond and vicinity including men, women, and children will be obliged to turn

over to the government such property as they cannot take to turn over to
the government such property as they cannot take with them and start
for the interior, probably for Kidjesireh or Momul where they will remain
until the end of the war. Upon their return after the war their goods will
be returned to them."

"It is impossible to convey an idea of the consternation and despair the
publication of this proclamation has produced upon the people. I have
seen strong, proud, wealthy men weep like children while they told me
that they had given their boys and girls to Persian and Turkish neighbors.
I know of one Armenian woman who is now in Dr. Crawford's house who
has become insane and two other such cases are reported in the same
vicinity. Many are providing themselves with poison which they will take
in case the order is not rescinded."

He then included the proclamation and begged President Wilson for
help. Help that didn't come.

There are so many more truths open to anyone who can bear to learn.
An Armenian student followed the leader of the Turkish extermination
whose name was Talaat Pasha all over the world after the genocide. It is
documented that he found this death mask of a man in Berlin and killed
him. He was freed on the grounds that Talaat Pasha was a free criminal
and he ordered the death and destruction along with Turkish extremists
Enver and Jermal. This Armenian college boy wasn't a murderer; he was a
haunted lost soul who couldn't rest until there was some justice.

Lord Bryce simply said, "Worse than any other." He knew how Turks
bound and murdered all the Armenian intellectuals, doctors, and leaders
by upside-down crucifixions. He knew that Armenian children were put
in garbage collecting trucks alive and thrown down the sides of hills. The
psychotic madness was so widespread that reports were coming in from
all over the world. When I was in Washington searching for evidence I
was finding so much that I had to take breaks so I could breathe. When
I recently found my old thesis I was shocked at all the horrors I reported
and then blocked out. I really did only use non- Armenians as my source.
I am forcing myself to put an excerpt that really helps show the ignorance
of Turkey's leaders. Turkish Ambassador Sukru Eleday declared in late
1981 to the Los Angeles World Affairs Council: "The accusations that the
Ottoman Turks [there is that ridiculous word again, accusation] sixty-five
years ago, during World War I, perpetuated systematic massacres of the

Armenian population in Turkey, to annihilate them and to seize their homeland is totally baseless." (CCIA, p.14.)

Wow, thank you for looking like a fool once again. America shields your atrocities but the rest of the world does not. He had it right and just needed to say, "I am sorry for my ancestors." Six words.

Winston Churchill described the Armenian Genocide in his work *The World Crisis* (1929): "In 1915 the Turkish Government began and ruthlessly carried out, the infamous general massacre and deportation of the Armenians in Asia Minor... the clearance of the race from Asia Minor was about as complete as such an act, on a scale so great, could well be. It is supposed that one and a quarter million of Armenians were involved, of whom more than half perished. There is no responsible doubt that his was planned and executed for political reasons."

In the official British *Blue Book*, Lord Bryce directed the compiling of information by historian, Arnold Toynbee:

"One can clearly see and feel the absolute hellish horror experienced by Armenians. Murder by bullet would have been a gift in comparison to what took place... In Harpout and Mezre the people have had to endure terrible tortures. They have had their eyebrows plucked out, their breasts cut off, their nails torn off; their torturers hew off their feet or else hammer nails into them, just as they do shoeing horses. This is all done at night time, and in order that the people may not hear their screams and know their agony the soldiers are stationed round the prisons, beating drums and blowing whistles... Harpout has become the cemetery of the Armenians."

Pope Francis was the one who had the courage all the way in Rome to shake open the vault that keeps getting closed. He got so much hassle for saying the truth. The Turks said they felt betrayed by him. Seriously? I still wonder why is it such a big deal to just say the truth. I turn the page and see on page eight on world news the far away look and pathetic words again! Mevlut Cavushoglu, Turkey's Foreign Minister, dismissed the comments as baseless. How is it that you can say such a bizarre comment with the same empty expression in 2015? Thanks to your callous inhuman response 100 years later, I dug up all the truth once again. If help is what you need, here it is. If you are that powerful that you can use words like baseless in 2015, I will never step foot in your world. Hopefully, you will not step in mine.

So, now that you have our land, our Holy Mountain, our churches that you chopped off and turned into mosques, you still haven't learned one bit. Now that is scary all the way here in sunny Los Angeles. Don't get me wrong; I am shuddering as I write, which is still weird. Your refusal to look in your past makes me feel like you are all still monsters underneath your nice suits. You all told my relatives my grandfather directly heard the same vulgar words. "Don't cry, nothing is happening." So, thanks to you I had to take my second self out of the boxes and into my life again. William Soroyan was really right: you just can't kill off these people no matter how hard you try. So, the more you deny the more you birth a nation. Thank you.

In case you don't read the papers I have included some frontpage papers from everywhere but Turkey during their extermination. Dear Turkey, to help you have a base, please read on. If you can.

The New York Times

MARCH 10, 1915

PREDICT A MASSACRE

Missionaries Arriving Here Make Charges Against the Turks.

American missionaries, who arrived yesterday from Jerusalem, via Piraeus,

MARCH 22, 1915

TURKS RENEW MASSACRES.

Sixty Christian Families in Village North of Smyrna Slain.

Special Cable to THE NEW YORK TIMES.
ATHENS, March 22. (Dispatch to the London Daily News.)—Additional Christian massacres are reported from the neighborhood of Aivali, on the Anatolian coast north of Smyrna.

Sixty families in the village of Kimerli were massacred.

MARCH 20, 1915

WHOLE PLAIN STREWN BY ARMENIAN BODIES

Turks and Kurds Reported to Have Massacred Men, Women and Children.

APRIL 18, 1915

TURKEY'S DREAM OF POWER.

Hopes by Alliance with Germany to Regain Lost Position in World.

Turkey dreams of regaining the Austro-German alliance of a world power, according

MAY 18, 1915 (3:4)

...DO ARMENIANS KILLED.

Turkish and Kurdish Atrocities a Van Rival Those of 1895.

Special Cable to THE NEW YORK TIMES.
LONDON, May 17.—Six thousand Armenians have been massacred at Van in Armenia, Asiatic Turkey, according to a dispatch received

APRIL 20, 1915

VON DER GOLTZ TO LEAD TURKS

German Field Marshal Will Head First Turkish Army.

CONSTANTINOPLE, April 19, (via London.)—Field Marshal Baron von der Goltz has been appointed commander... First Turkish Army.
...Field Marshal recently ...stantinople from Ber... went, according to ...many to send an army

The New York Tim

MONDAY, APRIL 26, 1915

KURDS MASSACRE MORE ARMENIANS

All Inhabitants in Ten Villages Near Van Said to Have Been Killed.

APPEAL SENT TO WILSON

By Head of Church—Evidences of Fearful Outrages Seen in Deserted Settlements.

STORY OF GREAT EXODUS

Flight from Persia Full of Suffering for Thousands Who Escaped the Sword.

APRIL 28, 1915.

APPEAL TO TURKEY TO STOP MASSACRES

Ambassador Morgenthau Instructed to Make Representations on Request of Russia.

WASHINGTON, April 27.—
for relief of Armenian C)

MAY 1, 1915 (1:7)

KURDS RENEW MASSACRES.

Attacks on Christians in Armenia Become Violent.

JULFA, Transcaucasia, April 20, via Petrograd and London, April 30.—A renewal of the recent massacres of Christians in Armenia is in progress in the whole district of Lake Van. Conflicts between the Armenians and Kurds are rapidly becoming more desperate. An encounter occurred today at Shahtakt.

MAY 10, 1915

MISSIONARIES IN VAN IN DANGER.

Americans in Van Threatened as Turks Overcome Armenians.

TIFLIS, (via London,) May 10.—American missionaries in the Vilayet of Van, where the Armenians appear to be weakening after a fierce resistance against attacking Turks and Kurds, are reported in grave danger.

The American missions are in the eastern suburbs of the village, where for fourteen days the hundred Armenian boys and girls and thirty American citizens have taken refuge in this quarter of the town.

The Turks have fired 17,000 shells upon the defenders in the fighting the last few days.

MAY 15, 191...

102

The New York Times

JULY 15, 1915

SEES GERMAN OFFICERS EVERYWHERE IN TURKEY

the Turks intend to retreat from that point. The Turks distributed 40,000 rifles among Kurds in Mush Valley for use against Armenians. Notwithstanding massacres and epidemics, the Armenians are resisting bravely. Their forces have been strengthened by the arrival of 100 Armenian volunteers from America.

JULY 19, 1915

SAYS GERMANS RULE TURKS.

Constantinople Under Sway of General von der Goltz, Says American.

Hugh Nettle, a Baltimore business man.

JULY 29, 1915

WHOLESALE MASSACRES OF ARMENIANS BY TURKS

AUGUST 4, 1915

REPORT TURKS SHOT WOMEN AND CHILDREN

Nine Thousand Armenians Massacred and Thrown Into Tigris, Socialist Committee Hears.

PARIS, Aug. 2.—B. Veradate, a member of

AUGUST 18, 1915

ARMENIANS ARE SENT TO PERISH IN DESERT

Turks Accused of Plan to Exterminate Whole Population—People of Karahissar Massacred.

Special Cable to

PLEAS FOR ARMENIANS.

State Department Inundated with Appeals for Their Protection.

WASHINGTON, May 14.— Replies are being prepared today at the Department to a flood of communications from various parts of the country that steps be taken to protect Christians in Armenian regions under Turkish control. Assurances will be given that the State is doing and will do all possible to aid the Armenian rep— been attacked.

JULY 17, 1915

TIED IN SACKS, DROWNED.

Old Punishment Revived for Enemies of Those in Power in Turkey.

Special Cable to THE NEW YORK TIMES.

ATHENS, July 16. (Dispatch to The London Daily Chronicle.)—Recently the Turkish Government expelled all —

JULY 15, 1915

ASK AID FOR ARMENIANS.

Relief Committee Tells of Sufferings Due to War.

appeal for aid for destitute non-combatants of Armenia was issued yesterday by the American Armenian Re—

JULY 29, 1915

REPORTED MASSACRES IN ARMENIA

VISCOUNT BRYCE asked the Lord President of the Council whether his Majesty's Government had any information regarding the massacres of the Christian inhabitants which were reported to have been committed by the Turks in the districts of Zeitum, Mush, Diarbekir, Bitlis, and elsewhere in the region inhabited by the Armenians; and regarding a

AUGUST 6, 1915

ARMENIAN HORRORS GROW.

Massacres Greater Than Under Abdul Hamid, London Paper Says.

Special Cable to THE NEW YORK TIMES.

LONDON, Friday, Aug. 6.The Daily Chronicle s— "A tragic—

BURN 1,000 ARMENIANS.

Turks Lock Them in a Wooden Building and Then Apply the Torch.

LONDON, Friday, Aug. 20.—A Reuter dispatch from Petrograd says:

"Almost unbelievable details of Turkish massacres of Armenians in Bitlis have reached Petrograd.

"In one village 1,000 men, women and children are reported to have been locked in a wooden building and burned to death.

"In another large village only thirty-six persons, it is said, escaped massacre.

"In still another instance it is asserted several scores of men and women were tied together by chains and thrown into Lake Van."

The Outlook

AN ILLUSTRATED WEEKLY JOURNAL
OF CURRENT EVENTS

OUTLOOK MAGAZINE [AUGUST 18, 1915]

THE ARMENIANS IN ASIA MINOR

On July 28, in the British House of Lords, the Earl of Crewe, Lord President of the Council, replying to a question by Viscount Bryce concerning the killing of Christians in Armenia, said that such crimes had increased both in number and in degree of atrocity. The Armenians have often suffered outrage and massacre, and the present war offers a new opportunity for oppression.

As far back as last January some one hundred thousand persons from the Turkish and

THE ARMENIANS IN PERSIA

We have been so accustomed to thinking of the Armenians as resident only in Turkey that we often lose sight of the fact that they also live in Russia and in Persia. The news which comes to hand from Persia is as ghastly in its detail as that which has been received from Asia Minor. The city of Salmast, for instance, has been completely destroyed by the Kurds. One of the survivors writes:

Hundreds of old people and children remained behind in the ill-omened "Valley of Blood,"

The New York Times

(3·3)

AUGUST 27, 1915

SEPTEMBER 3, 1915

TURKS DEPOPULATE TOWNS OF ARMENIA

Traveler Reports Christians of Great Territory Have Been Driven from Homes

600,000 STARVING ON ROAD

Adds That More Than 100,000 Greeks Have Been Deported from the Mediterranean Coast.

TURKS MASSACRE ARMENIANS OF ISMID

Burn the Asia Minor Port, Only 56 Miles from Constantinople.

LONDON, Sept. 2.—A dispatch to the Exchange Telegram Company from Athens says:

"Travelers arriving from Constantinople announce that on Friday last Turks burned the town of Ismid and massacred a large number of the Armenian inhabitants."

Ismid lies at the head of the Gulf of Ismid in Asia Minor, about fifty-six miles southeast of Constantinople. It has been the residence of both Greek and Armenian Archbishops. Its population is about 25,000.

The New York Times

(3:1)

SEPTEMBER 17, 1915

SEPTEMBER 5, 1915

MISSION BOARD TOLD OF TURKISH HORRORS

Correspondents Confirm the Reports of the Wiping Out of Armenians.

SCATTERED OVER EMPIRE

Christian Cities Cease to Exist as Such and Inhabitants Are Driven Far from Home.

SEPTEMBER 17, 1915

THE DEATH OF ARMENIA.

Her Land Has Been Devastated and the Few Survivors Driven Out.

To the Editor of The New York Times:

The deliberate murder of a nation is taking place in this twentieth century. Turkey is now in the act of murdering Armenia, and she has almost completed her work. There are no ablebodied male Armenians left anywhere in Turkey. They have either

SEPTEMBER 18, 1915

SEVERAL AMERICAN MISSIONARIES DEAD

And Survivors Reach Petrograd from Armenia After Terrible Sufferings on the Way.

1,500,000 ARMENIANS STARVE

Relief Committee Asks Aid for Victims of Turkish Decrees.

The American Armenian Relief Fund Committee has received two letters from Constantinople describing the horrors to which the Armenian Christians in Turkey are being subjected. One letter, dated June 15, says in part:

"The Turkish Government is executing today the plan of scattering the Armenians of the Armenian provinces, profiting from the troubles of the European powers and from the acquiescence of Germany and Austria.

"These people are being removed without any of their goods and chattels, and to places where the climate is totally unsuited to them. They are left without shelter, without food, and without clothing, depending only upon the morsels of bread which the Government will throw before them, a Government which is unable even to feed its own troops.

"It is impossible to read or to hear, without shedding tears, even the meagre details of these deportations. Most of the families have traveled on foot, old men and children have died on the way, young women in child-birth have been left on mountain passes, and at least ten deaths a day are recorded among them even in their place of exile victims of hunger and sickness. It has not been possible as yet to forward any help to Sultanieh, owing to the interdiction of the Government, in spite of the efforts of the American Ambassador, whose philanthropic and generous endeavors in aid of the Armenians are gratefully acknowledged."

The second letter, dated July 12, says:

"The condition of the Armenians is extremely aggravated since my last letter. It is not the Armenian population of Cilicia only which has been deported wholesale and exiled to the deserts. Armenian communities from all the provinces of Armenia, from Erzerum, Trebizond, Sivas, Harput, Bitlis, Van, and Diarbekir, also from Samsun, Caesarea, and Urfa—a population of 1,500,000 are marching today, the stick of forced pilgrimage in hand, toward the Mesopotamian wilderness, to live among Arabian and Kurdish savage tribes. Very few of them will be able to reach the spots designated for their exile, and those who do will perish from starvation, if no immediate relief reaches them.

"It is in the name of a starving population of 1,500,000 that urgent appeals should be made to the charitable public of America."

The Armenian Relief Fund Committee believes that unless immediate aid is forthcoming future efforts will be unavailing. The Treasurers of the committee are Brown Brothers Co., 59 Wall Street.

The New York Times

SEPTEMBER 25, 1915

BRYCE ASKS US TO AID ARMENIA

Says That All the Christians in Trebizond, Numbering 10,000, Were Drowned.

WOMEN SEIZED FOR HAREMS

Only Power That Can Stop the Massacres Is Germany, and We Might Persuade Her to Act.

LONDON, Sept. 20.—Viscount Bryce,

SAYS EXTINCTION MENACES ARMENIA

Dr. Gabriel Tells of More Than 450,000 Killed In Recent Massacres.

600,000 DRIVEN INTO EXILE

Unless Neutral Powers Intervene, Says Nubar Pasha, Almost the Whole People Is Doomed.

Dr. M. Simbad Gabriel, President of the Armenian General Progressive Association in the United States told a

The Independent

HAMILTON HOLT
Editor

HAROLD HOWLAND
Associate Editor

... ...
Literary Editor

EARL T. & HOWLAND
President

FREDERIC E. DICKINSON
Secretary

WESLEY W. ...
Treasurer

FOUNDED 1848

Independent Magazine
September 27, 1915

SEPTEMBER 24, 1915

500,000 ARMENIANS SAID TO HAVE PERISHED

THE DEPOPULATION OF ARMENIA

THE shocking news of the massacre, torture and deportation of Armenian Christians makes a special appeal to American sympathy and helpfulness. From numerous and reliable sources in Turkey it seems certain that this is not a matter of local disorders or petty oppression, but a systematic effort to extirpate the Armenian race. Thousands of families have been driven from their homes to starve upon the roads. Towns and villages have been divested of their inhabitants. Many are being put to torture to force them to renounce their Christian faith. Women are interned in the harems and children are sold as slaves.

Washington Asked to Stop Slaughter of Christians by Turks and Kurds.

Special to The New York Times.

WASHINGTON, Sept. 23.—Charles R. Crane of Chicago, a Director of Roberts College, Constantinople, and James L. Barton of Boston, Foreign Secretary of the American Board of Commissioners for Foreign Missions, visited the State Department today and confer...

The New York Times

(5:6,7)
SEPTEMBER 27, 1915

TALES OF ARMENIAN HORRORS CONFIRMED

Committee on Atrocities Says 500,000 Victims Have Suffered Already.

NATIONAL PROTEST URGED

Suggestion That Germany and Austria Be Held Responsible—Out-

TELL OF HORRORS DONE IN ARMENIA

Report of Eminent Americans Says They Are Unequaled in a Thousand Years.

TURKISH RECORD OUTDONE

ARMENIAN WOMEN PUT UP AT AUCTION

Refugee Tells of the Fate of Those in Turkish Hands.

SEPTEMBER, 30, 1915

WHOLESALE MURDER IN ARMENIA.

EXTERMINATING A RACE.

TALAAT BEY'S TREACHERY.

SEPTEMBER 30, 1915

ARMENIAN OFFICIALS MURDERED BY TURKS

Special Cable to THE NEW YORK TIMES.
LONDON, Sept. 29.—The Cairo correspondent of The Times, in a dispatch dated Sept. 27, says:
Confirmation has reached here of reports of Armenian atrocities of a nauseating and appalling character. Un-

ENTIRE VILLAGES SCATTERED

Men and Boys Massacred, Women and Girls Sold as Slaves and Distributed Among Moslems.

A Policy of Extermination Put in Effect Against a Helpless People.

The Outlook

OUTLOOK MAGAZINE
[Sept. 29, 1915]

THE TURKISH ATROCITIES IN ARMENIA

The New York Times

WEDNESDAY, OCTOBER, 6, 1915.

GERMAN DIRECTED THE TURKS AT VAN

Dr. Yarrow Says He Saw Him at Head of Troops Who Shelled the Armenians.

RED CROSS NO PROTECTION

And American Flags on the Mission Buildings Were Used as Targets, Returning Missionary Says.

Sixteen missionaries from Van, Turkish Armenia, arrived here yesterday on the Scandinavian-American liner Hellig Olav. They are members of the mission established by the American Board of Commissioners for Foreign Missions, and confirmed the reports that the Turks and Kurds are waging a "holy war" against the Armenians.

OCTOBER 7, 1915

MORGENTHAU GIVING RELIEF

American Consuls Will Also Do What They Can to Aid Armenians.

WASHINGTON, Oct. 5 —Many Armenians in this country have communi-

The New Yo

OCTOBER 7, 1915

800,000 ARMENIANS COUNTED DESTROYED

Viscount Bryce Tells House of Lords That Is the Probable Number of Turks' Victims.

10,000 DROWNED AT ONCE

Peers Are Told How Entire Christian Population of Trebizond Was Wiped Out.

ALREADY HAS $75,000 TO HELP ARMENIANS

Rockefeller Foundation Leads Donations to American Committee with $30,000.

The Nation

NATION MAGAZINE
OCTOBER 7, 1915

FOR ARMENIA

SURVEY MAGAZINE
OCTOBER 16, 1915

ARMENIAN APPEAL TO AMERICA FOR HELP

INHUMANITY AND RUTHLESSNESS, not of enemy invaders but of government officials, have spurred the latest appeal for American relief funds. This plea comes from the American Committee on Armenian Atrocities, consisting of Samuel T. Dutton, Cleveland H. Dodge, Rabbi Stephen S. Wise, Freder-

Thereafter cannon were trained on the Armenian quarter, while the Armenians on their side fortified their houses and dug trenches about them. Meanwhile 100,000 to 150,000 refugees from neighboring villages fled to Van before the Turks. Many of these were former orphans housed at the mission. Among them were little children treated at the mission hospital for dagger slashes in the abdomen.—Oct

74
HAMILTON HOLT
Editor

HAROLD HOWLAND
Associate Editor

EDWIN E. SLOSSON
Literary Editor

The Independent

FOUNDED 1848

KARL V. S. HOWLAND
President

FREDERIC E. DICKINSON
Secretary

WESLEY W. FERRIN
Treasurer

October 18, 1915

THE ASSASSINATION OF A RACE

THE HOPES AND THE THREATENED FATE OF THE ARMENIANS

THE Armenians in Turkey before the present onslaught upon them numbered about two millions, but their importance in the empire is not to be measured by their numbers. Intellectually and physically they are vastly superior

Just at the time when it seems that the tyranny of the Turk is about to be broken and the submerged Christian peoples given an opportunity to develop a national life of their own, the terrible news comes to us that the Armenians are being massacred

power to stay the gruesome tide of death, and we note with gratification that the public sentiment stirred by a knowledge of this tragedy is moving the President to protest in the name of humanity against such crimes against civilization.

New York Times

(3:2)

OCTOBER 18, 1915

Only One Man and One Woman Dissent from Resolutions Denouncing Outrages.

THOUSANDS PROTEST ARMENIAN MURDERS

TURKS HAVE KILLED 500,000

Evidence, Taken from State Department, Shows Quarter of a Million Women Violated.

The New York Times

OCTOBER 22, 1915

ONLY 200,000 ARMENIANS NOW LEFT IN TURKEY

More Than 1,000,000 Killed, Enslaved or Exiled, Says a Tiflis Paper.

TIFLIS, Transcaucasia, Oct. 19 (via Petrograd and London, Oct. 21).—The estimate is made by the Armenian newspaper Mshak that of the 1,200,000 Armenian inhabitants of Turkey before the war there remain not more than 200,000. This residue, the Mshak says, may disappear before the end of the war, on account of the Turkish policy of extermination.

The figures of the Mshak are based on the estimate of the Armenian Patriarch at Constantinople that 850,000 Armenians have been killed or enslaved by the Turks, in addition to which 200,000 Armenians are believed to have fled to Russia.

DECEMBER 9, 1915

POPE MAY MAKE NEW PLEA TO KAISER

T. P. O'Connor Hears He Will Be Asked to Take Action to Save the Armenians.

BRITISH COMMITTEE ACTIVE

Resolves to Work On Despite the Terrible Events That Have Stopped Its Work for Armenia.

Attempts to Send Food to Refugees Frustrated, Says the American Committee.

(1:2)
OCTOBER 26, 1915

SLAY ALL ARMENIANS IN CITY OF KERASUNT

Turks Wipe Out Entire Population in Town on the Black Sea.

LONDON, Tuesday, Oct. 26.—A dispatch to The Daily Mail from Odessa says:

"The Turks have massacred the entire Armenian population of Kerasunt (11, 6:5)

DECEMBER 12, 1915

WOMAN DESCRIBES ARMENIAN KILLINGS

German Missionary Says Turks Proclaimed Extermination as Their Aim.

FIENDS' WORK IN HARPUT

"Let Your Christ Help You!" the Cry as Torture Went On— Dr. Knapp a Victim.

(4:2)
NOVEMBER 1, 1915

AID FOR ARMENIANS BLOCKED BY TURKEY

PUTS VICTIMS AT 1,000,000

Careful Survey Shows 55,000 Persons Killed in the Vilayet of Van Alone.

110

The New York Times

(4:4)

SATURDAY, NOVEMBER 27, 1915.

ARMENIANS' HEROIC STAND IN MOUNTAINS

Men, Women, and Children Fought with Knives, Scythes, and Stones.

ALL FINALLY EXTERMINATED

Women Who Had Plunged Knives Into Turks Afterward Killed Themselves—Bryce Gets Report.

DECEMBER 10, 1915

MORE AID FOR ARMENIANS.

Relief Committee Issues Another Call for Funds.

Samuel T. Dutton, Secretary of the American Committee for Armenian and Syrian Relief, said yesterday that, although more than $100,000 had been sent to the sufferers, more relief was needed. He also said that the British and American committees were working together.

"... ... O'Connor, ... a member

JANUARY 15, 1916

500 ARMENIANS SLAIN UNDER TURKISH ORDER

Forced by Cold and Hunger to Surrender, Men, Women, and Children Were Put to Death.

LONDON, Jan. 14.—Armenian refugees arriving at Erivan, Russian Transcaucasia, state that 500 Sasun Armenians who were forced by cold and famine to surrender to the Turks under the Government amnesty, were killed by order of the Governor of Mush. The men were massacred and the women and children drowned in the Euphrates River. This news was telegraphed to Viscount Bryce by an Armenian refugee worker.

Commenting on the telegram to Viscount Bryce from the frontier of Russian Transcaucasia and Asiatic Turkey, the Armenian Refugees Committee in London says:

"This seems to indicate the final destruction of the unfortunate Armenian peasantry who fled to the mountains to escape massacre. They were the most manly part of the Armenian nation, leading a quiet life in the remote valleys of the Euphrates."

(3:5) DECEMBER 15, 1915

MILLION ARMENIANS KILLED OR IN EXILE

American Committee on Relief Says Victims of Turks Are Steadily Increasing.

POLICY OF EXTERMINATION

More Atrocities Detailed in Support of Charge That Turkey Is Acting Deliberately.

JANUARY 26, 1916

BRYCE ASKS AMERICA TO SUCCOR ARMENIANS

Refugees Will Starve on Syrian Plains if Not Quickly Fed— Page to Inform Washington.

THE LIVING AGE

FEBRUARY 5, 1916

THE MURDER OF ARMENIA.

Not the least service performed by Lord Bryce and Mr. Arnold Toynbee in their little pamphlet on "Armenian [illegible] (Hodd... [illegible]

They were driven forward by the blows and whips of their intolerable escort. Many of them had had their clothes [illegible]

committed by the gendarmes, brigands, and villagers." The people found themselves in the necessity of eating grass. [illegible]

THE AMERICAN
REVIEW OF REVIEWS

FEBRUARY, 1916

THE AMERICAN REVIEW OF REVIEWS

Photograph by Modern Photo Service   ARMENIAN GIRLS RESCUED FROM THE TURKS

THE FATE OF THE ARMENIANS

The New York Times

(II 9:3)
FEBRUARY 6, 1916

SAW ARMENIANS GO STARVING TO EXILE

Story of a Journey Through Turkey as Told to the Board of Missions.

WOMEN TIED TO DONKEYS

"The Slow Massacre of a Race," a Victim Calls It—Babies Thrown Into Rivers.

FEBRUARY 18, 1916

APPEALS FOR ARMENIANS.

Dr. W. A. Shedd Urges Secretary Lansing to Protest to Turkey.

FEBRUARY 13, 1916

RANSOMS ARMENIAN GIRLS.

American Committee Asks Funds to be Paid to Turks.

FEBRUARY 8, 1916

AMERICAN BURNED ALIVE BY TURKS

Missionary Tells How He Himself Escaped a Similar Fate

AIDED SICK BEFORE FLIGHT

Women and Children Are Victims of Wholesale Butchery, He Says.

PETROGRAD, Jan. 13. (Correspondence of The Associated Press.)—Dr. Jacob Sargis, an American Methodist medical missionary, who has arrived in Petrograd after narrowly escaping death at the hands of the Turks and Kurds in Urumiah, Persian Armenia, asserts that among the outrages committed against the Christian refugees was the burning to death of an American doctor named Simeon of Shimmun, as he was known there. His identity was not established further, but the story of the outrage, as told by Dr. Sargis, was as follows:

"Dr. Shimmun was in the village of Supurghan, when the Turks attacked that place. He was among those who took refuge on a mountain near the lakes. His life was captured and told that since he had been a good doctor and had helped the wounded, they would not kill him, but that he must accept the Mohammedan faith. He refused, as almost all Christians did. They poured oil on him, and, before applying the torch, gave him another chance to forsake his religion. Again he refused, and they set his clothes afire. While fleeing in agony due to the flames the Turks shot him several times. After he fell to the ground unconscious they hacked his head off. Mr. Allen, an American missionary, who went from village to village burying the victims of this butchery, found the body of Shimmun half eaten by dogs."

GREAT MASSACRE BY KURDS

40,000 Armenians Driven from Erzerum and Killed, According to Petrograd.

(3:7)
FEBRUARY 7, 1916

TELLS OF GREAT PLAIN BLACK WITH REFUGEES

Agonies of Armenians Described by Dr. Richard Hill In Letter From Caucasus.

A letter written by Dr. Richard Hill,

DAY, MARCH 6, 1916

RUSSIANS SLAUGHTER TURKISH THIRD ARMY

Give No Quarter to Men Held Responsible for the Massacre of Armenians

LONDON, March 5.—The Russian soldiers at Bitlis, according to a Petrograd dispatch to the Morning Post, took a terrible revenge on the Turkish troops for the cruelty which the Turks were alleged to have practised toward the Armenians in that district. The correspondent says:

"Terrible slaughter followed the capture of the Turkish positions at Bitlis. The Russian troops had witnessed at Van, Mush, and many other places, an appalling sight, the massacre; namely, by Turkish fanatics of tens of thousands of Armenian Christian men, women, and children. It was unlikely after such deeds that any quarter should be given. This colossal killing completed the destruction of the Turkish third army."

MARCH 2, 1916

DETAIL ARMENIANS' PLIGHT.

German Nurses Declare 550 Bodies Were Buried in One Day

Dr. Samuel T. Dutton, Secretary of

MARCH 5, 1916

PLEA FOR THE ARMENIANS.

Dinner Speaker Says America Should Protest Against Massacres.

Reminding his hearers that in 1895

113

HE LITERARY DIGEST

PUBLIC OPINION (New York) combined with THE LITERARY DIGEST

al y Funk & Wagnalls Company (Adam W. Wagnalls, Pres.; Wilfred J. Funk, Vice-Pres.; Robert J. Cuddihy, Treas.; William Neisel, Sec'y), 354-360 Fourth Ave., New York

---

The Literary Digest for September 1, 1917

WO IS ARMENIA!

SO LITTLE FIRST-HAND INFORMATION concerning the sufferings of the Armenian peoples reaches us that the letter of a British officer, printed in the New York *Evening Post*, deserves notice. The source of the letter is Bombay and the writer, who is ill in hospital there, declares that before he got his wound in the fighting beyond Bagdad he came in contact on several occasions with a highly educated Armenian who had escaped from the Turks and was being employed as an interpreter. The stories he told of the inhumanities inflicted upon his compatriots were so appalling that the officer made notes of his conversations and reproduces them "in something like his own language," so that "you can get at the heart of the man and realize what he and all educated Armenians feel." This is his story:

"What you have read and heard about Armenia is not a hundredth part of the truth. Dante's 'Inferno' was a heaven compared with the hell that the Turks have made of my country. Something of the awful reality of the past twelve months I have myself seen in passing through on the way to the front.

"At Aleppo there are four factories in which, under the supervision of deported Armenians, two thousand Armenian women are being employed under terrible conditions. The women are all deportees. One of them said to me: 'On a halt during our deportations I saw a *gendarme* bury a sick woman alive. Cold-blooded murders were an every-day occurrence. Our guards had orders to kill on the spot any one who lagged a pace behind on the journey. Often several were killed at once, and there was no separate grave for them—the bodies were just thrown into a ditch together and covered. It was all horrible to behold, but our eyes eventually became hardened to the sight.'

"Bab, Mesaguene, and Zor are three places never to be forgotten by us Armenians. I have visited them. Do you know what happened there a few months since? By the order of Governor Afif, nearly one hundred thousand of my brothers were murdered, massacred by armed Circassians.

"At Bosanti, I saw six railway-trucks of little Armenian children being dispatched 'to an unknown destination.' What had these little innocents done to offend? Was it the mere fact of being alive and children of our thrice unhappy race?"

The German soldiers that one sees around the stations in Armenia, he describes as "generally of a low type and not far behind the Turks in their disregard for the rights of our people":

"Their cruelty is a little different from that of the Turk, but the difference is only one of kind. The Turk, for example, often respects certain things which we have learned to associate with our religious or racial beliefs; the German has no respect for anything, nothing is too sacred for his profane hands. The Turk frequently used to show some respect and deference to the upper-class Armenians, the educated people, regarding them as perhaps capable of being useful even in a Turkish dominion. The German, as soon as he arrived here, pointed out the educated Armenian as the most dangerous of all, and instigated the Turks into organizing a ruthless persecution of the intellectual classes of Armenians.

ARMENIAN WOMAN. A good illustration of the Armenian type. The head-dress is that usually found in the Caucasus. The Armenian women, as a rule, are fine looking, with intelligent faces and womanly bearing. This is especially noticeable in the case of old women. Among the oriental races, as a rule, the old women are not handsome, but the reverse is true of the Armenian women

CHRISTIAN GIRLS AND THEIR CHILDREN RESCUED FROM MOSLEM HAREMS

THE LITERARY DIGEST

PUBLIC OPINION (New York) combined with THE LITERARY DIGEST

179 Published by Funk & Wagnalls Company (Adam W. Wagnalls, Pres.; Wilfred J. Funk, Vice-Pres.; Robert J. Cuddihy, Treas.; William Neisel, Sec'y), 354-360 Fourth Ave., New York

A CALL TO RESCUE ARMENIA

OVER TWO MILLION wretched victims of war are reported actually destitute and in need of daily food in western Asia. Of this number four hundred thousand are orphans. This is the body of people that the American

Staggering as to the war, it is c cable dispatches workers returning

WHITHER DOES THE WAY LEAD?
One of the thousand bands of deported Armenians sent out on an aimless journey to the trackless desert.

SIGNS OF THEIR PASSING.
The deserts of Asia Minor are strewn with heaps of bones cleared by the wild beasts along the routes of the hopeless Armenian caravans.

THE LITERA

181 PUBLIC OPINION (New York) comb
Published by Funk & Wagnalls Company (Adam W. Wagnalls, Pres.; Wilfred J. Funk, Vic

October 6, 1917

GERMANY'S SINS INDICTED BY A GERMAN

THE RESPONSIBILITY for the slaughter of Armenia

The Literary Digest for Octo

GERMAN GUILT FOR ARMENIAN BLOOD

The New York Times

A MONTHLY MAGAZINE O
The New York Times

Current History

PUBLISHED BY THE NEW YORK TIMES COMPANY, TIMES SQUARE, NEW YORK, N. Y.

Current History Magazine
November, 1916

Lord Bryce, Former British Ambassador to the United States,
Has Followed Up His Report on Belgium with a
Still More Harrowing Story of Armenian Sufferings.

Lord Bryce's Report on Turkish Atrocities in Armenia

Most appalling of all the documents of the world war is the record of Turkey's wholesale massacres of the Christian men, women, and children of Armenia, as revealed in a detailed report prepared by Lord Bryce, the former British Ambassador to the United States, which fills a volume of 600 pages. Lord Bryce's material, much of which was furnished by American and other neutral workers in Armenia, is edited by Arnold J. Toynbee, late Fellow of Balliol College, Oxford. The volume contains 150 documents, all the authentic evidence obtainable up to July, 1916, as to the massacres and deportations of Armenians and other Christians dwelling in Asia Minor and the northwestern corner of Persia invaded by Turkish troops. All the evidence goes to show the deliberate purpose of the Turkish authorities to exterminate the Armenian Nation, the most colossal crime, says Lord Bryce, in the history of the world. CURRENT HISTORY MAGAZINE herewith presents the more striking portions of the report.

The New York Times

FEBRUARY 3, 1919
(1:4)

SAW ARMENIANS DROWNED IN GROUPS

American Woman Whom Elkus Helped Tells Her Story of Massacres.

VICTIMS BOUND TOGETHER

And Then Thrown Into a River—
Mrs. Das Amarian Saved By

APRIL 19, 1919

STILL MURDER ARMENIANS.

Armistice Makes No Change in Turk Methods, Says Finley.

Withdrawal of the American Red Cross

(4:3)
JANUARY 3, 1919

TELLS OF TURK ATROCITIES.

French Writer Says 50,000 Armenians Were Slain at One Place.

us.)—In giving
massacres in

(14:1)
JUNE 1, 1919

ARMENIAN GIRLS TELL OF MASSACRES

Escaped Victims of Turkish and Circassian Cruelty Recount Their Experience.

HELD NAKED AND STARVING

Hundreds Slaughtered with Clubs at Parties Up to 5,000 Were Taken to Syrian Desert.

THE MISSIONARY
REVIEW of the WORLD

MISSIONARY REVIEW [NOVEMBER, 1917]

EDITORIAL COMMENT

THE RESCUE OF ARMENIA

OVER a million Armenians have been murdered or have died as a result of the fiendish policy of the Turkish government. These million men, women and children are beyond human aid and beyond earthly want. But there are over two million surviving victims of Turkish cruelty who may be rescued by the prompt help of Christians.

The Independent

HAMILTON HOLT
Editor

HAROLD HOWLAND
Associate Editor

EDWIN E. SLOSSON
Literary Editor

FOUNDED 1848

KARL V. S. HOWLAND
President

FREDERIC E. DICKINSON
Secretary

WESLEY W. FERRIN
Treasurer

THE STORY OF THE WEEK

The Armenian Massacres

The photographs given here show how one small band of Armen-

THE GREAT WAR

November 29—Bulgars capture Pris-

Bryce is the head reports that the extent of the massacres and the cruelties practised are greater than at first supposed. Since last May 800,000 Armen-

THE FLIGHT INTO EGYPT OF THE CHRISTIANS, FROM ANTIOCH

One of the most moving incidents of the Great War is the marvelous escape from massacre of a body of Armenians from six villages just west of Antioch. Notified that they were to be banished to the deserts of Mesopotamia within eight days and knowing that this would mean death for most of them, they fled to the hills overlooking the Gulf of Alexandretta. Here they defended themselves for fifty-three days against an overwhelming force of Turks until finally their Red Cross flag caught the attention of a passing French cruiser which carried them to Port Said and safety. Those rescued included a thousand men, fourteen hundred women and eleven hundred children and four hundred babies

119

AMBASSADOR MORGENTHAU'S STORY

...and is this the way many exiles prepared themselves for death... to lie down and wait? *

In the desert of Der-el-Zor. Why there are no living Armenians in the Armenian provinces in Turkey. *

Above: One of many young orphans who trail the exile caravans in search of scraps of food or shelter.

Below: Photo of the heads of eight Armenian professors who were massacred by the Turks.

"Horrible scenes of Turkish and German brutality." *

THE LITERARY DIGEST

PUBLIC OPINION (New York) combined with THE LITERARY DIGEST

Published by Funk & Wagnalls Company (Adam W. Wagnalls, Pres.; Wilfred J. Funk, Vice-Pres.; Robert J. Cuddihy, Treas.; William Neisel, Sec'y), 354-360 Fourth Ave., New York

EXTERMINATING THE ARMENIANS

NAMELESS HORRORS are being perpetrated in the interior of Turkey in Asia upon the Armenians, one of the oldest and most faithful Christian nations of the world. The accounts of reliable eye-witnesses are now filtering through, and they contain descriptions of scenes too revolting to be included in anything but official reports. We learn from the press that Mr. Morgenthau, American Ambassador at Constantinople, has protested in vain against this organized extermination of the Armenians by their Moslem neighbors, and, as a result of his last protests, we are told that seven of the most prominent Armenians in Constantinople were taken and hanged in the streets. American missionaries in Asia Minor report that they are unable to afford more than temporary protection to their Armenian pupils, as Turkish soldiers have entered the missions and slaughtered the Armenians before their eyes. In a recent article the *Journal de Genève* says:

"The extermination is being carried out by three means: massacre, deportation, and forced conversion to Islam. Throughout the whole of the country it is the same story. . . . The Government has released from prison criminals whom it has organized and enrolled. It is these criminals who are in charge of the Armenian convoys, and there is no brutality they do not commit."

The *Manchester Guardian* learns from a Swiss correspondent recently returned from Turkey that in Constantinople—

"In the street the insolence of the Mussulmans toward the Christians knows no limit; the sons of Turkish families gather in bands and go to the houses of Armenians to decide which of

MAKING PREPARATIONS.

"Children, now there will be surely another winter campaign. See, they are collecting the oven-doors already."

— *O Simplicissimus* (Munich).

the young women they will have. In the same way Turkish housewives choose their future residence in Armenian houses under the eyes of the owners. Hooligans threaten and insult Christians in the street. Massacres are stated, on reliable authority, to have already taken place in the city. No Armenians dare to leave their houses. . . . . .

"In the provinces the violence of events surpasses all that can be imagined. Whole towns have been sacked and the inhabitants sent to the interior. At Marsivan the men were told they need not take provisions with them; they would be fed on the way. Before their eyes the town was then burned, and they were taken to a series of graves already prepared, and poleaxed. Some escaped, but were caught. 'Kill us with your

ARMENIANS FIGHTING FOR THEIR LIVES.

Armenian entrenchments in "The Gardens," a suburb of Van, in Asiatic Turkey, during the recent siege by the Turks. Taken unawares and many of them massacred, the Armenians fled to the American Mission Compound, fortified it, and directed their fight against the Turks from that place until the Turks retired.

guns,' they said, as they were taken back. 'Never,' was the answer; 'a bullet costs a hundred paras; you aren't worth it; better as it is.' As for the women, they were sold in all the villages on the way to Mosul, so that at the end there were only left cripples, hunchbacks, and other deformed people."

The Italian Consul at Trebizond, Signor Corrini, who returned home on the outbreak of war between his country and Turkey, recounts his experiences in the Rome *Messaggero*:

"From June 24 the Armenians in Trebizond were interned, they were then sent under escort to distant regions, but the fate of at least four-fifths of them was death. The local authorities, and even some of the Mohammedan population, tried to resist and to decrease the number of victims by hiding them, but in vain. The orders from Constantinople were categorical and all had to obey. . . . The scenes of desolation, tears, curses, suicides to save honor, sudden insanity, fires, shooting in the streets, in the houses, are impossible to describe."

Signor Corrini concludes with an eloquent appeal to neutral Christian nations:

"When one has witnessed for a month daily scenes of this terrible character without being in a position to do anything, one wonders—Have all the wild beasts of the world congregated in Constantinople? Such massacres cry out for the vengeance of all Christendom. If people knew what I know, had seen what I have seen, and heard what I have heard, then all the Christian Powers yet neutral would rise against Turkey and cry anathema against that barbarous Government."

The New York Times

Current History

A MONTHLY MAGAZINE OF
The New York Times

PUBLISHED BY THE NEW YORK TIMES COMPANY, TIMES SQUARE, NEW YORK, N. Y.

CURRENT HISTORY MAGAZINE [NOV. 1917]

Armenians Killed With Axes by Turks
Harrowing Account by President of Anatolia College

AMBASSADOR MORGENTHAU'S STORY

THOSE WHO FELL BY THE WAYSIDE

OUT OF 18,000 ARMENIANS ONLY 150 SURVIVE

Remains of murder by the Turks.

THE RIGHT
TO
LIFE

Everyone has the right to life, liberty and the security of person.

— ARTICLE 3 OF THE UNIVERSAL DECLARATION
OF HUMAN RIGHTS

"The Result of Turkish Rule"

Taken from National Archives, Dept. of State Rec. Group 59, Decimal File No. 867.4016/417

"The Turk has trodden this land, all is in ruins".   **—VICTOR HUGO**

A scene of mass murder. (Mesopotamia, 1915. Photograph by a German Officer in Turkey).

A group of starved women and children. A monument for the glorification of Turkish Racism.   (Photograph by a Viennese Officer, 1916.)

After slaughter

The child shall have full opportunity for play and recreation...

THE CHILD SHALL PLAY

PRINCIPLE 7 OF THE DECLARATION OF THE RIGHTS OF THE CHILD

"The Turk has trodden this land, all is in ruins".

—VICTOR HUGO

In the desert of Der-el-Zor. Why there are no living Armenians in the Armenian provinces in Turkey.

"To serve Armenia is to serve civilization".

An Armenian Deported Mother and her Child
Taken from National Archives, Dept. of State
Rec. Group 59, Decimal File No. 867.4016/417

A public square of Erzindjan in Turkey. (An Armenian theatre had been planned for this square, now the remains of the murdered Armenians act the roles of their tragedy.)

"The Turk has trodden this land, all is in ruins". —VICTOR HUGO

The bones of hundreds of thousands Armenians whom the Turks murdered, by gathering them together, pouring gasoline on them, and then setting them to fire alive. No pen can truly depict the horrors inflicted by the Turkish monsters.

"To serve Armenia is to serve civilization". —W. E. GLADSTONE

Last days of starving children. (Arabian Desert. Photograph by a German Officer in Turkey.)

"The Turk has trodden this land, all is in ruins". —VICTOR HUGO

After slaughter

The New York Times

A MONTHLY MAGAZINE OF
The New York Times

Current History

PUBLISHED BY THE NEW YORK TIMES COMPANY, TIMES SQUARE, NEW YORK, N. Y.

CURRENT HISTORY MAGAZINE [NOV. 1917]

Armenians Killed With Axes by Turks

Harrowing Account by President of Anatolia College

THE slaughter of all the Armenian Faculty members of Anatolia College, Marsovan, Northern Asia Minor, with 1,200 others, by Turkish peasants, whose pay for the work was the privilege of stripping the clothing off their victims' bodies, was described by the Rev. George E. White, President of the college, upon his return to the United States in the Autumn of 1917. The massacres were committed at night by order of the Turkish Government, he said, the Armenians being sent out in lots of a hundred or two hundred to their doom and their bodies rolled into prepared burial trenches.

"One group of our college boys asked permission to sing before they died and they sang 'Nearer, My God, to Thee,' then they were struck down," Dr. White said. The number of Armenians who have been massacred is estimated by the American Committee for Armenian and Syrian Relief in New York City at from 500,000 to 1,000,000, while there are a million still living in need of immediate aid. Dr. White, who is now living in Minneapolis, was ordered to leave Marsovan by the Turkish Government. He was formerly pastor of the Congregational Church in Waverley, Iowa.

"The situation for Armenia," he said, "became excessively acute in the Spring of 1915, when the Turks determined to eliminate the Armenian question by eliminating the Armenians. The Armenian questions arise from political and religious causes.

"On the pretext of searching for deserting soldiers, concealed bombs, weapons, seditious literature or revolutionists, the Turkish officers arrested about 1,200 Armenian men at Marsovan, accompanying their investigations by horrible brutalities. There was no revolutionary activity in our region whatever. The men were sent out in lots of one or two hundred in night 'deportations' to the mountains, where trenches had been prepared. Coarse peasants, who were employed to do what was done, said it was a 'pity to waste bullets,' and they used axes.

"Then the Turks turned on the women and children, the old men and little boys. Scores of oxcarts were gathered, and in the early dawn as they passed the squeaking of their wheels left memories that make the blood curdle even now. Thousands of women and children were swept

"I received word from Ambassador Morgenthau that our premises would not be interfered with. Next morning the Chief of Police came with armed men and demanded surrender of all Armenians connected with the college, girls' school, and hospital. We claimed the right to control our grounds as American citizens. More than two hours we held them at bay. They brought more armed men. They again demanded surrender of the Armenians. I refused. They challenged me for resisting the Turkish Government. They said any one who did so was liable to immediate execution.

"They broke open our gates, brought in ox carts, and asked where the Armenians were. I refused to tell. They went through the buildings, smashing down the doors. Then our Armenian friends, feeling that further attempt on our part to save them would bring more harm probably than good, came forth, professed themselves loyal Turkish subjects, and offered to do what was required.

"An oxcart was assigned each family, with a meagre supply of food, bedding, and clothing. The mother sat on the load with her children about her, the father prepared to walk beside the cart. I offered prayer, and then the sad procession, carrying seventy-two persons from the college and hospital, moved away.

"These teachers were men of character, education, ability, and usefulness, several of them representing the fine type of graduates from American or European universities. The company went in safety for about fifty miles. Then the men were separated from the women, their hands were bound behind their backs, and they were led away. The eight Armenian members of the staff of instruction of Anatolia College were among the slain. The women and children were moved on and on. No one knows where, and no one knows how many of them are still living.

"The Government officers plowed the Armenian cemetery in Marsovan and sowed it with grain as a symbol that no Armenian should live or die to be buried there. No Armenian student or teacher was left to Anatolia College, and of the Protestant congregation in the city of

"To serve Armenia is to serve civilization".　　—W. E. GLADSTONE

First Ally: These from a London Zeppelin raid.
Second Ally: These from the Armenians.

(Harpers Weekly)

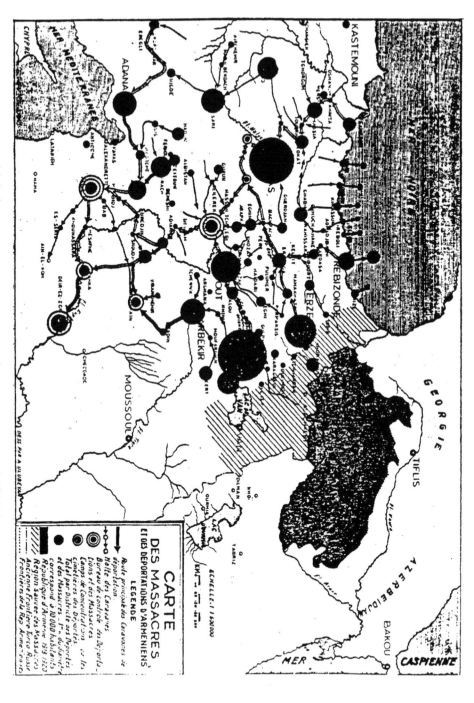

MAP OF THE ARMENIAN MASSACRES AND DEPORTATIONS

Telegram of English Translation
Regarding Progress of the Armenian Massacre

Ministry of Internal Affairs
Superintendent of the Imperial Possessions No. 33
Director of Office, date of dispatch
April 21 (1915), hour: 3, minute 43
Director of Information: Mehmen Fakhri,
Place of dispatch: Erzerum, No, 2597,
Number of words: 20, charge: 36.

To His Excellency Sabit Bey, Governor General of El-Aziz
No. 5, to be delivered to Nazim Bey

          Are the Armenians deported from there wiped out?
Inform me of their massacre and extermination.
Are the dangerous persons massacred
or only expelled from the town and deported?
Let me know it clearly, my brother.
April 21, 1915
April 21. 1915 at Erzerum
The President for the Special Organization:
Behaeddin Shakir.*

---

    * Photostatic telegram in the file of the martial court;
signed by Dr. Dehaeddin Shakir Bey, President of the Special
Organization. The telegram is addressed, through the Agency
of Tahsin Bey, Vali of Erzerum, to Sabit Bey, Vali of Harpout,
to be delivered to Nazem of Resne, Executive Delegate of the
Union and Progress Party in Mamouret-Ul-Aziz.

CONSULAR BUREAU
AUG 12 1915
DEPT. OF STATE

Copy for Department.

AMERICAN CONSULATE

TREBIZOND TURKEY, June 26, 1915.

AUG 10 1915
DIVISION OF
NEAR EASTERN AFFAIRS

Honorable Henry Morgenthau,

American Ambassador,

Constantinople.

Sir:

I have the honor to enclose herewith for the information
of the Embassy a copy of the proclamation which has been
posted up in public places by the local authorities notifying
the Armenians that within five days from its date, namely, on
Thursday, July 1st, the entire Armenian population of Trebizond
and vicinity including men, women and children will be obliged
to turn over to the government such property as they cannot take
with them and start for the interior, probably for Kidjezireh
or Mosul where they will remain until the end of the war.
Upon their return after the war their goods will be returned
to them.

It is impossible to convey an idea of the consternation
and despair the publication of this proclamation has produced
upon the people. I have seen strong, proud, wealthy men
weep like children while they told me that they had given
their boys and girls to Persian and Turkish neighbors.
I know of one Armenian woman who is now in Dr. Crawford's
house who has become insane and two other such cases are
reported in the same vicinity. Many are providing themselves
with poison which they will take in case the order is not
rescinded.

Honorable Henry Morganthau

    American Ambassador,

        Constantinople.

Sir:

    I have the honor to enclose herewith for the information of the Embassy a <u>copy of the proclamation which has been</u> <u>posted up in public places by the local authorities notifying</u> <u>the Armenians that within five days from its date, namely, on</u> <u>Thursday, July 1st, the entire Armenian population of Trebisond</u> <u>and vicinity including men, women and children will be obliged</u> <u>to turn over to the government such property as they cannot take</u> <u>with them and start for the interior</u>, probably for Kidjesireh or Momul where they will remain until the end of the war. Upon their return after the war their goods will be returned to them.

    It is impossible to convey an idea of the consternation and despair the publication of this proclamation has produced upon the people. <u>I have seen strong, proud, wealthy men</u> <u>weep like children</u> while they told me that they had given their boys and girls to Persian and Turkish neighbors. I know of one Armenian woman who is now in Dr. Crawford's house who has become insane and two other such cases are reported in the same vicinity. Many are providing themselves with poison which they will take in case the order is not rescinded.

"Official Proclamation"

1. Five days from the date of the present all Armenians, except the sick, are required to start by sections and villages under the guard of gendarmes.

2. When they go they may take with them any portable goods that they desire to take but it is forbidden to sell any property or extra household goods or to hand them over to any other persons to keep for them, because the deportation being temporary, the portable and unportable goods will be made into bales and kept under the protection of the government in large strong buildings and will be given back, just as they are, to the owners on their return. Those who buy, sell or keep, contrary to this order, portable or unportable goods or property, will be sent to the Court Martial. Any goods that are necessary for the army may be sold by the owner to the government.

3. Hans and proper buildings are prepared on the roads to secure their comfort and all measures are completed for their safety from any offensive act or injury and for their safe arrival at their temporary places of abode.

4. The guards will use arms against those who threaten the life or goods of one or more of the Armenian population or dishonor any of them. Any such person will be at once arrested, sent to Court Martial and condemned to death. This measure, which is the sad result of the leading astray of the Armenians, has no connection in any way with other divisions of the population and they must not therefore interfere in any manner in this affair.

5. Armenians are compelled to obey the government's decision. If there be any persons among them who dare to have arms against soldiers or gendarmes, arms will be used against such persons and they shall be "arrested dead." Likewise those who refuse to depart, disobeying the government's decision and hinding themselves here and there, and those persons who hide them in their houses or feed them or help them to hide, will also be sent to Court Martial to be condemned to death.

6. Armenians being prohibited to carry any fire arms, they must surrender to the government all kinds of arms, pistols, bombs and daggers that they have hidden in their houses or out of doors. The government has been informed about the quantity of these arms, and those persons who try to secrete them instead of delivering them up to the government will be very severely punished when the arms are discovered by the government.

7. The soldiers and gendarmes acting as escort are permitted and required to use arms and to kill those who try to seize by force or plunder the Armenians on the roads or in villages.

8. Those who are in debt to the Imperial Ottoman Bank, may leave their goods in the depot of the bank as security for their debts, but the government reserves the right when it considers such goods necessary for military purposes to buy them from the Bank by paying the debt for which they are left as security and deliver same to the military commission. In accordance with this condition, goods may be left as security for debts to other persons but the correctness of the debts must be certified by the government. The merchants' corroborated books are the best evidences required for this purpose.

9. Large or small animals, that cannot be taken along, will be bought by the government in the name of the army.

10. The officials of villages, towns, districts and provinces on the way must assist the Armenians as much as possible.

Trebizond, Turkey
(Old style) June 12/ (New Style) June 26, 1916.

National Archives, Washington D.C. 807.4016/85, pages 1, 2, 3.

Chapter Sixteen

IT IS SO STRANGE how the human language becomes so infinite in meaning and word formation when it regards a tragedy, marriage, death, or extermination. That a word casts pages of reactions that must now be responded to like a duel stroke to stroke. Pope Francis says "slaughter" and the Turkish representative uses one word back: "baseless." Most people will read the soundbites and remember two things: "slaughter" and "baseless," a perfect conflict, as opposing as Heaven and Hell.

Grandfather Galoust, I am submerging into the deep muddy hell again as I write. They are marching you all deeper into Turkish areas. Somehow you heard that the pushing of these starving and broken people was to an area called Kamakh. Once you arrived the Turks left the sick and more children behind. "I saw a Turk cut a pregnant woman's abdomen with a knife. They took out the baby from her abdomen and threw it away. They wanted to take away a nice looking young mother with a baby about four to five months old she was still carrying in her arms; she resisted. They grabbed the baby from her, held it by the feet, and knocked it down on the stones. Then, they dragged the screaming mother away. The poor woman screamed, yelled, and pulled her hair apart; but nothing helped. To this day and moment her voice sounds in my ears. My heart breaks into pieces with pain. What could I do! I only sobbed. I passed and told my mom, my sister, all the rest wept and damned them. They said that God does not see, what can we do?"

I didn't know you heard these voices. I didn't know there were echoes but Grandpa I felt them. They are with me right now. I am resting their names on each gossamer page. That they can be seen in the light of day just once more helps their unmet cries for help. I hear the word "baseless" and my soul curdles with rage at the ignorance that still reigns. I am not a rageful being and I know I must bury our ghosts Grandpa. Only then will I be free.

"We walked dragging our feet. We walked at the bank starving, thirsty, and exhausted. My little brother Haroution was exhausted and could no longer walk. He asked me. 'Brother, will you clasp me a little?' I picked him up on my shoulders, walked a little, and put him down. I could not walk. I was consumed with exhaustion, too. After two hours, we witnessed another cruelty. Landord Peto's three daughters-in-law from our village were walking together. They were nice looking women. They had no children. The Turks gave us a short break. Three Turks came up to take them away. The youngest, Marguerite, was my uncle Neshan's daughter. The three of them hugged and kissed. They resisted. The turks [this is all I can do, Marguerite, is use a lower case t to deminish the value of the word] began to beat them. They made us move on. How did their bitter situation end? I did not know."

You saw an Armenian woman curse the Turks as she ran into the Euphrates river with her gold rings, and purse with gold inside. As she ran into the river to drown she cursed Mohammed. But it was not Mohammed that did these horrific deeds, it was criminals that dishonored Mohammed.

Another Kurd came up to you and held you by your arm. He figured out you were a boy. You began to cry and so did your precious brave mother. She told the Kurd that they have taken all her sons and now they want her last son. The Kurdish man warned her and said, "My sister, they'll slaughter you all and throw you into the Euphrates river. I don't have a son. You should be happy that your son has a chance to stay alive." He convinced her as well as your sister that this was the best thing to do. He also told her if she resisted that he would take my Grandfather by force. There it is again: force. This Kurd gave your mother some cheese and took you away. There were only three of your family members left. Your mother, your sister and your brother. You all cried and the Kurd had you in his hands holding you with a tight grip, and you write: "Where they stayed it's dark for me this day. I am haunted to this day by one thing and that is that I couldn't carry my little brother, I feel bad to this day. This moment never leaves my mind.

"I shall never forget, for as long as I am alive, the Armenian Genocide. Days and nights, I feel remorse at the sufferings of my family and everything else I had witnessed and experienced during the deportation. These were my sufferings. After this I shall continue about my loneliness; bereaved from father and mother; deprived from relatives; and longing for them all the time."

Don't you know Grandpa I felt something I couldn't explain that tortured me all my life too. I didn't know until now what it was. What an irony that after you were killed by that degenerate hit and run driver I went mad with grief. I found out he told the police that it was a dog that tore his windshield, but it was you. Blood everywhere. A witness said that you flew so high in the air that it looked like a white plastic bag in the sky. Then my agony turned into a refuge to help in some small way the thousands of Armenians once again left on the streets with dead children in buildings that no one could climb into. The black market cement made nine-story buildings fall like cardboard, one floor on top of another. The people were in shock. The doctors had lost their whole families but were working and saving the ones they could get to without modern conveniences. I walked into hell, a modern hell in March 1989. It looked like a nuclear bomb had gone off. I saw nothing but anguish, grief, and terror in survivor's eyes. Very little help occurred after the major earthquake of December 7, 1988. So much of the aid was being diverted into Russia.

The Armenian people whispered, "Please don't tell anyone, they will make it worse for us." I was in shock at the level of indifference. To this day if I see any form of demolished buildings I am back in Armenia. I found the people, as a whole, illuminating in spirit. I still treasure and grieve when I look at a hair barrette a mother gave me from her hair. It was all she had. I begged her to not give it. She wept so much. She wanted to repay me in some way for helping the children in the hospital. These people are so resilient, so powerful in their faith. They begged me for a page of the Bible. They believed and had nothing to read. I had smuggled in some small icons and children's Bibles. At that time it was not allowed. I was mobbed once while they screamed for a small picture of anything spiritual. It seems we need to look at something so other worldly for meditation in order to feel we will be heard in the Heavens. Grandpa I wrote my dissertation on treating Post-Traumatic Stress Disorder plaguing the Armenian children. The ones that survived lost everything. Little did I know that once again I was researching and writing about you, my mother, my father, my loved ones, and lastly me. The Armenian children taught me so much about overcoming grief. There they were, at least a hundred kids in a makeshift hospital. The actual hospital that had just been completed was destroyed in the earthquake. This was an old school. There was one of me and over a hundred of them. I decided to work in groups. I had paper, markers, small buildings that were therapeutic toys.

I had a big bag of little people and trees. There was no clock Grandpa. I had a watch. Each day those children somehow knew when it was 10 a.m. Each group would be waiting for me. The mothers were living with them like homeless Armenians in your time. The only difference was no one was trying to kill us. At first the children only used the red and black markers. They drew the devastation. Then within days they began to take colors and paint fish in the water, and draw flowers in their new home. One day they wanted to hear themselves on my tape recorder so one by one they told their story and listened to it on the playback. I never planned this. They showed me what they needed. Within a week they were singing their school songs and dancing in the stark and barren room. They were so beautiful. They have eyes that have direct paths to angels. Then they were ready to dip into the bag. They together spontaneously built a beautiful city. One girl held a small house intact in her hands and they all aggressively destroyed the city. They did this three times. Then meticulously rebuilt the city, trees, people, and this time the girl put the house into the rest of the city and it was done. They were back again. I could see it in their eyes they were O.K.! Then I realized it was Easter. We had nothing but paper and markers. I had brought some tape from America. We all made Easter eggs and taped them on the ugly walls and the room was happy! We celebrated Easter together.

Grandpa I always asked you when I would meet my soul mate. You always said the same thing. "*Gagad a Ger.*" (Your destiny is written on your forehead.) You simply believed if I was to meet the person that was for me that it would happen without my searching, hoping, wondering. Alas, I let it go. In a million years I would have never imagined that through the horrible loss of you that broke my heart and obliterated my will that I would meet the most life-changing human being. Unbeknownst to me was a clinician who saw me working with the children in Armenia and came back and told his dearest friend. He called me, Grandpa, and I knew on the phone that a peace beyond any words came over me. I had enough life experience to not be fooled by feelings. This was different. It was strong, it made my soul soar in breath, it changed my life. He was not Armenian. Grandpa, he was not what you said you wanted. But I know that for 24 years I feel the same flight in my soul every minute of every day. Even you Grandpa understood that no one can control *Gagad a Ger* not even my love for you.

Thank you precious Grandfather for being in my life. For watching me when I was a baby. For taking care of all of us and never once telling us of your ongoing survivor guilt and agony. I go to school to treat the very thing you had and never told me. I wonder what I would have been if I hadn't loved you all so much, and if you had told us all along.

I suppose this too is *Gagad a Ger*.

Chapter Seventeen

"IF OUR CHILDREN FORGET this much evil, let the whole world read insult to the Armenians. This is my commandment to you all my dear sweet children, grandchildren. Love each other as I loved you."—Galoust

I didn't know this would be the fire that lit my soul with light again. As I wrote "Turning Point" I stayed in the mud and wondered why this story would be important to continue. Then I see your commandment, for the critical need to surface above and beyond the Euphrates where I have stopped. That when there is this much evil we must remember as a nation, as humanity. Somehow it will be absorbed in our DNA; it will fuse in our memories and carry on the hope that one day there will be no more genocides. Greed is the poison that fuels it all.

"When the Kurd took me to his house, I discovered he had one mother, and two wives. The first wife had no children. That childless woman told the man, 'Mahmoud, the Armenian boy you brought will be my son.' That man loved his first wife very much."

I am cringing from the depth of your capacity for compassion. This man just stole you away from your mother for cheese, and brought you home like a pet for his first wife. You write as to her choosing your name. "I shall call you Ali." The reason was that they believed in Allah more than in Mohammed. She fed you and let you sleep. You slept for 20 hours. The next morning she woke you called you by your new name. She then fed you breakfast. You were required to work now. You were sent out to help the cattle graze right in the spot where the Kurd took you away from your mother and siblings. They were all gone now. You began crying and you wanted to run away. You were out with the elderly mother of one of the wives and for the first time you received some empathy. The elderly woman told you that there was nowhere for you to go that the Turks killed your mother and all the rest of the Armenians by throwing them in the Euphrates river. You got very scared when she told you this and she then took her apron off and put it on the grass, so that you could take a nap. I want to hug her in thanks that she let you cry and take a nap. A little while later she woke you up to have lunch. Someone had brought flour and Khashil and churned milk. You did not join them and eat. You were a child and told the man that your people ate this food with butter and not churned milk. The man muttered that from now on you eat what they serve. I read for the first time you having a conversation inside your head. You tried to snap into focus, and say you didn't know where you were or what was happening but you had to snap into focus because you would next be drowned in the river.

You write about having to adapt to this new life. You ate their food and each day you did your duties. My heart sinks as I see that within three weeks the Turk beast returned for more blood. You felt that even the Euphrates rising from the number of dead Armenians was not enough: the Turks returned for more carnage. It is so clear to me about the wish to eradicate Armenians from the earth. After all the mayhem and death they wanted more death. Another order by the Turkish government was issued to the Kurds. If they were hiding any Armenian women, men, boys, or girls over the age of three, they would be condemned. Even the Turks who had taken Armenians for their pleasure and slavery were threatened by the proclamation. You were not aware of the new order. Instead you would look forward to meeting an Armenian hostage who was much older than you 18 to 20 years of age. I sigh; you were so young, so very young. You both would speak Armenian and didn't care that the Kurds heard your tongue. One night he disappeared and you would look everywhere for him but only with your eyes, never words. You couldn't remember his sweet name in your diaries and you felt so bad. One morning you were out in the fields with the cattle and you saw a pretty maiden who was around 17 years old singing in Armenian.

"Are you Armenian, young girl?"

"Yes, dear brother, I am Armenian."

"Aren't you afraid to sing, even in Armenian?"

"Why should I be? If they kill me it's better for me to be dead than to stay alive."

She told you her story that she was engaged to be married and so in love. That while the Turks marched them all to their deaths her fiancé was grabbed and murdered in front of her. The Turks dragged her to where she was now. She told you, precious Grandpa, that she was embarrassed to say that any Turk that wanted her had her and "wouldn't it be better to die, and be finished from this torture and disgrace?" She left and you left but you were late getting back. The master wanted to punish you but he wouldn't in front of the wife who adopted you. He just warned you not to be late.

How you knew the time without a watch or the Ghartal Stone in your old village is beyond me. But, somehow you knew when you were late. That evening while you returned from your duties you learned of the new order.

It sounds so biblical: three years old and older. The Armenian slave told Galoust that his master told him that he would protect the Armenian slave as long as he was alive. Slave.

Baseless.

You write how you wished you were him. As you ate dinner with your adoptive mother you looked sad and she inquired as to why. The master of the house Mahmoud upon learning that you knew told you not to worry. That he will not let anyone take you away. Mahmoud promised to take you to Kamakh City, to a Turkish official named Sarekh Pek. He would tell him to release you. (Then Ali the Christian would come back to his new home.) In the morning the prayers began and your new mother told you to get ready to go to the city. Mahmoud told you that when you see the Turkish official you kneel down and kiss his feet. So, strange here is Mahmoud praying for God's help. It is like religions are fighting siblings with God, shouting "I am better!" Then the other faction shouts "No of course God chose us, we are better!" I always felt that there is enough room for all siblings.

You got to the city and went to this building and inside people came and ate in groups of 10 to 20 people at a time. You saw food coming from the kitchen through wooden-made pipes. As you sat a man came up and told your master Mahmoud that the Pek was calling for you. The Pek was on the second floor and was standing at the edge of the stairs. He called out to you and told you to go upstairs with him. Your master went downstairs. You write how there were two stairs left before you reached the top floor but this man ordered you to stop and wait. I don't want you to kiss his feet Grandpa. You write that you couldn't kiss his feet because he told you to wait. He then asked how old you were you told him you were thirteen years old. He then wanted to know whose son you were.

You answered Mahmoud's son. (For a second I thought you would say Tateos.) He then said to tell him whose son were you before? Were you an Armenian's son? You answered, "Yes." He then told you to tell him your father's name. "Tateos." You remember how he then told you that if he released you would you be the legitimate son of Mahmoud? Grandpa I am sad but glad you sad yes.

"We bowed, bent, we almost kissed the ground. But, we turned back and came out of the room happy. We headed for home. Entering the house, the woman rejoiced saying, 'My son came home.'"

She hugged you and you all began the work of the day. Time passed and each day you worked the fields. Then once again an order came. That anyone keeping an Armenian as young as even one year old had to turn them over to the government. If they did not they too would be burned alive. Everyone was scared again. The fellow Armenian slave told you what was about to happen and he still believed that his master would protect him. Your new father and mother promised to take you away to Dersim.

(Years later you saw this Armenian slave in Vladicaucasus at Assetins' village. You write how seeing him made you feel such joy that someone else escaped the hell that you were all in.)

Mahmoud decided to take you to another Kurd named Atash. Atash always escorted Armenians to Dersim. Supposedly Armenians that could make it there would survive. You write so poetically Grandpa. "The father, like an obscure cloud; the woman like a sweet moon. Cloud and moon clutched each other." Your new parents had to make a decision. In the end you had to go.

You figured out the month you were in because of the heat during the day. That the moon was your enemy because the illumination made you fugitives more visible in the dark. Darkness always made you feel safer. There were two Kurds walking with a gun guiding an Armenian woman and her child. Mahmoud was still with you and wanted to hold the child because of the danger everyone would be in if the child cried out. You were all near the bridge. The mother pleaded not to take her baby, that she would silence the baby if it cried. The Kurd had compassion knowing he would be killed by the Turks near the bridge and he still let her carry the baby. The Kurd went ahead and came back to report that the Turkish soldiers had built a fire and were laughing and talking. He believed that the fire would obscure seeing them. But the moon was bright. Then all of a sudden the moon ducked behind a cloud and you write how God heard your prayers. As you four tiptoed onto the bridge you could hear a Turk say that he could hear footsteps. Another one told him no way. Yet the other Turk said that maybe those gyavours escaped. While they argued you all made it across the bridge! Just then stones began to tumble down from all the footsteps and the Turks began shooting from below.

The Kurdish escorts got you all across and over to yet another Kurd named Aydatash. He was hiding two groups of Armenians. You remember exactly how many in each group. The three of you remained with that man who was resting under a prune tree. Mahmoud gave you some coins—*ghouroush*—and he told you to keep them with you in case you need to bribe someone or find refuge. I realize now that he really loved his first wife. He risked his life for her and for you. After you put them safely inside your pocket he left never to be seen again. The Kurd Aydatash told you three to sleep because the next morning you would begin the next part of your voyage.

You had barely fallen asleep and the sun came up and you were all told to follow him to his fields. There he had two groups of Armenians who were being worked in the fields. One group had seven people, the other eight people. He kept the fifteen of you for one day working hard in the fields for him. He brought you bread at noon; two clay pots and two big cups' they were filled to capacity with churned milk in a buckle. One pot was passed around the one group and the second passed around your group of eight. You were all given a loaf of maize (corn) bread. Each person was allowed to cut a piece of bread and put it in your mouth then the clay pot was passed to each person and they would sip the churned milk into the corn bread waiting inside your mouths. As long as there was bread more churned milk was poured into these pots. Then back to working in the field. You all slept under the stars. In the morning you all got up and for the first time I read the words "we felt free." You were all hurrying down narrow paths in a mountainous region to get to a place called Dersim. If you looked down there was an abyss you would fall into. Very steep paths through forest. You all walked very carefully. You would all clutch each other at times for courage and balance. Grandpa you had the courage to ask the Kurdish man escorting you all to please tell you where you all were going.

"Dersim, a region called Bazgaroushakh." The escort stated this without any more discussion. That word comes to me again. Baseless. How murderous in behavior even now.

You asked the Armenian woman how she came to be able to join him on this journey to nowhere. She told you that one of the Kurds taking them was in close relations with Armenians. That her husband had been a close friend. This same Kurd protected her husband when he took to the mountains after killing some of the Turks that were slaughtering everyone. He helped her husband get to Dersim. The Kurdish man promised her husband that he would protect this very woman and their only child and bring them to Dersim to join him. I sigh at this type of valor. Atash, may others know your name and your courage to help friends no matter what.

The Kurds used to go to the mountains during the summer for almost five months. They knew the mountains well. When night fell you all reached the summit. A tent was put up and for five long days with no bread and very little churned milk you all survived feeling abandoned and alone. Grandpa you had no cover, just a stone to sleep on.

In the morning a Kurd walked up to you and asked you if you wanted to work. Asked you? I can't believe my ears. You said yes, and asked what you should do? He told you to mix the sheep and goats and take them out to pasture. I am thinking you are thirteen in a foreign land. How are you supposed to do such a thing, but off you go into the forest. The child clinician side of me just shakes at the anxiety a child would feel. As you walked them into the forest they all scattered and disappeared. You remember shouting for help from the Heavens and a shepherd heard you and came to your aid. He told you not to worry, that he would help you gather them up and return them to their owners. Another stranger being so kind while you were in utter misery.

When noon arrived the shepherd simply whistled and the sheep and goats came together. You drove them back—and you write the word—home. Home, it really isn't where we live; it is knowing there is a place waiting for our return. Now, I understand better why material things never mattered to you. You only cared about where all of your loved ones were. You had a piece of paper with all of our names and every birthday or anniversary of someone you loved. You would honor their special day in various ways. I remember you would always give me an envelope and birthday card with Armenian writing inside along with a $5.00. You always wrote how you loved me and wished me happiness. You did this for all of us. There were so many. I continue to understand your message decades after I lost you so suddenly. Live each day to its fullest. Every day is a lifetime so live it as though each minute mattered.

For two days you did this kind of work, you learned fast the way of the Kurdish field worker. But, once again you were told to go that there was no more work. If there was no work there was no food for you. Once again you slept outside on a stone, so cold and all alone. In the blur of the early morning sunrise you looked up and saw yet another Kurdish man. He pointed to a resort. He told you to go to the other mountain and find a rich man there named Houseyin Pek.

This landlord was a very good man and perhaps he could help this poor Armenian lad. You got up and walked to the landlord's resort. He had a rich man's tent and he was called Hassan. The people there told you he was not there. A woman sympathized with you very much. You write how she was a goodhearted woman. She gave you food and bread. "I ate it all up and had a good sleep that night. I got up in the morning, and she gave me my breakfast. I ate. She assigned me work all that day. I collected dried cattle dung to burn under the tinplate so that they could bake bread, cook food, and boil milk."

You write how just this little empathy made you feel you had a king's life. You got into a routine of caring for the cattle and sheep, but alas your royal life did not last long. Within a week the kind woman's husband returned. He was happy she had found you and allowed you to sleep in the rear of the tent. In the middle of the night you saw two armed men come in and you were terrified they were Turkish soldiers. You hid under the blanket and peeked out from underneath. They all sat and had dinner then put out the light. You heard the husband say that he was taking you into the village the next day so that you could work for "them."

Morning came and the Arab man took you to the village. You were sad because your new master wanted to give you to his brother. You pleaded with him that you liked working for him and that there were Armenians you could speak with. He lied and promised he would bring you back to his tent in a fortnight (fourteen days). You were treated horribly there. The elder brother passed away and you stayed there as a working child slave for the whole winter. You were not allowed to rest and in the freezing cold. Instead you had to take care of a multitude of cattle by finding food for them, cleaning their stable, and moving the dung to the dump. You slept with the sheep.

"It was cold as ice. I had no shoes on. I wore worn out sandals, I bandaged my feet with cloths. I used to raise one leg to warm, then the other. I climbed up a tree. In the evenings I had to bring wood on my back. If the master's wife would not give bread, she would beat me instead."

One day a wolf devoured a goat. The cruel woman kept counting the sheep and one goat was missing. She began to beat you with a stick. Her own son told her to stop beating you, but she had no heart. Her deceased husband had brought his lover's son to stay with them and when he died she treated that poor boy worse than you. This boy would steal bread in the night and bring it to you and together you ate the bread. Soon she figured out that bread was missing and locked the window. This woman would not stop demanding to locate this goat. She threatened to exterminate both of you boys. She starved you both, and then an epidemic illness started in her sheep and they began to die every day. There was another goat that you loved because it looked just like the one your father Tateos had brought home from Erzroum. You write how this goat had two kids a year. This goat got sick and she was going to slaughter it and you begged her to give you a chance to save her. She wouldn't listen until her son told her to give you a chance. You did save the goat's life, and after that this woman saw you a little differently. When her pretty eighteen year-old daughter fell and passed out in front of you this very same woman asked you to pray for her. That because you were Armenian she was certain you could read. She asked you to read a prayer and the girl woke up and was better. Keeping you hungry continued. Your good deeds were in no way repaid by some food and civility.

There was a tradition amongst the Kurds. If a region's Pek died, bread would be made with a lot of flour and distributed to the people living in the perished tombs. An old Kurdish man secretly would give you bread he brought back from the tombs. He sympathized with your horrible situation. He was impressed that you could now speak Kurdish as well as Turkish and Armenian. He spoke of a kind Kurdish man that lived through the forest and as you would climb up to the summit of the mountain there would be two homes. He instructed you to ask for this man and he would welcome you. He encouraged you to run away.

Run away. I remember my mother telling me, "You began running away when you were six years old." I had to look it up, it seems so obvious but I have to look it up. "Run away, leave or escape from a place, person, or situation of danger." You want to run away, and it makes so much sense to me because you are really running to something you need. I would run away to find the same thing you wanted, kindness, love, and safety. I loved my parents so much and I still do with every cell in my body, but they could be so ruthless to a child. I read, I drew, I never once said please come home I miss you. Never. They had to work every day into the night. They never took a dollar from this great country; that is why my mother loathed people that would come to their market and use food stamps like coupons. My mother would lecture them and tell them this is a country where everyone can make something of themselves. That they were stealing from this country making a lifestyle out of their dependency. She saw how they would trade them for booze. She would not sell them cigarettes or alcohol. My parents worked themselves to death but had such pride and sincere appreciation for America. This country gave them a home. In their lives they always gave back. Interestingly they didn't think that my brother and I needed them home with us. We needed guidance, and their love. But, such is the life of many children of immigrants. I flash back to that night I ran away. I was six and my dad told me to watch the string beans on the stove. So, I did. I watched them so closely even while the smoke started in this huge pot and the firemen came and all the fans were turned on and my father raged at me for causing such a mess. I ran away right around the corner to the Japanese family I loved. They were so quiet and contented in their lives. I just stood in front of their home in the dark. Soon I saw my mother come around the corner in our white Mercury and tell me to get in. Decades later she would say how I ran away beginning at age six yet never sounded like she had a hint of curiosity as to why. Behaviors were judged independently of the cause. Instead it was the child that baffled them. Grandpa I never told you. But, we were so alike. I saw your softness when you spoke to me and I never was scared of you. But, I was of them. So, we both ran away for the same thing. How sad when one's own family is so damaged from war and loss that they too perpetuate the same behaviors that were done to them.

Two days passed and you got up enough courage to run away. You followed the old Kurdish man's guidance and went up the middle of the forest and reached the summit where the house he described sat! You entered and the wife told you that you could wait for her husband. She fed you, and you waited and waited and now it was after 5 p.m. and the door opened. It was the son of your master. You write that when you saw him you began to faint. "I was dead."

The son called you horrible names and grabbed you by your arm to stand. The kind woman gave you food but she too feared these harsh and crude Kurds. You were certain he would kill you in the forest as he mounted you on his horse. You were their property. They didn't purchase you but you were their slave. When you got back the woman wanted to beat you but the same son stopped her. You got back to work in the stable taking care of the cattle. Back to sleeping in the stable, with the sheep at night. The old Kurdish man heard about your recapture and told you how sorry he was for you and that he would help you find a better place for refuge.

A week had gone by and this dear Kurdish old man told you about an Armenian tailor that had come into the town you were in. He went on to tell you that he told the tailor about you and that you should go to the inn where he works and speak to him. He warned to be careful and not be caught again.

You did it, you found the Armenian man and while he sewed he quietly told you to run away and come to him. That he would take you to a man that would protect you from these brutal masters. It was spring now. It was a sweet and sunny day so you did all your morning chores and drove the sheep into the field. The old Kurdish man had shown you the road to take and off you went. I am scared for you Grandpa; I am thinking what about those sheep? She is going to go mad when they don't return. You found the Armenian's house by evening. Once again the person you wanted to see wasn't home. The landlord told you to be patient and rest. I am so relieved when I read that he showed up and took you to the Pek of the region. The Armenian man told you that this Arab man would treat you like his son. That he was a very goodhearted person. It was getting dark and you set off to meet this Pek. He welcomed you both and talked with both of you. He spoke Turkish perfectly. He told you that he would treat you like his own son if you stayed.

The official's wife did something that is making me smile from my soul as I write. She showed you kindness Grandpa. She heated a bowl of water and bathed you. Then you had dinner and she gently made a bed for you, a real bed for you. You slept until 10 a.m. the next day. When you awoke it was like a fairytale: she had bought you new clothes and had put them next to you. "There was no limit to my joy. I told that Saripek, 'Papa, what if my master comes to take me away. What am I to do?'" His new father told him that if they came you must verbally tell them that you will not go with them. If you refuse to go they cannot take you away. That if you do not renounce them verbally that he himself can do nothing.

With this you ask them what you should do for them as far as work. They told you to relax and rest. He then told you later if you choose (if you choose!) you can go to the forest and bring wood so that your mama could cook food. So later that day you went into the forest and did collect wood for the fire. As you felt stronger and safer you began to do chores all around the property. Armenians churned milk with clay. The Kurds used goatskin and they churned milk to get butter. You helped by putting hay in the stable so that the animals could sleep more comfortably than you had in the past two years. You had a broom in your hand when you saw the son of your master come to the home. They found you yet again. You went into your new parents' home and sat in the guest-room. They called you in. A bearded man sat between your two masters (so you didn't think he was your new father after all); he then asked you why you had run away and come to this house. You told him that your previous master beat you and didn't treat you well. The bearded man became furious and pulled a gun out and aimed it at you. He called you a son of a bitch. Your new master, Saripek, jumped up and told this cruel creature that he had no right to try and kill this boy. To take account where he is and that if the boy says he doesn't want to go back that he cannot make him. "I showed the old Kurd my old clothes and told him that I wore these clothes all through winter. You better butcher me before I go." The old Kurd threatened you and yet you got to stay with your new master. The word "baseless" floods my veins with rage.

You write about your new master and his wife. He would tell you that when you grew up that he would get you a lovely wife. He would ask you, must it be an Armenian girl? That if you would take his daughter he would give you a house, and cattle, and sheep and your own field where you would live safely and be happy.

This was truly a turning point my beloved Grandfather.

Chapter Eighteen

IT WAS JULY 1916. It is July 2015. Grandfather if you were here you would be terrified of the ignorance that continues in mankind. Not the animal kingdom which continues to dwindle thanks to humans. People using atrocities to self-promote their supposed fierceness are just little men brutalizing innocent people. They are called criminals not religious groups. If one has to kill another for power they have just murdered countless people that will take an eye for an eye as restitution until their death. With all the brilliance walking around in minds all over the world we still can't seem to find a way to overcome violence as a way of sounding off. Old truths still remain as resonant as they were thousands of years ago. Violence begets violence. During Christ's time scholars wrote in code. They painted in code.

Yet in certain parts of the world sections of the Bible are taken literally. Cut your hand off (yourself) was written if one hand offend the other. It wasn't literal. It was a plea to begin a process of remorse, and build a conscience. The vulgar vapor of these disgusting criminals is simple. The criminals want a war so that they can loot and rob and create mass genocides everywhere. They poke the bear in order to push those who have a conscience to madness and to join them. Under the cloak of war, looting, stealing, killing masses of people is so much easier. We must not let the visuals that are done to provoke primitive blood-curdling rage to win. They are the bugs that come and sniff for opportunity. Grandfather I read today the same brutal murders of your day. Only more often, and wider spread.

The only difference is the articles don't stab the wounds by saying "alleged," nor do they say "Baseless."

Never the less they are just as bloody and just as evil.

On your sunny day in July 1916 a miracle happened. While you were tending the fields of your master you noticed people began gathering at his house. It was very hot while almost 200 workers reaped his fields. Your job was to take care of your master's horse. You also needed to take water in a jar to the workers.

"Suddenly, I heard an Armenian voice. I turned my head and saw lots of Armenians coming down the mountain. I dropped the jar, my work, and ran to them. I saw women, men all dressed in trousers that were made of jean material and it surprised me I had never seen women dressed in trousers. It was such a big surprise! Oh Lord! What a vision I saw! Finally I asked a question to those people.

"'Brother, are you Armenians?' 'Yes. We are Armenians.'

"'Where are you coming from? Where are you going to?'

"They told me, 'Haven't you learned anything?'"

You told them that you were very isolated and have heard no news of the plight of the Armenians. They told you that the Russians came and were occupying the lands that the Turks stole. That the Turks had run away from Yerzenga.

You felt your eyes were open for the first time since the massacres began. Tears ran down your face and you shook with joy. You were miles away until you heard the workers shouting out for water. You felt light-headed and very wobbly as you walked. You were so disoriented that the workers asked you what was wrong. You didn't tell them what you learned because you feared that they would tell your master.

There was a boy a couple years older than you who was a field worker. His name was the same as yours—Galoust. I love your name, "the light comes forth." You told him about the Armenians and he told you that you were wasting your time thinking about it. How would you find a better situation than the one you were in? You were so torn inside that it showed to your new father and mother. They truly did adopt you as their son. They only had one daughter and a son was so important for Arab families. Your new father and mother asked you why you looked so sad. With great reservation you told them both what you had seen earlier in the day.

They reasoned with you as parents not as masters. They told you that even if this were true all your family has been murdered. That your village was surely destroyed by now. That it would be gravely dangerous to embark on such a journey. They themselves did not believe that the Russians had come and that the Turks had run. You protested that you had to go back and if there were no one left that you would return to them.

These adoptive parents were Muslim. Their humanity was as pure as any Armenian and Christian. The character we have when we profess that we believe in something greater is the true filter of our behavior, not the written word. Their character was beautiful and loving because they suffered as you begged them to go back. Your new father said that since he couldn't convince you to stay, he would arrange for your journey back to your village.

I love your adoptive parents Grandpa. I wish I knew their offspring. You found out that those very Armenians were sponsored by your new father! They had been freed for one piece of gold per person! Your new father asked you if you would be interested to go see your new sister who had married someone in another village. You did want to say goodbye to her. Your new mother was told to cook a feast for you; by now you could speak and understand the Kurdish language well. She killed a cock, and cooked it along with halva and cake. She packed a basket of food to take to your elder sister from your new family.

You safely arrived to her village dressed in the fineries of Kurdish custom. She welcomed you and was genuinely sad when you told her of your plan to return to your motherland. She asked you if her parents mistreated you. You told her they were wonderful and also fed you. Food becomes so synonymous with love when one is starved for affection. What was so beautiful was that your new sister agreed with you. That you had a right to go back and see if any of your loved ones survived. As you bade her goodbye you used the word "sister" for the first time since the slaughtering began. She called out to you as you were walking out the door to come back and let her kiss you goodbye. You both cried and that was the first time in years you felt a kiss of love on your cheek.

You write in a detached way about returning to your new home one more time. "I reached home. The mother inquired about the daughter and I told her she was alright."

You speak of this new father's good deeds and his influence amongst the Kurdish people. Eureka! Grandpa I am frozen with clarity. That is who you learned the power of kindness and influence: it was your new Kurdish father! He was a man that showed his strength by being gentle and firm in his words and behavior. I wish you wrote his last name and I would search for his offspring to thank them. He always checked on you and asked if the other Kurdish boys gave you any trouble when you were in the fields. That is what a father does!

I had another sign today. Our family ghosts came to me once again to give me courage to keep writing. My first sign was my letter that I sent far away to London. I made an error and instead of May 1st I wrote June 1st. I was embarrassed that I wrote the wrong month and wondered how I could have made such an error. I had never proofed a letter and got the month wrong in my life! When the publishers sent back the letter of interest in our work Grandpa I went out to the mailbox and though their date was different I received it on June 1st. I always want to shrug it off as a coincidence. But just now when I realized that your Kurdish father is the one who influenced you the most I got up for a break to breathe in the realization and walked by my picture of a bird with the word joy written on it and saw it was illuminating during the day. Somehow the battery operated candle that holds the page up was on! I never turn it on, I use it as a stand for the picture! I just had a miracle. Thank you ghosts of my ancestry. Thank you Grandpa.

Your new father was so protective of you that the other Kurdish workers got scared when a boy's rock struck your leg and you began to limp. The older men begged you to walk straight and not limp. You kept trying but the pain was so great that your new father saw it and was enraged at your misfortune. He grabbed a weapon and went to the worker's home. You spoke up to your new parents and you finally were heard. Your new father accepted that it was an accident and no harm came to the family. How ironic: now an accident that causes you to limp is causing a life risk to a Kurdish worker. We are all the same underneath; we are one, we are each other.

Your new father would take his grain and collect you to go with him as he delivered it to others in need. Your new father was honored and respected by all who knew him and now the Kurdish people respected and honored you his son.

I notice it has been a while since you brought up returning to your homeland. You go back and forth Grandpa trying so hard to let this man's love and care make him your father but you do not succeed. Sometimes you refer to him as new father; most of the time you write your master Saripek.

One day Saripek took you with him out into the forest. He gave you a gun and told you if some primitive Kurds try to attack you both that you were to run in the bushes and shoot in the air. Off you both went to the peak of a mountain to a small village that had ten houses. You both entered a home where you were served food and soon after Saripek told you it was time to go down to the abyss. It was very dangerous terrain; as you both carefully walked four men with guns jumped out of a bush. They told you both to surrender and put down your guns. You both put down your guns and raised your hands. Saripek was brave: he warned them that if they did not allow you both to take your weapons they would be very sorry. The men told you both to get out but would not give back your weapons. You asked Saripek if they would kill you both and he surprised you by saying: "You don't worry, tomorrow or after tomorrow they themselves will bring back our guns. They will beg, even those troublesome Kurds will give us a bribe. They don't know who I am."

When you returned home your new mother shouted at Saripek as to why he would allow those donkey Kurds to cause him dishonor by taking his weapons. Saripek answered that he had no choice, that you both were suddenly ambushed. He explained that you both would have been murdered and by tomorrow they will be back begging for forgiveness.

The very next morning four different Kurds came with two sheep and your master's weapons. You say "papa" this time as your master refuses the apology and sheep. He wants the four Kurds who ambushed you both to come in person to him and to you. The fathers of the Kurds that ambushed you both came with four osmain gold pieces and two sheep. They begged for pardon that their sons knew no better. Saripek turned to his wife and wanted her to understand that her yelling and anger had been unfounded. He wanted her to learn that if he reacted they would have died. Now she can see their honor is being restored completely. They all apologized and the same kind of elderly people who beat you Grandfather came to your feet this time. They gave you four gold pieces and begged you for your forgiveness. You write how this time you did not fall at their feet but remained quiet and kept your dignity.

Your time had come to risk going back to your homeland. An Armenian brigade leader who was called the Mountain Lion gave an order that for every Armenian returned he would give one gold piece. He was called Mourat Pasha or General Mourat. So a local Pek, not your new father, gathered some Armenians from Dersim and sent them to Yerzenga (Armenian land). He then received the gold as promised. This created a desire by more Kurds to return Armenians for gold. Your new father told you it was time for you to get your wish. He gave you twelve *ghouroush* and a secret hand signal to be used only by you after you reached your destination. That if you signaled the men that were patrolling the area, word would get back to your adoptive father that you made it. Your new father gave you his horse and told the Kurds that were escorting you to let you be on the horse so you wouldn't get too tired. That once you reached the border the Kurds were to return the horse to your master.

His last words to you were so loving. That if you found loved ones stay. If you did not, come home for you are his son now. "I bade them goodbye and they kissed me. That woman cried like she was my legitimate mother."

Grandpa can this be true? When I discovered the candle had turned on by itself, I kissed the candle, I kissed the word Joy and I kissed the bird on the picture. I looked at the clock: it was 4 p.m. Deep down inside I am too pragmatic; I tell myself thank God no one can see me. I dare not write this down—someone will think I am crazy. It was a whisper of a voice because I really know that no one touched that candle. No one is here to touch it. Now I come to the journey starting for you again. You write the words "It was 4 o'clock..." That is it. I believe. I will continue the journey with you.

"In the evening when we reached a deep abyss there flew a russet. I saw two Russian soldiers standing in the water. Seeing us, they were suspicious. They had lost their way. There was somebody among us from Chimishghale. He had been in Russia before and he knew the language. He spoke to the soldiers and when they finished talking the lost Russian soldiers joined us. We reached the deep abyss in the evening when it was dark."

The Kurds told you that they could guide you no further. That the border was near and that you should join the Russians. The Kurds began to leave and you gave them the sign to give your precious new father. You had it all Grandpa and yet you had nothing. These Kurds feared you, a child, because of your new father and his authority, and you finally were safe and not beaten by the Turks. Your birth father struck you on many occasions. Yet, you had to go back. I know I would have. I am gasping again as I watch you in the cold freezing temperatures in December 1917.

When nightfall came the escapees began a fire and you wanted to warm yourself and as you got near the fire an Armenian man began to beat you. He shouted that you came to rob them! You had a voice now and you said you were cold and you would never rob anyone. An Armenian woman was with him and spit in his face telling him what an animal he was to beat you. I love strong women Grandpa. She yelled, "You man, aren't you ashamed to beat this poor boy. What do you have that he might steal? Kurds must have killed and exterminated an Armenian like you." She was brave Grandpa.

I just remembered a time I was terrified but I had to fight these big teen boys that were pelting birds on the beach. They had succeeded in hurting them enough that they couldn't fly. I turned into a hawk and screamed and ran at them shouting at the top of my voice to get out! I was eight; they were all around 18. I was unafraid once I became brave like a hawk. Another time I was walking in elementary school. I loved to go to school. It was my home. I protected the weak kids that others teased. I was teased for having long black hair but I could split that off if I saw anyone hurting. I hated cruelty and I hate it more with each passing year I live. I can't take someone laughing at someone else, period. This day I saw a huge group of children in a circle out on the grass right near the cafeteria. I had never seen a group of kids in a perfect circle inches deep. I broke into the circle and in the center was one boy named Dale. He had a dead bird by its tail and was spinning it around while the blood dripped down and the children laughed. They laughed and laughed. I went mad with anger and grabbed the dead bird out of his hands and shouted at him for being so cruel I didn't care that he was the school bully I know I would have flattened him that day if he tried to take the bird back. Only one girl followed me. One girl, my age, around seven years old. She had pure eyes. I went under the bushes and dug a grave. We buried that bird and put stones around the grave with a cross in the center and left. None of those children ever said a word and neither did I. That flashbulb memory says it all to me. Somehow many watch as a few murder and kill. I don't understand it until now.

The Armenian woman took you and put you between everyone huddled for warmth. You bless her in your diary; I bless her this moment. In the morning some of the people sat around a large pan and ate with big spoons while you starved again. One man had something up to his ear and he was talking. You thought he was crazy. But one of the soldiers laughed at you for not knowing what a walkie-talkie was. He was really talking to soldiers up at the border. You kept thinking he was mad and talking to himself.

Grandfather, if you could see life today in 2015. Everywhere I walk or drive people are talking to themselves. It used to be that you were psychotic when this happened; now it is an epidemic. I think to myself this open air is shared it is not your private bathroom or dwelling. I imagine everyone carrying old-fashioned phones with cords and how silly they would look. They still look silly and ridiculous. The people that are more sophisticated and do not walk in tunnel vision never have strangers listening to the sounds of their own voice. Talking on the phone is a personal and a private gesture. Now it is a way to be noticed. Still so many small-minded people in the world with low self-esteem and lack of respect for others. So little changes for the better with humanity. Always a few doing most of the work. A text message by its very definition is to intrude upon. I drive, Grandpa, and each day I help people as they text and crash and drive with no regard for the stranger behind them. How could they care? Their friend and pretty sounds override the awareness of others. All I can do is avoid them and pray for them. The addiction is more for the sounds the object makes. That lovely sound that something has arrived. So, one swerves out of their lane into mine hoping that they got a treasure in that sound. I am not in a violent war but in a different kind of battle. If I want the respect of the stranger in front of me driving, I cannot have it if their phone makes a magical sound. I am invisible when that happens. So children end up in hospitals with horrible injuries while their parents model distraction and beg them to behave.

Grandpa you would have frowned on the silliness of those that have it all. I am happy for the mentally ill for now they don't get pointed at when they walk and talk to themselves. The number one reason children end up in hospitals now is from distracted adults. In your time the children thrived and learned instruments and theatre, and weaving and most of all loving their families.

So the soldiers taught you what a telephone is. It amazed you and I still have your blue old-fashioned phone you had with the numbers dial on the top and the receiver that weighed a ton. I learn that *ghouroush* is Kurdish for money. You all were brought to Yerzenga and handed over to Mourad from Sebastia. You slept in the headquarters and was fed for that night. Another Armenian boy that survived like you asked if you wanted to work for 12 *ghouroush* a day. You said, "Yes." This man you worked for paid you both very well. He felt sorry for you two and though he did not promise to feed you dinner he changed his mind. You both had done a great job and he was grateful. You write how it saved you money and this man knew everyone around him. He had recaptured his fields from the Turks. This man survived the horrors of 1915 and knew his town very well.

He was broken inside but asked you both to return the next day. You told him you would if you both were able. I realize you have no one now. Just this boy and the headquarters you were sleeping in. In the morning you couldn't move your arms. You were so scared but the boy helped you figure out what was wrong. He asked you if you had ever worked the fields using a scythe before. You told him never. He helped you understand that your muscles were frozen from the new experience. I looked up a scythe and it looks like a long pole with a long curved blade at the end. There was no way you could return today. The sweet boy would not go without you. He chose to stay and rest with you.

When you wanted to treat your friend to a meal for his kindness he took you both to a Turkish eatery. You thought you would surely have enough money to pay for the meal and it turned out putting your money together did not cover your meal. You were stunned and bewildered that a whole day's work didn't even cover one meal. You had some of your adoptive father's money and that is what saved you both. You knew you had to risk moving out further from the headquarters to survive. The next day you found two people from Boul village and asked if you could join them as they journeyed to your birthplace, Terjan. You were with Armenians again. It was so strange walking through the ghoulish hell that you once saw and head back to your beginnings. You had no money again and risking your life just to know if anyone survived.

You met a young man with the same name as your beloved brother Haroutioun who perished at the river. This man was responsible for saving your life. He risked his to get you out of the Turkish village you were trapped in. Once you got closer to your father's land you recognized some of your animals that had been pillaged from all of you. You must have been fourteen now and you were brave enough to go to the Russian headquarters and you complained! You told the commander that you saw animals that were stolen by the Turks during their slaughter and the Turks had them out in the fields. He actually gave you a document saying that if you thought they were yours that you had the right to take them back. Back where Grandpa? But you had to start somewhere. The Armenian brothers and their sister whom they had come for joined you as you gathered two cows, and ox and a donkey. The Turks could not stop you now. You slept in an abandoned stable and got a fever and became very ill. You were asleep from the heat and fever for a long time. When you awoke you saw the two brothers arguing. One brother wanted to leave you there and the other brother was telling him that it would be on his conscience to leave a boy who survived the horrific massacre just to be abandoned when he was so sick. If they left you the Turks would kill you. They kept arguing but the younger brother won. He wanted you to sit on the ox and they would drive the animals forward. You quietly prayed while they slept on the grass. Once again you didn't know what would happen next even though you were with Armenians.

You slept and the next morning the kind brother woke you up and neither brother knew that you had heard everything. The younger brother was to never disobey the wishes of the eldest but this young man in his early 20's was your angel that day. He got you up and told you to get ready for the long journey home. You were so weak but he kept you going with stories and encouragement. The terrain was very hard to cross and you all had to go down a steep abyss as you made your way up again. You all slept one night in a Kurdish village. No one hurt you that night. In the morning you all set out again. Another long day walking through paths leading up to yet another mountain and then it happened. Near dusk you looked up ahead and saw Ghartal Stone (The time-reading boulder). You were filled with strength even though you were still ill. You spoke honestly to the younger brother who saved your life. You told him that you heard the argument and that his brother wanted to leave you for the Turks.

"He was hearing all this and kept his head bent, mute. 'My share, the calf belongs to you. Perhaps one day we will meet again. There is the village Mants. I had a relative there. I shall go there to stay for the night in Mants. The next day I'll go to our village. Goodbye.'

"I began running down the mountain to the Mants village. I reached Mants, and inquired about my relatives. They told me that Hakop from the Peto family had survived. Near that village is their house. I went to their house and knocked at the door. A strange woman came out."

You announced your name and that you were Tateos' son of the Moloyents family. "Moloyent?" I never knew that name before Grandpa. She told you that Hakop was her nephew. You told her you were set free in Dersim. Then the door opened and it was Hakop your cousin. She told Hakop, "Don't you recognize this boy?" Hakop did not. "He is Tateos' son from Khoumlar, your uncle's son!" The young man cried and you both hugged. Then he told you that your other uncle's son survived as well. They were sons of your father's brothers that were all murdered. He too came into the house and wept and hugged you in gratitude that someone else survived.

They were looking for wives to begin a family. Most of the Armenian girls had perished during the extermination. Mkrtich also told you that your mother's brother survived and was in Vartouk village. You were loaned a horse and found your way to Vartouk village. When you found your relative's house another strange woman answered the door. She was odd and distant and questioned you as to your reason for being there. You felt so uncomfortable there. You write that she sat with a chain around her neck with a watch hanging from it. She survived the massacre and remarried. You write how she was acting like a king's wife. Maybe Grandpa she was mentally sick from what she endured. But she made you feel most unwelcome and you got through the night with a clear sense that you would leave at daybreak and take your chances going home. It had been a year and a half since your departure. You had forgotten the shallow part of the river so that you could pass by horseback. Across the way you saw Russian carts and soldiers on the way to Yerzenga. You were terrified and began praying that they would not catch you. You left the horse and began on foot. You took off your clothes and sandals and rolled them up and put them above your head as you crossed. You were crossing back in the same river that was a grave to so many you loved. As the cold current swept around you the memory returned of the shallow part and you moved towards it and you were able to cross the river.

"I then, put on my clothes. The village was already near. I walked three versts [Russian measure, 0.66 miles] and went to the village. First, I went to our house with Kurdish clothes on me. I saw our haylofts were destroyed. All the wood [logs] were taken away. One long, thick log was left, which they could not take away nor cut. They had left it on the ground. I turned to the side of the large room to see it was all destroyed. The kitchen and the tounir room were still standing. I turned to face the guest room. They hadn't destroyed it. They had only taken away the door. It appeared that the Russians had put up a new door. Without knocking I opened it and went in to see somebody sleeping on his back with his hands under his head while a soldier was cleaning. I didn't know who they were. It came out that the sleeping man was a commander and the cleaner his servant.

They called him Denshik, in Russian. He started to shout at my face. I didn't understand. I only said in Armenian, 'This is our house.'"

Grandpa there was no ours anymore, just you. "I then said in Turkish that this was our home. I crossed my face. They didn't want to understand. The lying man got angry and shouted at the servant. He shouted so loud that I was trembling. The servant turned to me and slapped me once or twice. He caught me by the arm and threw me out. I cried. I pondered what I could do."

Grandpa you would have never been able to bear what the Turks in power still say in 2015. Baseless. I hope one of these individuals is reading this. I am not this imaginative and neither are you.

The sun began setting and you headed towards the church. So much had happened at that church. It was a place to worship and run to for hope. For many it was a place to die. Today you saw Russian soldiers cooking a meal in big pans near the church wall. As you entered the church of your family you saw the animal droppings everywhere. You were so wounded at this sight and lifted your hands up and called out to the Lord. You were still a child at heart and called out to God that his house was sinned upon by the shameful treatment of this sacred place. As you left the church you saw the beloved fountain still flowing with water day and night. You washed yourself the best you could. You looked up and saw a woman dressed in red, sitting on a Turk's rooftop. It was chilling to see but you walked in her direction towards the home of your baptismal Godfather. You saw a man walking towards you. As he got closer you recognised him: it was Drtad your Godfather! You ran to him and hugged him and cried but he did not recognize you. The last time he saw you was when you were nine years old. He had left your village and gone to Romania. The tired man asked who you were and when you told him both of you broke into tears and he held you close to his heart. He told you that he lived in a Turk's house. There were no Armenian houses. They had all been destroyed. Your Godfather told you how your uncle Mkrtich went looking for you in Vartouk. You didn't want to say how cold and unwelcoming your relatives there were and just stayed silent as to why you got up and left to come home again. Your brother-in-law named Armenak also survived; he too was out looking for you, dear Grandfather. Your loved ones, my loved ones, scattered in the ruins. Hundreds of villages gone from the face of the earth. You lived with 13 people that returned to look for loved ones that were no longer alive. You were all willing to die in order to know what happened. "The damn Turk devoured all of them. What could we do?" You all slept and in the morning you awoke before everyone else and ran to your destroyed home, certain your loved ones were there. "I went and sat in the destroyed house. I cried recollecting my past. It seemed to me that my mother would come from her whereabouts now. I saw Armenak standing by me. He tried to talk with me but nothing helped." For weeks you kept flashing back to memories before the extermination and couldn't rest or sleep. Armenak you brother-in-law was getting angry with you. But of course you would be having memories of all the places you played and all the things you did with your playmates. What re-directed you was Armenak telling you that you had no document as to who you were. Without this, once again you would be in danger. So, off you both went to Mamakhatoun, only now there was a Russian Commander with a Turkish translator. After much struggling to be understood the document was given to you. You are Armenian from the village of Khoumlar. That your father was slaughtered and you are now returning after the genocide to locate any loved ones who may have survived. Now you had an identification card.

The Tatarian translator followed you and told you that there was an Armenian refugee office. You searched until you found it. When you opened the door you shuddered because you were still scared when you saw military men. You had walked many places looking for this office and for the first time since the extermination you felt safer. The military men were Armenian! They wanted to know what you wanted and once you told them you survived the genocide they told you to stay with them. Out of respect you returned to your brother-in-law to tell him your plan and ask for his blessing. Both were given. Upon your return the Armenian man who was the official took you to a room full of clothes!

He asked you to pick whatever you liked and clean up. When you came out he was pleased. He told you that soon more survivors would start coming to this very office. Your job would be to protect the office and help him feed the arriving survivors. Together you would go and bring supplies. After the survivors were fed and clothed they would be sent to Erzroum. Grandpa I see the names of villages that were destroyed. It is like pesticide was sprayed and you all could return to the ruins and rebuild.

One night around 10 p.m. two men came from Koter. They tried to tempt you to sell the clothes to them. You would not. You were afraid they would come back and steal but they didn't. The Armenian military man who took a liking to you wanted you to be safe. This is the only time you write that you regretted a decision you made. He told you that the job you had was coming to an end. He wanted to send you to Russia to be with his parents and that you would be sent to school and looked after. You chose to stay and ponder continuing your father's family lineage.

Chapter Nineteen

YOU TRIED WORKING IN an eatery. You taught yourself Russian and the soldiers liked you. You were trying to find your identity while you got pushed around by the older Armenians. Your mother's brother survived the genocide because he lived outside the region. He came for you. I read how yet another relative wants to take you and give you a home and you decline. You are all alone but you decline several offers to adopt you and raise you. It was like you wanted respect and to be treated as an equal and others just pitied you, tried to take you home and you refused. At one point you had learned that you had an uncle in Russia. Some fellow helped you buy a ticket for a train and you arrived at the station. "We went to Sarighaish and from there we went to Kars." This fellow traveler helped you locate your uncle's home. I am relieved Grandpa that you found someone that made you feel truly welcome. You write that your uncle's eyes shined like the world was given to him. So you ate and slept in, and stayed there for one month. However, once again you walked around sad, wanting to go home. People would get angry, they didn't understand you wanted to go back to your motherland. You felt homesick every day. But, there was no home to return to. No matter what they said you could not be dissuaded. In the end you returned once again.

I am trying so hard to understand your next decision. It makes me vulnerable because I should see your reasoning clearly, but I don't. As people began connecting the dots of who survived and where a loved one may be you could not submit to the natural need of survival. You were nearly sixteen now and the only survivor left from your family. The people you saw were furious that you decided to join the army. No one could understand your reasoning. That after all the heartache and now a chance to rebuild your life you chose to be the one with the weapon this time. In psychology we call it reaction formation or identification with the aggressor. I ponder this all night. I remember how angry I was at my own father when I learned he wanted to leave my mother and me when I was just a baby to go fight with the Americans in Korea. I couldn't understand this reaction! He lost everything during World War II, just like you did Grandpa. You lost everything twice. He lost his home, his mother, and he traveled on horseback all over Europe with his father who had no parental instinct. Finally his miracle came. He arrived to America, met my mother, had a child—and then wants to go to war. His reasoning was that he was grateful to America for taking him in and he wanted to help his new country. He used to joke on the level that he couldn't go with the Americans because he had a baby and young wife. I knew inside he wasn't kidding like he pretended. All his life he loved guns. Even though he was nearly hung as a 12 year old with countless others in Germany because the law at the time was if one German soldier was killed by a sniper one hundred people at random would be hung. Some friends of his father saw him in the long line and distracted the officer allowing the man in the back of this truck to pull him into the vehicle. This type of horror, and Dad you used to say, "The ropes were so white," as if you were looking at "art." I think hell has a way of being romanticized in order to file it away. He had guns pointed at him, countless times of starving, and his resolve was John Wayne movies and the collection of guns. This is the same man that would put a bandage on a pigeon and nurse it back to health in the back of his market and then let it go. What a contradiction you were Dad. But I understand the need to feel safe by owning the very things that destroyed you.

Now you Grandpa chose the Russian army instead of rebuilding your life. You were feeling mistreated and disrespected by your own relatives. Seeing such bloodshed made you a man in a youth's body. In all the chaos you now chose to be part of a group that had rules, routines, and held the order and power in the region. I also think you were too young to marry and too old to be treated like a child. As you visited your few relatives, and bade your goodbyes they were shocked at your decision. Again, no one could dissuade you from joining the Russian army. As you put on your uniform and held your gun, riding away from your beloved now destroyed village, you said out loud, "Goodbye bloody birthplace and Khoumlar Village.' I shot three bullets towards the village and wondered if I would ever see it again." He didn't.

The Russian army had brave Armenian soldiers coming to your ravaged villages trying to create some order. Of course they would influence your decision. They were your role model now. It is now November 1917 and the massacres were still occurring but more randomly by Turks and Kurds coming down into the valleys like bandits. The soldiers would keep them at bay. When the Turks retreated the Kurds retreated. As I read these words I see you waiting in the cold for the next step in your life. You go to Sarghay village and see a few friends. You tell of how you all ate and sang revolutionary songs, "Andranik the brave with his friends, he wants to combat he waits for spring..."

All my life I heard of General Andranik. My parents spoke of him like a relative. You never did Grandpa. All my life I heard songs dedicated to him but he was a distant name to me until now. (Never in my life did I think he would be next to me while I am writing these words.) Here is one of the greatest heroes in the Armenian heritage and I am reading that you and the youths are singing his name. You were far from believing that you would be meeting him in the near future. Let alone joining his army! It is 2015 and both my parents have passed over. I haven't touched their home in over three years. How can I touch their body, their Armenia, their rebirth? A realtor tells me, isn't there anything you want from this house? I say, nothing but the pictures. It is all too painful. I never understood it all, until you were both gone. All your pain, all your wishes, are in that house. On the very same day that I stated that I wanted nothing from the house I left carrying a painting in a simple frame that I was never interested in. As I read about General Andranik in your diaries Grandpa, I instantly knew who that painting was in the house. An oil painting of a simple looking man in a simple uniform. No adornments, no medals, yet a face with the most soulful eyes I have ever seen, second only to my husband's. It is General Andranik. No names but I know it is him. He has big beautiful brown eyes like a poet's. He has thick white hair and a full mustache that is grey and white. It is whispy like William Saroyan's mustache. He has his hand gently touching the side of his face in a contemplative position and exactly like my favorite picture of my father's. His uniform is dark green with goldish-yellow plain epaulets on each shoulder. He is warm and comforting to look at. I see he has a long narrow leather strap of some kind that he wears over and across his shoulder down the front of his uniform. A silver buckle attaches a sword as he gallantly looks out at me while I write. I make yet another discovery. My father's beloved heirloom that he treasured was not a horse leather strap as antique specialists told me because it is the same width and style as the general's. It is from the Armenian army after all. He is with me now. I have placed your general's painting near you Grandpa and know with both of you at my side I can do some justice to the rest of your journey.

When you awoke the next morning in Sarghay village you all felt you had been to a wedding. You were happy, and joyous for the first time in years. You continued forward on horseback for nearly a month until you reached Fem town in the Keghy region. You were taken to the military barracks. Alas, there were no beds. Once again you had to improvise by using hay for pillows and hay for a mattress. The mattresses were called "*Nar.*" Soldiers slept on nars. You were lucky that your barrack had a stove. It could warm the barracks. The commander told you youths to eat and sleep. You tell us that you finally had a military blanket for cover. The Russian government allowed the Armenians to be together in training, and because of their fluency in Armenian and Turkish they were very useful as the army continued to try and bring some order to a very debilitated land. In the morning you all trained, exercised, and learned the daily routines of military life. Your jobs were mainly to guard roads and supplies. One day, for the first time your corporal told you that you would be guarding a bridge that had open air storage of flour, sugar, rusk (toasted bread) and ammunitions. This was a big task for a young youth.

It was bitterly cold at night with freezing temperatures but your job was to guard the supplies. You were to stay overnight. Two Armenian soldiers were mailmen, and they got caught in a storm, and were frozen to death. As you guarded the supplies you also watched over these two precious youths' corpses as they were in the process of being transported to Yerzenka for burial. Grandpa, at least some civility was beginning. Some respect for the dead. You were assigned advanced sentry of places that put you at more risk. Because of your courage and valor the day came where your commander assigned six soldiers to be under your care. The mission was to go to Shakar Dagh (Sugar Mountain) and locate a hut in the valley. There your job would be to prevent the enemy from coming in and slaughtering the soldiers stationed inside the building. You were told that there would be a parole (military password) and that you were the commander of the guard. No one could sleep the whole night and you would rotate two guards every two hours. If anyone approached your station you were to call out "Parole," which had a secret code that the person approaching stated. You write how there was a human chain. There were other soldiers also stationed a half of kilometer apart. They too rotated guards all night. The Turks were still slithering into the night and killing and looting. There was a guardhouse along with trenches. Four at a time slept inside while two at a time guarded their posts. One night two men started approaching you while on duty. You shouted, "'Who are you? What are you? Say the parole.' They did not answer. I repeated my commands, and shouted do not come forward. I aimed my rifle. 'Tell me the night parole or else I'll shoot.' The captain immediately said the night parole and he turned away from his friends and said, 'Good for you. You are a brave man.' He turned to his friends and said, 'He is 17 years old. See the way he accomplishes our commands completely without complaints.'" I love you Grandpa. You never told me. You were too humble all your life.

One day there came an order to send a soldier to every Turk's house and burn fire in their furnaces so that smoke would rise up through the chimneys. This event was a very important one. It was the documented attempt of the Armenian soldiers under Russian authority trying to make intercessions. Turkish delegates were coming to this town called Fem. The lit chimneys was a clever way of making it look like many Russian and Armenian soldiers were staying in those houses. The truth was there were a few soldiers and a very few Russian and Armenian officials. The rough estimate was under 300 soldiers for the whole region! They stayed calm and the smoke was now wafting through the small town. It was now December 1917. The ground was covered in snow. The moment came when the Turks were approaching. Grandpa you watched as they broke the snow and continued their journey down the side of the mountain. You recalled there were Kurdish porters, Kurds, Turks and three officials among them. All of you were on edge because this gesture could be an empty one just to see your military status. There were at least 60 military men coming down the mountain. Clearly they were in the advantage. It was psychological warfare. Once they came into the town they promenaded through the city in the officials' coaches. There was no way to know what nationality they were. Armenian? Russian? Tatarian? Turkish? It turned out to be Turkish delegates and they were not helpful in any way. They all left in 2 days. Once again it got too quiet. The worry began that all this posturing was to set up an attack from three sides. Once the soldiers stayed in the town they knew how few soldiers were mobilized for the Armenians.

Within days it was evident that once again the Turks wanted blood. An Armenian corporal who was sent from Sarhgaya shouted to finish dinner and run to the mountains. Twelve of you were sent to Mouskhanly and Karabolaty mountains and the neighboring Shakar Dagh (Sugar Mountain). It was a bitter cold night. The snow kept falling around you young soldiers. The valley was white with snow, and the mountains were filled with serpents that you all had to face. You young soldiers created a human chain strategy, holding your rifles ready to shoot.

"We were looking towards the enemy, anticipating every moment that the Turks could attack us. After an hour, the dawn came. There was nothing on our side. The battle began in the city. The regular Turkish army and Kurdish crowds that were nomads seized the city from three directions two kilometers from us with 150 men from Yerzenga. The Kurdish nomads had entered into the center of the city. Our men stayed as war prisoners. They didn't know what had happened; there was no way to communicate with them. We began to help the soldiers who were in the city. The Kurds retreated, thinking that there was enough power from Erzeroum to help us. The road opened, and our men fled the city. Only one Armenian man from Garabagh was killed. This Armenian soldier ran out of bullets and died after his last bullet was shot. Karapet from Koter who was a dear friend was shot in the belly. His guts had spilled out. His friends and cousin Serop had collected him and bandaged his wound and put him on a horse. He was my most trustworthy friend. It is now February 1918 and it is snowing and cold. The morning light opened. Our people left Fem and were coming towards us. I knew my friends were in the battle all night. They were hungry. All the stores were being looted by the Turks and Kurds. I ran to a store and grabbed two loaves of bread. I knew my friends were starving and weak. I then ran towards my friends Drtat Nersissian, Greigor Kirakossian, Tigran Sarkissian, and Serop Kotertsi (from Koter). 'Where is Karapet?' Serop began to cry, 'There is Karapet, Galoust, he is seriously injured. We bandaged his belly and put his guts back inside with clothes. Karapet was face down now.'

"I said, brother Serop, when Serop Pasha was battling, his son was killed. He cried, but his wife's sister Sosse, got angry at Serop Pasha saying, 'All these are your sons.'

"Now, we all are here your cousins, brothers. At this point our fate is subject to this situation. We are now here talking. We don't know what will happen to us in the next fifteen minutes. It's all unknown. You take care of Karapet. Be with him and drive the horse slowly. We will come, covering you as we are surrounded from three sides: from West, South, North. Only the road to Karin, Erzroum is open.'

"The Turkish regular army was coming behind us and kurds were attacking from both sides. We were lucky there were Armenian powers in front of us. The Kurdish crowds could not block our way. We barely reached Melik Kent village of Kghy region by nightfall. I immediately went and found our injured friend Karapet. Serop had laid him in a house near the Armenian church where the furnace was burning. The house was well heated. He was sitting near him doing whatever the sick man wanted. He was so seriously injured that he could barely talk. I came in with my hands and feet frozen. My corporal came in, and told me to keep guard for two hours: what could I do? It was a military order. It was important to defend ourselves. We were trapped from three sides in fire. We had to come out of this horrible fire to survive. I immediately got ready. I took my rifle and went out to fulfill my duty. [Grandpa I wish I could wrap you in warm blankets and lift you above this hellish fire you are in again.] I stood at the place my corporal had told me. I watched through the darkness. I was too cold to sleep. I walked up and down so that my feet wouldn't freeze and so that I would be able to walk in the morning. The commander of the guard brought a reliever after two hours. I went home to my injured friend to learn about his condition. When I entered, I asked Serop, 'Please take off my shoes I am burning.' This cruel Serop sitting near me would not help me and take off my frozen shoes."

I am cringing again Grandpa. Serop's heart is frozen. You are so hurt by his lack of empathy and support but not everyone had your fortitude. I can see the madness setting in from being hunted down for years inside some of your friends. You asked Serop to please bring you water and he wouldn't and the worse part was that poor Karapet a youth your age is asking for water as his dying wish and Serop won't bring it to him. You tried to reason with him, and tell Serop that their friend was dying and surely giving him water was a small way of quenching his wish for something other than life itself. He finally snapped to and agreed with you. As you put the cup of cool water up to Karapet's lips he blessed your father and your mother. He spoke spiritually and said that let light shine on the graves of your parents. I watch you as you put a pillow you found in the house under his head. Then Karpet turned his eyes on to you both. Tears rand down his face. He spoke for the last time. "I so much wanted to see my relatives, friends, and my beloved motherland, your longing stayed in me. I stay alone, goodbye." You and Serop were quiet as he took his last breath. Then voices shook you back to the present moment.

There were people outside and a lot of tense murmurings all around. It was your commander and you both wrapped Karapet and took him to the Armenian church and near the Holy wall you both buried him under the snow. These loose Kurds were trying to attack you both right outside the church, yet you could feel they were somewhat afraid of you both. The Kurdish nomads would get scared that the Turks would retreat and they would be killed. It was truly mouse chasing mouse, while all of you worth living for fought to make sense of the next move. You were also on foot again. The snow was coming down steadily which made every step a challenge. Then nightfall came and you all had to walk in the dark exhausted and hungry in hopes of reaching the village called Baskov. Once your small group of soldiers arrived to Baskov you discovered it was completely abandoned. How lost you must have felt. Like the world became a wasteland. Hundreds of villages scattered everywhere and no way of knowing what the situation was right before you entered. You write that you all quietly wanted one thing to save your own lives by escaping. But escape where? As you continued to walk the bag on your shoulders was getting heavier and heavier. It was full of bullets, and a little food. Your rifle was still in your hands and the very thing that could save your life felt like an albatross around your being. I watch you lay down your bag in the delirious thinking of taking a quick nap while the men behind you caught up. You almost died. You were frozen and under the snow when a fellow soldier shook you awake. You shouted for him to stop beating you, but this time it was Trdat Nerssissian from Chekhlouss, and he was saving your life. He shouted at you until you could get up; he kept encouraging you by saying that you were all near the next village. He carried your bag for you dear Grandpa until you regained some strength. I am reading Russian village names now. Pashkovka village was a military barrack and it was heated! Grigor Nerssissian from Dzaghgar came and took off your shoes and clothes. He washed your clothes and hung them near the stove to dry. He brought you some food and you ate and fell into the deepest sleep. "I awoke in the morning and we were ordered to leave. I thanked both men for their care and kindness and most of all their brotherly love." Your regiment had captured Turks and Kurds that had originally come down the mountain and attacked all of you. You all had to march forward towards Erzroum. It was exhausting and the prisoners were also marched in lines to the next destination which was Tashakhly at the foot of the mountain. The village was abandoned and had a few people living there. You were told that assistance would come to you all from Erzroum. To hold on the best you all could until morning. You had to guard your men from a post for a two hour rotation. All four sides of the village had this strategy. When you fulfilled your duty and went back to the makeshift barracks you used your overcoat as a blanket and your bag as a pillow and slept until early morning.

"Get out! Get ready! Get your breakfast!" You all finally got a moment to wash up, and eat. Outside it was cold with snow on the ground but a clear day. The news was that relief support was coming from Erzroum. As you all got into formation the command was given and there it is again, the word "Boys." I have to remember you few soldiers were boys. Your commander said, "Boys, an order came that we should go to the other side of this mountain. The army coming to reinforce us is there and you'll stay there together with them. But be watchful, do not dismiss the presence of Turks."

With the Kurds in line in front of you the army of boys slowly made it to the summit of the mountain. As you stood on top of the mountain you could see the city of Erzroum below. (I know Erzroum is Armenian.) I am watching you tired boys slide down the mountain to the place called Tarkdarasy. There is a thick blanket of snow. You are all the first to make long strings of paths as you sail down to the bottom. Then it was awful again. The snow was so high on the ground below that your legs sank into the thick mounds of snow like quicksand. It became very hard to walk, let alone guard the prisoners. You were each ordered to take guard of one Kurd. You write how the Kurd you had to manage was huge and monstrous in his attitude. He turned and began to seize your rifle from you; the word "hit" was shouted and you instantly, reflexively stabbed him in the belly with the end of the bayonet, along with one shot from the rifle. He let go and fell into the snow. You felt horrible but had no choice. You told your commander that your strength was not enough as the prisoner went for your rifle. You were a boy, he was a huge man, end of discussion. Self-defense. I am pleased that you all exercised conscience and sorted out the situation rather than an eye for an eye. Soon you all entered the city of Erzroum by passing through the Kharbert door. Armenian towns at last.

Grandpa you call Armenian officials of higher rank "pasha." I look it up and it is to identify Turkish high ranking officials. To see their names next to the word pasha and it tells me how close you all were, that you don't see the contradiction in your own diaries.

You sing praises to Mourat, a leader in the Armenian quest to prevail against all odds. You were reunited with some neighbors that were kin through marriage. You are so happy because you see familiar faces again. Your leader Mourat tells you boys that he is aware of how hard he has been on all of you. That now he wants to listen to your needs, your impressions, your ideas for survival. That his strictness was to keep you all fighting for your people that may still be alive somewhere. Your group went to the town of Ilijay in Jermouk. "*Jermouk*" means "white." Whenever I drink water from these ancient Armenian water springs I think of you. You were there.

One day news spread that General Andranik was going to arrive at Ilijay to hold a meeting to talk to the disobedient Armenians. The Armenian soldiers in the Russian army of Eastern Armenia (about 300 soldiers) had revolted; they did not want to stay at the Erzroum front. They did not think they needed Erzroum as the center of fighting for their land. They thought they should go to Gharaourghan. This is where they felt they could defend their motherland. These survivors of the genocide are now having to fight without a chance to even grieve.

(It was the same madness in Armenia in 1989 when I was trying to help the countless families that had lost everything again. The doctors lost their whole families and were having to work under primitive conditions and the only therapy they had was vodka. They did not believe in mental health. They told me they drank and slept and got up in the morning and tried to save some lives in the squalid conditions they were working in. Decades after the genocide I saw horrors and no help that could reach over 250 villages, let alone the cities that were devastated. I will never forget the two men that drove to the hospital. One got out with an amputated leg from crush syndrome during the earthquake and as we sat outside to take a breath he came over to us with a large butcher knife and started threatening us. He looked psychotic. He kept shouting that he would kill us because we were not taking care of his daughter inside. One of the nurses shouted back at him. She shamed him and he got back into the passenger seat and they left. I must say I was visibly shaken. It is one thing to bypass meals and sleep; it is another to have a raging man waving a butcher knife. But once again Armenia has risen out of the ashes and ruins. They are such a mighty race, even if they never win their big battles.)

Grandpa your hero was coming to the very city you were in. You wanted to see him with all your heart. You were able to talk to a fellow soldier and dear friend and you made a plan that he would cover for you at your post so that you could meet your hero. Your wish came true. "We went to General Andranik and saluted him. We were about to cry from happiness but we felt ashamed to. We exchanged glances with each other. Oh, how lucky we were to have the merit of meeting him. All soldiers came together, divided in two groups, and stood in line. He stood in front of those 300 people with the others on the sides. We waited to see what General Andranik had to say. He was not tall, but rather of middle height with a generous moustache. His uniform was decorated with medals, crosses, and golden stripes were on his shoulders. [My painting is General Andranik in repose and without all the medals.] He wore a fluffy poukhalka [fur hat]. General Andranik was standing with his hands folded on his chest like a cross. He said, 'Listen to me, dear brothers, brave Armenian soldiers, I am Andranik. Thanks to your support, if it weren't for you I wouldn't have been Andranik. The nation has sent me to this front to defend our motherland, our fathers, mothers, and our brothers, and sisters. We must do this together. What do you say? Do you agree?'

"There were some soldiers that shouted, 'No.' He continued to try and rally them but still these men said the word no, again and again. The soldiers began to talk in a disgruntled way and unrest was filling the air. General Andranik unsheathed his sword and gave the command to feed the men for up to three days and then let them leave. They would need to turn in their weapons. The General admonished them by saying, 'Shame on all of you who lay down your weapons.' General Andranik returned to Erzroum [Karin]. Many did lay down their weapons and then headed toward another town in Ilijay. Those that abandoned serving General Andranik were seen by the Russian general Perjanpakov while he traveled with his cavalry. These Armenian soldiers promised to serve him and only him. The Russian general told the men that it would be days before the meetings were over and a plan made as to the next step."

Grandpa you stayed, but I also see how these men were so defeated that even an Armenian general they all admired was not enough to mobilize them to risk sure death. Somehow this more powerful known entity gave them strength to serve. Inbetween the finality of war there are a hundred miles of uncertainty and decay. That process brings the finality of something not the other way around.

You slept Grandpa and then you heard the corporal shouting to get up because you were all surrounded. Your old teacher Haourtioun's son Toross went mad and began screaming and crying and attacking his own men. He was tied and sent forward to the next city. You were told to join the other 47 soldiers and fight for your life. You were all sent out of the village and to the front line. It was dark and foggy, with no visibility. Somehow you all managed to dig trenches in the dark. The snow kept falling down. You were ordered to make a human chain and not to shoot.

The Turks cannons were roaring. There was no noise from your side. "We waited for a long time. First Sergeant Yeznik Kotertsi [from Koter] said that he would go to the headquarters and find out what to do next. He never returned. Then the corporal said the same thing and left and never returned. Lastly, my half-brother Yeghia Manoukian. (He called himself my half-brother because my sister breastfed him as an infant in order to save his life; Yeghia could only bring himself to say the word 'missing' with regards to Oghik, but underneath everyone knew the Turks devoured her.)"

Yeghia said that he too would go and return and you all told him that if he went he was never coming back like the other two. But, he did. Yeghia was shaken and crying while telling you all that the headquarters had been destroyed, that there was no one out there. The Turks had raided and killed everyone once again. He wept that all of you were prisoners trapped in trenches. He closed with saying that the only open road was the road to Erzroum. Yeghia was a volunteer soldier like the rest of the boy heroes. He was a sergeant and the only veteran among you. All of you began to ask him for guidance. Your one idea was that 20 of the men go to the wall and begin shooting towards the Turks' side. You Grandpa were one of these men. The Turks retreated and then created a wall of fire right behind you all. You still managed to cross the bridge towards Erzroum. There were a few hundred people walking towards Erzroum. It was like a scene out of Exodus in the Bible. There were some mothers holding children, sick people, elderly people, soldiers, and men. General Perjanpakov stopped the procession of people and told them to wait! He wanted women, elders and children to enter the city first. You watched and most of the people were not listening. The snow had fallen and closed the road. People were struggling to walk. Mothers clutching their children. Now, the elders were giving up and couldn't walk anymore.

"The weather cleared and the sun shone behind the clouds. The Turks had turned the cannon, and began bombarding forward. This made people retreat. People ran forward, some to the left, some to the right. No bomb fell on the people. There was one who said, "The artillerist or commander is a Christian because they fired a bomb that does not fall on the people." "But there doesn't come the voice of artillery from Erezroum. Our Armenian artillerists had dismantled the cannons so that they would not fight.""

"Artillerist and machine-gunners were eastern Armenian men serving in the Russian army and were well trained. Western Armenian soldiers had no concept about those things. Just give the weapon and let them shoot. This was the situation."

People tried to reach and enter the city of Erzroum. They saw it as a place of refuge. Grandpa I watch your tired being as you turn to see a young man crying for help in the snow. "No one was helping him, they just passed by." The voice sounded familiar to you. This young man was a villager from Vejan of Terjan district and an acquaintance of yours. This young man had a wounded leg that prevented him from walking. You got some men to help you and you all hoisted him onto a horse that was headed to the city. You never saw him again.

"Fighting, with much torture amongst the people. We somehow came to Erzroum's small train station together. In the Russian language it was called 'Koukoushka station'. It was two or 3 o'clock in the afternoon. The folk went to the city, but they didn't allow the soldiers to enter. He who could slip secretly into the crowd would be free from going to the front."

You didn't try to sneak away Grandpa. You got into the lines and waited. Then all of a sudden you heard the roar of "Attention!" Right before your eyes you saw the fabled and beloved General Andranik coming in your direction in a car. He stepped out and with food in boxes he piled them on the snow. He said, "Dear brothers, brave soldiers, what do you think? What ideal do you serve? You have all fled here and now are gathered together. Don't you have a father, mother, sister, brother, relatives? Don't you worry about them?"

I really can't believe he didn't talk about the fact you were all being asked to fight when the opposite had occurred. You didn't have any relatives or family left. You were fighting to survive, and now there were weapons in your hands. Yet, I do understand that no matter what had occurred there were still some who survived and that you boys had to start somewhere. He then left bread, meat, tobacco, and asked you all to eat and go back to the front. If you all went back to the front the Turks would retreat and flee to Kaz village. The General then left his car and mounted a horse and moved in front of you all. This action mobilized you boys and you remember everyone saying to hurry. You all ate and followed your leader to the front. General Andranik was right: the Turks retreated this time.

The majority of soldiers were Eastern Armenians and they didn't want to try and reclaim Erzroum. They wanted to go to Charaourghan border to defend Sarighamish, Kars. Once again there was chaos in the managing of these bewildered and untrained soldiers who had volunteered. I think that word is finally hitting me: "volunteered" is not the same as a fully trained member of an army. These young youths wanted refuge. At the time it made sense to join, but the constant facing of death after the brutalities they had suffered was truly a psychological nightmare that caused major internal conflict.

The bullets were flying around General Andranik like hail. He shouted "*En Avant!*"—no one would listen. The boy soldiers were fleeing the rain of bullets. Poor Andranik, he shouted that he never turned his back from the Turks until now. General Andranik kept shouting at the men to fight but they wouldn't. Deep inside, Grandpa, was it because they couldn't? The famous General went back to the city while the boy soldiers ran for cover in many directions. The rest of you came back to the mouth of the valley. The corporal had you all surround this first opening to the valley like a human chain. There were iron-made thorns two meters wide that had been cut. The sun set and in the darkness you all sat while it rained and then snowed all night.

I have a blanket over me and I am up before the sun came out. Grandpa I ask myself why? I should sleep but, as I am all bundled up I realize: how can I sleep while you are freezing with the clothes on your back? The least I can do is join you from the comforts of being free. I can never complain again about anything I face. My father was right when he would say that we could never know how lucky we were. He was an artist in the making and had to become a butcher in America so that I could have the luxuries of freedom.

Grandpa that night you started shouting out the names of your friends, relatives, and co-villagers. You were reprimanded by the guards. You were calling out names of very specific people; Armenak your brother-in-law, your godfather Trdat, brother Yeghia, and Uncle Manouk. It took courage to breathe a word in the dark. I get it now. As soon as you stopped calling out for loved ones you all heard someone crying out for help. "Help me, I'm dying." The voice was a familiar one as you approached him near the bridge you recognized him. It was Khnkanoss from Camour Dara. He was a relative from your father's side of the family. He was dying and wanted you to save his life. You bravely first went and saluted your officer. I remember how I went to an ancient castle this year and saw the armour that soldiers wore centuries ago. I was struck by the fact that the tradition of saluting came from these medieval soldiers. They had to wear such heavy head armour that when they wanted to honor their leader they opened and closed the front of the helmet that covered their faces. How such a gesture transferred its current into every soldier's stance I will never know. The past is alive, the future is being fused by today.

Your commander stood in front of you waiting for your next move. You told him your friend was sick and lying in the mud. You asked him permission to help him. The permission was given. You were given clear instructions as to your limits in helping this dying friend. You could try and move him as far away from the front as you could, then you were to return for duty. As you got your friend up from the mud and snow he put his arm around your neck. I see you struggling to stay on your own feet. A guard shouted at you both to stop; he thought you were fleeing your duty. He didn't believe you when you told him you were given permission. The guard got clearance and now I watch you from the sky as you drag his tired being through the snow to the Erzroum train station. There you knew of underground military premises. Once you got in you saw newly arrived Russian soldiers. There was a stove and you found a small kettle. You brought snow from outside and used it to make hot tea. Then this lad's cousin Khachatour came in and found you two. The rich treasure of drinking hot tea together is what followed.

How unworldly it must have been just walking around empty houses as you began your journey back to your post. No matter how much you sought to be near order of some kind, things changed constantly. As you left the barracks with the sick youth's cousin Khachatour you were told that there was no post to return to. Everyone kept moving to this side of the city. The situation had changed; he told you that the guards would not let them back across now. You both ventured out into the darkness again.

The ill relative stayed in the underground barracks for now. You both found a large house that clearly belonged to a wealthy Armenian family.

You both found the quarter where some of the refugees from your own village were. There were migrants from Terjan—your region—Papert and Yerzenka. This large two-story house appeared abandoned. When you both entered you went up to the second floor and like the loaded treasures inside a pyramid you saw household belongings stacked up high all along the floors. Food was piled so high that it resembled haystacks to you. The stove was burning and an old man was lying on the couch. Bewildered, you asked him where the people of the house were. He told you that he was asked to watch these belongings while his family left promising to return soon. They never did. He also whispered that a Turk is in the house, that he fled downstairs when he heard your voices which scared him. He did not know how many people came into the house.

Grandpa I want to leave this next part out but I won't. I will say the truth as I was taught to do my whole life. You and your fellow volunteer go downstairs and kill him. I know you had to but it is still so hard for me to read. I am reading out of context. I try to stay with you every minute. I am spared because you do not say how you killed him you say only that you both finished him. He was the enemy and he would have killed the old man. If he knew how many you were he would have tried to kill you the second you entered. But, I still think that we were all babies once, being held by loved ones rejoicing in our birth. He was someone's son.

I am snapping back to focus now, and I am watching you walk through the momentary quiet and see you light a candle while reaching out to take an Armenian book down from the shelf to read. You move towards the window and for the first time since 1914 you have a moment of repose, and I am sighing with relief.

The old man felt more secure for you both had just saved his life. He would ask questions from time to time and you would gently answer. Then it happened. Loud explosions from outside shook the windows and you began to hear people screaming. The old man told you to open the window and ask the people passing by for information. When you opened the window you could see flames of smoke rising in the dark. The people shouted up to you saying to stay calm and that nothing was happening. (How strange people behave when they are in shock. It is like they are calming themselves by those words which have nothing to do with reality.) You asked your friend to cover for you so that you could sleep and by morning he shook you awake telling you that the city had been evacuated. People were in disarray running in all directions now. You thought like a soldier and asked old Khnkanoss where the gate to Kars was. He pointed and off you went. You saw a horse coach that was heading towards the gate and there were children and adults on it. A Turk shot an acquaintance of yours from your home town Terjan. He just fell and died instantly. Somehow you both reached the Kars gate. I know that word "Kars" is Armenian. I heard it throughout my life but just like the sacred word "Van" where the most traditional Armenians lived it was a word that was tender but I knew nothing about its value in your life until now.

Once you crossed under the gate you once again entered a gruesome hell.

"Oh, Lord what a scene it was. What an infernal, hellish place it was. Crowded people, the sick, the elderly, children, hundreds of burdened women clutching their children, some with frost-bitten legs and hands. They were not able to walk so they dove into the snow to die. God bless their souls.

"General Andranik and gallant Mourat Sebastatsy from Sebastia, Sepouh Papirtis (from Papirt), stood at the gate, and were shouting to the soldiers, to let the children and women pass first. The crowds would not listen; the gate was overcrowded and masses of people were frantically trying to get out. There was no waiting for anyone. The Turks had entered the city from the Yerzenka gate and had occupied half of the city.

"The Turks were chasing us heavily. People were climbing up the fence wall to get away. Fences began to be pulled down. No one cared about 'children and women first.' General Andranik, Mourad, Sepouh shouted and screamed from the gate and no one listened. Finally, the people passed through the gate and went out into the wilderness with nowhere to go. The national heroes got into a military car and were transported to another location. Those poor miserable, helpless people. They were like bewildered sheep that remained unprotected, unbacked. These people kept walking. I also left my friends and dropped everything in my bag so that it wasn't heavy. My feet were aching. I could not walk. I only kept my weapon and a few bullets. I hadn't many things with me. Whatever I had, I put them in my pockets. In a similar situation only your weapon is your friend and nothing else. I went on my way, step by step."

You haven't eaten for two days and walking nonstop Grandpa. We lucky ones starve between meals. "I'm starving" is a catchphrase but none of us have truly known what it is to fight for our lives despite us dying at the same time. You had to find ways to survive. You jumped on the back of a cart. The Russian man told you to get off. You told him you were starving and that your feet were so sore and that you would not get off. They stopped their demands to get off and forward you went into the unknown. You had found a few friends again and they told you they were trying to reach Ghalay (Castle). No one had a plan. If ever the saying "one day at time" could be illustrated this was it. Everyone just pointing themselves forward and walking with the name of a place as their motivation. We are hard-wired to walk, and really to walk in a big circle. I truly see that mechanism in full view right now.

You had told one of the Russian men driving the cart that you wanted to go to Kouby Koy ("village" in Turkish). They told you when the road divided that was where you would get off.

They called you little brother. They pointed you in the direction of Kouby Koy. (Ahh, that word again the dear Turkish delegates like to use popped into my head again, "Baseless.") You got on a cart that was heavy laden with supplies and animals. You saw loaves of bread and took two of them. Your friend jumped off, and the man started yelling at you to get off the cart because the oxen were so tired. You did and that day you both ate bread.

By nightfall you and your friend reached Korby Koy. A miracle happened. In this town all was destroyed. People were trying to build tents and stay warm. You found a corner and slept. In the morning you began to look around and heard a man shout your name. He was telling Armenak your beloved brother-in-law that he saw a young man that looked like Galoust. Armenak got upset because he had been told by a co-villager that Galoust was dead and that he himself buried him. I think it was an honest mistake but things got heated. Once Armenak looked into your eyes he knew it was true—you were alive! He was enraged at the man who had told him that he buried you with his own hands. You calmed everyone down and tears of joy streamed down all of your faces. This friend of yours disappeared and you never saw him again. This happened quite frequently: it was like you had a guardian angel that helped you walk a few feet, and then they were gone. Armenak said the plan was to continue walking towards the Russian border that was called Gharaourghal. It took days of walking to finally arrive.

"I recollected the arrival of General Andranik, God bless his soul. To those 300 Armenian now-trained warriors in King Nikolai's army who said, 'We don't need Western Armenia, we'll go to the Russian border to defend our Armenia.' Those Western Armenians who died, and those that survived, survived."

So many survivors had frostbite. No help, no food. You had hoped to rest for a couple days but that was not to be. After two short days a panic rose among the refugees. All of the people began to flee. The Turks were coming to slaughter yet again. So on you went Grandpa. You and Armenak reached Sarighamish. You stayed there for only three or four days. There was certain death if you stayed. Your only hope now was to go to Eastern Armenia or the deep parts of Russia.

"We suffered very much, and were exhausted. We had become soulless. We could not endure or persist any more. We could not tolerate these tortures. No one cared about the refugees, they just wanted our weapons. We would not give them. We hid them in our clothes on our back. We had a cart now and we loaded the weapons with some of our collective belongings. We let weak people sit on the cart and people took turns all the way to the next village called Malakan near Kars."

You walked slowly with the cart and a few hidden Russian rifles that were called Mosins. You all knew you would be running into Turks in this village. There were Russian soldiers that were yelling at you all. They warned that you couldn't pass unless you gave them your weapons. You told them you had no weapons but they wanted to search your cart that was still far behind you. You told them that of course they could search your cart. Quickly you decided to talk in a relaxed way and warn Armenik, Yeghia, and Vartan, a relative through marriage. The men pulled out the weapons and told the Russian soldiers they would not hand them over. The Armenian men told them that they knew how dangerous the roads were and that when they arrived safely to the next city they would return them if they so wanted. Armenik spoke truthfully that death would greet them either way so take your pick. Amazingly the soldiers let them pass.

You finally reached Kars. Grandpa it seems the will to move forward never stops. Kars was just as dangerous as every other village you all had gone to. But, in survival mode the mind says the next place will be better. It wasn't.

In Kars (a pure Armenian word) mayhem was going on. People of all kinds were fighting, stealing, and pushing each other in these mass crowds of chaos. You and your small group continued on to Mazra village. None of you could understand the cruel way the locals treated you all.

I am uncertain if they were only Armenians at this time. All I know is that they were extremely hostile and would not sell you anything. You write there were many refugees now and you all continued walking to Sandramish. The refugees kept up with you and your group. You write that you stayed in a dale (a valley).

There was a large group of you all now. Together you created a human wall outside and started a fire to try and cook food. Some tried going back into the village to pay for food; no one would open their doors. It was another hard night but you all withstood the cold and the cruel behavior of these locals. The next morning the walk continued to Paltourvan village. You all were begging, asking, praying while you searched for hope. You found vacant barracks for rent. They were ruins but you all pitched in together and found corners to claim as your own. Collectively people shared what they had brought with them: a few rugs, cushions, and other items that could help get through the night. You were all so exhausted that food was not a concern. People were too fatigued to want to eat. Little by little the group began to gain some strength and in a couple days you all sat at your own meeting. Each person was given tasks that were based on their strengths. Armenak your brother-in-law was told he was adroit at gathering things so he should go into the village and figure out how to get food. Yeghia was told to go find things that are combustible. Mkrtich was told to go and prepare a fire-place. You Grandpa were told to go and find water. You were to find a spring or a fountain. In the mean time you were to fill a jar with water and come back so the people could begin to wash. I am watching and shaking my head. William Saroyan was so right when he spoke of the spirit of the Armenians. No matter how many nations have tried to obliterate them they truly rise up through the ruins and rebuild Armenia even if there are two people left.

The day came where you had to leave Armenik because everyone had to separate and continue the march towards hope. It was decided that you should find your one uncle who left your village long before the extermination started. He had killed a Turk in self-defense and had to flee to survive. He lived in a village called Gouyoyjogh. He left his child and wife when he escaped and after twelve years she remarried and so did he. The elders in the barracks felt that since you had a living relative your mother's brother, you should find him and let them care for you until you got your strength back. As much as Armenik grieved for your leaving you could not change your mind. Your sweet sister Oghik's husband found solace in your eyes. She saved your life, but lost her own. You left once again and walked until you reached your uncle's village. Thank God they welcomed you with open arms. You had your first real bath in years. Your first pajamas, and your first real bed to sleep in. You stayed there for nearly three weeks.

You did not feel rested yet when bad news broke out. The Turks were coming to slaughter this village too. The people were fleeing their homes once again. So did you Grandpa. You all found a great-hearted wealthy Armenian man named Kayl Vahan. He took all of you in and continued to feed refugees around the clock. There was unrest amongst the Armenians. All this crowding and the need to survive created a sort of madness amongst the people. Grandpa you write how it is an abomination that the gunshots that were coming from across the river were from Armenian bullets. But, I could see the madness occurring very easily. Everyone was in constant flux. No home or village was safe. Armenians would see Turks coming into a village and they would try to defend the area. There were no leaders in close proximity. No way to communicate. General Karekin Njdeh came into the village because he was enraged that the Zeitoun and Moush villagers arrested and imprisoned a few of his soldiers that were giving trouble to the people. He ordered large and long willow branches to be brought and one by one he ordered elderlies to drop their trousers and lay flat on the ground while they each got twenty five lashes. This was an Armenian general! He was telling the people to never ever arrest his soldiers. When he got to Kayl Vahan you couldn't take it Grandpa and you ran up to him and saluted him. He asked you what you wanted and you told him that the man he was ready to lash had been feeding Armenians for over a week around the clock and that he was a great man. For your courage this sweet man was spared. Kayl Vahan thanked you for your valor and courage. He told you he did not think he could have survived the beating. You were very demoralized by this treatment of your own people. I wonder why the elderly? Was it to provoke guilt so that order would resume? People were coping the best they could in the constant threat of annihilation. You stayed with this kind man for almost a week, then the day came you had to leave once more. This time your small group walked towards Yerevan. In 2015 Yerevan is the capital of a free Armenia. One evening you reached Tsitilyakova village where an Armenian priest lived. He welcomed you all with great happiness: you quietly thank him, and wonder to yourself, "Where shall we end up?"

Chapter Twenty

I FEEL LIKE I have taken a break to exhale from this journey with you. It has been 24 hours and my arms are very heavy but thinking only of returning to this stream with you. I read some of the next volume and split off from my body in order to sleep. I can't believe what I read. I can't believe it is happening again. I can't register this in my mind. I sleep in my own barracks to gather strength to write this most horrific scene that I embraced last night. I hid in my comfortable bed. I felt guilty for having the easy part which is to write. I then tell myself it isn't easy for me. It is all relative. I must continue.

Grandpa, all my life since I was a child I read biographies and auto-biographies of great women and men. The ones that changed the world with their persistence and commitment. I read the commandment you wrote to your children and grandchildren last night. It is as though a great writer wrote this to us. It reminds me of the purity of the Dalai Lama. All this time your 400 pages sat next to me for over 20 years, and I couldn't bring myself to re-enter. I kept your words near me as I read countless biographies, autobiographies. I call myself a biography junkie. I love it. I go back thousands of years or last year. I just discovered a German scholar who single handedly changed the face of Hieroglyphics and Egyptology by his persistent passion of learning and traveling and journaling. I am in awe at the number of languages he spoke. I ordered his translated journals from the 1800's, and then it hits me. Your writing is one of the best auto-biographies I have ever read in my life. Not because of your relationship to me, but because you're so interesting to read. You are honest and don't hold back. I am pained as I read but I can't wait to climb back in once I regain my strength. You remember names, cities, and let the ones who can listen be enriched by the truth which does feed our souls, and clearly gives us strength and wisdom.

I do not understand it yet. As I walk through the valley of death with you I can sleep again. I feel like I have laid down some of the corpses. When I penned your parents' names together and sent it to our Holy Church I felt nearly certain they would say no. It is odd, I feared they would judge me and tell me they were not real and that is why they cannot have a plaque. Or that these two died a long time ago, and never came to the church in question. It was all so strange that I was ready to defend my gesture when the call came. I thought, here it is. They will tell me to find another path to honor them. Somehow I felt they would say it was inappropriate. Instead all I heard was to come and proof read the words for the plaque. What would happen if we all did the same thing? We would have to build another church to hold all your names and your kin. Soon, Great-great-grandfather, I will honor you and your beloved wife. You were murdered in the 1895 looting massacre, along with your two sons. Your dear wife was murdered in 1915 only after she fell on the corpse of her son the priest. I will also make a plaque for all the rest of you I have grown to love. There are so many of you as I walk this journey. I hope and pray that this dare-I-say book will be your funeral so that the readers can be near you during your last hours on earth. We are all 1914, 15, 16, 17, and now 2015. In my lifetime I have witnessed genocides that continue to occur like rains of murder to so many innocent people who just want the right to live with dignity.

Where you ended up was Tsitiankov. This village was one of several at the skirts of Alakiaz. The backside was a mountain, while the front part was fields and adobe. The water came to the village from the Alakiaz Mountains. The villagers had prepared ample places to live, and had dug a ditch where waters were reserved. You Grandpa had been fighting a fever for weeks. There was a water spring that sprang up from beneath the ground and was called a "Goula". There was even a manmade lake for the cattle. There was a deep valley on one side of the village where water flowed. They called it mill water. Along the way there were small mills powered by water. The inhabitants of this village belonged to two declarations of faith. One was called the illuminators and was the majority. The other was called Frangs which were Armenian Catholics. There were two churches right across from each other, one for the Catholics and the other for the Illuminators. An Armenian priest gave you refuge in his home. You were still in great pain throughout your body. You ventured into the streets and spoke with the locals. It lifted your spirits. You continued to heal and break the fever. You were free to come and go as you please. It was like a dream, you write. Then the dream turned into a bloodbath again. The Turks came to this beautiful village and brought the reign of terror with them. The Armenian villagers were distraught and listened passively to the Turk pasha. The priest you were living with took bread, water, and salt which was the sign of surrender. You heard the people shouting "Do not slaughter us Pasha! Let us live! We surrender! Let the King's sword be sharp and we pledge!" The commander put soft pillows under the head of the priest as he begged for his people. "Very well, I accept your bread, salt, and water. I respect you. I will not allow soldiers to come into the village. Go collect weapons of your village and bring them to me. I'll assign some teams of soldiers as defendants. Then, I will leave." This is the unbearable part in the next volume. Give us your weapons. There it is again! Aleksan had approximately 150 to 160 households. The Turkish pasha lied of course and gave the people two hours to return with any and all arms. They began to tell on each other. One old man kept pointing to the men that had rifles and he would tell the pasha how many they had. Grandpa you quietly told him to stop it. You told him say one rifle not three. Keep one for your safety. He betrayed you and shouted that you Western Armenians were nothing but trouble. He told you cruel words that you remembered 67 years later. He actually told you to get out or he would have you exterminated like a dog. Little did he know what was to come. You gave up and returned to the stable, pulled a blanket over your head and slept. During the time you slept because you were still weak, much had happened. The people brought their weapons and handed them over one by one. The very same night when the darkness covered the houses the evil Turks came down to massacre once again. You heard screaming, and gun shots everywhere. Your fever was burning you up and keeping you weak. An old man was in the stable hiding with you. You heard the neighbors screaming as Turks came in and dragged a bride out of her home and then raped her. You could hear her begging them to stop. Her husband and brother-in-law stood there as the guns were pointed at them. Finally you hear the husband shout at the Turk and after two shots both Turks were dead. Then you heard the young man shoot himself and die. At that instant it began to rain heavily. You write how this was luck for the people.

In the morning a Turk came into the stable and began to slap you. He didn't have a gun with him. He told you if he had his gun he would shoot you. He stole your clothes and the ring you wore for your friend who died during the massacres. He stole what bedding was there. You were completely alone and without clothes. The ring was for the fiancé of your friend that died. He wanted you to give it to her if by chance you made it to freedom. The Turk kept calling you a son of a gyavour. Then another Turk came in and he had a rifle probably from all the arms they stole from the people. The first Turk demanded the rifle so he could shoot you and the second one told him why shoot a sick boy he is a corpse anyway. You thank him for saving your life. But, he didn't think you were worth a bullet. Within 10 minutes Kurdish outlaws joined in with the first Turk and emptied the house. They did not harm you. "My God, give me some hope."

The old Armenian man was hiding with the cattle. You tried to give him hope. You felt bad for the hungry animals. You always cared about animals and their pains. The old man found you some clothes in the house nursery. You told him that the only option was to try and run away. You covered your head with a white cloth. You took an old blanket and wrapped it around your body and you no longer looked Armenian. It was your only chance. As you both left the stable some Turks took the old man and threw him in a well. They let you pass because you spoke perfect Turkish and they thought you were one of them. Humans are so primitive. They see you with a white cloth around your head and call you brother. They spoke kindly to you because you were not a Christian. They counted on you to join them in the stealing and pillaging of innocent people. One Turk told you to drive the cattle which was not theirs to begin with. You agreed to help them. They told you to hurry back after grazing them. You ran away down among the rocks. You sat down to take a breath and turned to the village to see...

"My God! What a scene I was witnessing! They had brought together the village population that had remained there in the three barracks and two churches: one of the Illuminators', the other of the Frangs' church. They had set fire to the three barracks, and had the machine guns set on those barracks. The people were burned alive and those that escaped were shot by the machine guns. The same thing was going on in the other churches. They had set the machine guns and were slaughtering the people. People ran from the Illuminators' church to the church of the Frangs, from there to the Illuminators' church. They shot them uninterruptedly."

Ethnic cleansing. What a sick way of putting it. How about mass steal-ing from thy neighbor because you are lazy and undisciplined? Whatever day one person decides to steal and murder his fellow neighbor in order to take what is not theirs, that day becomes a genocide for a family. Anyone who claims to do it for God is truly just a criminal. People kill one gun at a time then they deplore the name of their own God while wounding all of humanity. A personal God somehow becomes the reason to plough through countless people because the one destroying is superior? Sounds like insanity of the soulless minds of others.

There are two things groups like this who want money and power. The most disgusting thing of all is to continue to resolve a horrific part in one's own history by simply saying it never happened. This would lead me to believe it will happen again. Killings in smaller groups and under the radar. I wish these miserable little groups would drop the religion and just do the stealing. Because they hurt true believers who start reading about religion as the root and this feeds in to the separations of great faiths that should work together in harmony. A very pure Muslim man in Paris who saved the lives of innocent people in his local kosher deli where he worked said it best. When asked how he felt about fellow Muslims doing such a horrific act. He simply said that those were not Muslims, they were criminals.

So I will state that the Turks during the time of the Ottoman Empire's decay chose to mass-murder a group that had been their neighbors for thousands of years because they wanted their stuff. Period; end of subject. Today they still don't want to return our stuff. So, like criminals, they say it never happened. What would it look like if there was restitution? Would we be fighting for destroyed homes? Money? Too little too late. How about the wall I wrote about? How about writing about the genocide in your history books? How about not killing reporters and teachers who want to talk about it? How about that? How about people in your own country getting to ask what really happened? How about a monument that holds all the names of those that perished? Granted it would be a huge monument but we can write small. You still keep the stuff.

The hardest thing in the world is to get a murderer on death row to say he or she did it. Maybe you are waiting for your own elderly to die. The ones who participated in the extermination. Perhaps you have many Turks that live in our ancestral homes and live in the countless Armenian villages. Don't you know that if I carry corpses and live with ghosts all the way in Sunny California, then so do you? There are millions of Turks who know the truth. You know what happened. Some of your blood is Armenian. Your own grandmothers were Christian. The countless Armenian girls sold at auction—I have seen the pictures, pretty dead looking girls—they would have survived. Why don't you speak up?

Wow, still afraid of the Turks after all these years. It took this writing process for me to get what was missing. The third heat has been those of you still alive Turkey who won't talk because you are scared. I see us all in a huge convention in Turkey. One million and a half Turks say: "I am a survivor of the Armenian genocide." Then all the dead will be buried, all the marches will end, and you can stop pretending you have mental amnesia at the pasha level.

What if Turkey is the chosen one to teach the rest of the world to stop genocides?

Chapter Twenty-One

THE ACHING SCENE OF the Armenians running back and forth between the two churches and being mowed down right before your eyes froze my pen. I was so hungry today because I hadn't eaten and it was 2 p.m. I felt light-headed and so weak and couldn't help but thinking of you Grandpa. My hunger was due to time constraints and most of my country is on a diet. Here we beg people to walk for 30 minutes a day. We have so much food we are starving ourselves so we don't gain weight. I felt your pain if only in my imagination. I had a headache and I was shaky and it was so great to have a good meal and regain my baseline of inner peace.

As I begin the second volume of your diary I am overwhelmed of how much more you endured. I have walked through many villages with you. The miracles that would happen and the hell that would happen were side by side like a land mine. You never knew which would happen. Some Armenians were so kind; some were as ignorant as the Turks that were destroying the soul of Armenia one village at a time. You starved so much of the time. Speaking Turkish saved your life as well as others many times. It also made Armenians suspicious of you. They didn't know how you could speak Turkish so well. It is years now of uncertainty, one day to the next. You find your mother's brother twice! He left you in his home while he escaped with his wife and child. But he risked his life coming in the dark to save you. What valor. You tell him to leave because your fever was so great that both of you would die. He cries and prays for you and leaves. Yet, within a month you are in another village and you see him again. He fell to the ground in shock at God's mercy. That He saved his family and he got his nephew back as well. At this point you leave again, wandering from place to place while starving. One family feeds you, another family ignores you. You had a fever that would not leave and you finally learned you had typhoid. You found a loaf of bread and two people begged you for it so you gave it to them. One Armenian man pulled it from your hands and fell into the mud eating it and people began to attack him and you shouted to stop hurting him. It was your bread and he was hungry: what is the difference? Everyone is hungry. I better understand why bread was so important to you and my father. You wouldn't eat a meal all my life if there wasn't bread on the table. Everyone in my family loved bread more than any other food. There was always such bountiful food in our house. Too much. It was the most important item to give to others and to have plenty of at home. Once again, too much. I understand now.

It is now May 28th 1918 and a miracle has happened. A few states signed a declaration that Armenia was to be a free republic. The Turks also signed this declaration. After all, most of the Armenian nation was dead. You write that after 600 years of slavery deliverance finally came. It was shortlived. Within less than two years with the rise of Lenin and Stalin in the Soviet Union the Republic of Armenia imploded to dust. You decided to rejoin the army again. You had been pushed forward to Leninakan. I see the word and I truly sit astonished that of all the 250 villages devastated during the December 1988 earthquake in Armenia I ended up in Leninakan. The whole city flattened. Nine-story apartment buildings sitting stacked like cardboard blocks one on top of the other. I saw what you saw Grandpa but from nature and not a genocide. It felt the same. I remember the paranoia and fear everywhere. Armenians were telling me to keep quiet in America. That soon after the major earthquake occurred military men showed up for the first and only time then disappeared. They believed there were missiles that were stored underneath the ground in their region. When the massive earthquake occurred it set off an avalanche of destruction aided from below. They truly believed it. What was scary is I did too. I saw the tanks back in Yerevan circling to terrorize us to be quiet. I felt like I was in a nightmare. Grandpa the children were gone. Schools that had 1,100 kids were now less than half full. The people were so brave so kind, so beautiful I will never forget them. I know fear Grandpa, I know what it is like to see massive destruction, but I have never been hunted for. This I do not know.

Today it rained even though it is summer. As the rain pelted down I stood under it and cleaned. I wanted to feel the vulnerability you must have felt sitting in the rain all night. I realize the rain is sweet and I love it on my being, I accept I will never get a glimpse of your life growing up. It is beyond the sphere of humanity as I know it. But, I do know I can step on a plane and enter hell on earth right now in several parts of the world. It is the 21st century and humans are becoming robotic or primitive. I stand in between.

The Armenian section of the army loved having you back in the army because of your vast experience and your ability to speak multiple languages. You could now speak some Russian, Armenian, Kurdish, and Turkish. You wanted to serve your people but your uncle thought you were mad to join again. Your own Armenian commander struck you to the point of severe injury just because someone stole a loaf of bread in the barracks and it was your turn to guard the door. Some in the new group of Armenian superiors were interested in your story. You told them all of it and then your military service ordeals.

It is now 1919: you are sent to a village that was occupied primarily by Turks with a small population of Kurds. You were instructed to take an order to the chief of the village so that your barrack could purchase meat for the soldiers. There were many stables filled with animals that the Turks stole from the Armenians. The chief was so degenerative in mind that he took you to a poor old woman's house. She had one calf and that was all. She was Kurdish. She wept and pleaded with you Grandpa that this one calf was all that she had in the world. Where would she get milk? You felt a strange presentiment as she kissed your legs. You felt your sister Oghik's spirit around you. Oghik saved your life and though this woman was an enemy you wanted to spare her grief. You remembered that a Kurd saved your life during the march. You can't take the tears and begging and you ask her who has the most cattle. She tells you of a Mullah named Hassan. You tell the chief to take you there and I am trembling at your verve and tenacity at eighteen years old. You did go to the Mullah's stable and you released a fatty calf. Then you drove it back to the barracks. One day your commander shouted to get ready that the President of Armenia, Khatissian and the commander in chief, General Nazaekov, were coming to your barracks. There were a total of 50 volunteer soldiers in your barracks. The general shouted at all the dirty soldiers because you were the only one that was clean. You had been secretly helping an Armenian family by taking them meat and they in turn washed your clothes for you. When you were clean you got in trouble and when you were dirty you got in trouble.

It was now May 1920: your regiment moved to Meternick. You are still having to do military exercises. You weren't a big fan but you had to do them. There were two Armenian families that lived in this village. You used to visit them for comfort and they would churn soup from donkey's milk. All of you would laugh about it but food was food. You returned to your garrison and had just fallen asleep when you heard,

"On Foot!" A mutiny was beginning within the Armenian army. The commander and sergeant were now pulling the men from the line and beating them one by one with their bare hands. None of you knew what was occurring. A soldier grabbed the sergeant and threatened to kill him if he touched him. Within two weeks order was resumed throughout the barracks of soldiers. It is as if a single murmur starts a flame that then rages as the soldiers sublimate their unspoken grief into a tsunami of disturbance in the face of their own choosing to join the army. It is like their own unconscious minds flooded and they wanted to be free, but there was nowhere to go.

Life in the army had its own challenges. The soldiers were from every walk of life, some were hostile, emotionally unstable and would fly off in a rage or want to take something from you. This one Armenian man wanted your one utensil that had a spoon on one side and a fork on the other. He wanted blood because you would not let him take it. From that moment it ends up with you being forced to stand in one position holding a bag of bricks along with your rifle for punishment as you tried to defend yourself from this soldier. It was so hot and you were miserable but also stubborn as you tried to hold on to your integrity. The commander came in and immediately told you to put the bag down. You wouldn't. The commander then reprimanded the sergeant for giving you such a harsh punishment. He was reprimanded for going outside of his rank. You only put the bag down when the sergeant told you to. Then the sergeant was punished for five days. Sometimes there was justice and most times there was not.

In June 1920, a Turkish official came to Meternik. The depth of vulgarity of the Turks never stopped. This official told the commander he was on the Armenians' side. Of course he was checking things out again. Within a short time the Turks were planning another massacre. This time they were coming for tired boy soldiers with Russian influence. The Turks were now having to plan an attack versus setting everyone on fire because the Russians were close to the Armenians now.

There was a hero in your battalion. His name was Hokin Sirem. "*Sirem*" in Armenian means to like or to love. You were all told to start walking through a forest to get to the place where your regiment was to protect your border. You all felt it was way too quiet. The boy soldiers heard the gun shots spraying at you all. The Turks had dug trenches and were shooting above your heads because of their position and ignorance. Your Commander shouted, "Retreat!" You boys were stunned at the rain of gunshots but it was a miracle that they continued to spray above your heads. The commander was shouting in Russian to retreat and dear brave Hokin shouted out for you all to stop running! That running back would lead you all out on an open field again: this is where you would all be gunned down. The other boys shouted, "Hurray!" The Turks then fled the trenches and the army gunner from Garabagh would not shoot. He was frozen and the Turks were running into the forest and fields: this was one time the slithering evil didn't win. Smbat the Greek repositioned the tommy gun and some of the Turks were gunned down. All the soldiers were saved thanks to Hokin which means "soul." One meaning of this boy's name is Soulful love. He ended up being taken to the military high office and raised to the rank of Corporal. Heroes amongst the boys who fought for their motherland. I wish I could write their names on the wall that Turkey should build.

How you blush Grandpa. You had such sensitivity and decorum. Because of the squalid living conditions you all had things like lice and other maladies which would attack at a moment's notice. You bless the soul of your commander because he gave you gasoline to kill off these horrible flesh-eating pests. You would suffer in silence for days before you would muster courage due to embarrassment to ask for help. The strange thing is you all knew cures that really worked and you applied it for two days and were cured.

I blush at ever complaining about anything in my life. We are all so lucky. We worry about tomorrow when all you ever got was a moment by moment chance to walk into the fog of hoping you would survive.

It seems the commander was really trusting you more and assigning you to more critical posts. He chose you to protect a village and then gave you the high position of Chief Guard. You are still in your teens. You were told the night password, and instructed to guard a group of seven soldiers: that the hope and safety of the whole army which was positioned behind your post was in your hands. There were four ranks of soldiers. There was an abyss and you had to stand guard in the open air. You learned that Turks were on the other side of the valley. You say that in the dark you all talked openly. It was a catharsis for all of you. Your job was to rotate the guards every hour. The other six men could sleep but not you. There is often the sweet innocence of a kitten or a bird amongst the battalion that reminds the soldiers of what reality is. The twisted mindstate that is required to maintain an order of killing the enemy is a complex paradigm. There must be a unified hatred, fear, and the hope for deliverance as tonic for sleep.

Your battalion had a young lad, born handsome, kind, and wanting to grow up too fast. He was the captain's son. After the first wave of massacres he wanted to follow his father. He was the only person allowed to do what he wanted when he wanted. He was like the little prince. You all loved him but felt fear because it was an unspoken rule to keep him safe from all harm. He did act invincible. But, he cheered you all up like the kitten you all needed. One day he went missing. You were all stationed in a dangerous mountainous region called Vaskout near Oti. This area was considered the front now. There were no roads just steep rock filled ground. The boy was last seen with a soldier that was driving the few cattle the army had for grazing. He just disappeared. (Grandpa my right rib side hurts so much that I can barely write. It has to be from the stress wafting down into my body. I feel centered and calm yet in pain. A pain that must be emotional in origin. I am very aware of my being as I write. It is strange. I feel like I am looking out into a dangerous vista. I am writing no matter what.) This boy caused you great joy and pain. I say caused because you loved this child. He reminded you of yourself before the blood that stained your innocence. Your captain appointed you to find him in the dark! You told him it was dangerous but he didn't care. You were allowed to choose two other boy soldiers to accompany you. He ordered you to return with his child. There was a section of the mountain that was so steep that you all called it an abyss. The Turks lay wait on the other side of the mountain, God only knew where. You chose the soldiers and off you went into darkness. You all held the rocks as you skid down the sides of the mountain. There was a cave and you ordered the two youths to go inside and rest. Then you continued searching the best you could.

The moonlight helped you see the trees straight ahead. Once you got close to the trees you saw the military kettle on the ground. You followed it past the fallen bag of apples, pears, black plums, and mulberries. Writing the names of the fruit feels so heavenly. The simplest things feel so life-affirming when one is walking in the valley of death. There was a small stream of blood on the ground you followed it to the sight of this boy hunched over the stream as if he were drinking water. When you touched him he fell over onto his back. He was dead and his beautiful Armenian eyes were still open. The Turks killed him and he had crawled as far as he could before he died. You went and got the two soldiers. No stretcher. There was no way to carry him up the sides of the mountain. It was daybreak now. The two soldiers were crying from the heartbreak of what they saw. The boy was collecting a bag of fruit to bring back to the soldiers. He loved to surprise them. Grandpa I watch you reach the highest point of the mountain and take out your handkerchief. It was a rag but it was all you had. You tied it to the end of your rifle and you told yourself somehow the soldiers must figure out where you all are. One shot was heard and seen by the soldiers. I shuddered that the Turks saw the handkerchief and heard the bullet as well. It did work because they arrived with a stretcher. You write how you felt so bad tying the boy in the stretcher but it was the only way to get him up the side of the mountain.

My dearest friend just died. I too had that strange reaction when the undertakers bumped his feet on the wall. So I took his feet in my hands as they ushered him out to the van. I wouldn't let them bump him anymore. I know it didn't matter but it did to me. It is as if their bodies are in process of leaving and should be honored exactly as they were when they were alive.

What happens next is beyond me. You all get this boy back to the barracks. You didn't sleep for 24 hours, and I really know what that message means now. Don't shoot the messenger?! You were instructed to stay awake again and guard the body. I am thinking from what? The father's grief? Then at five in the afternoon the next day the corporal came and told you that the captain was assigning a punishment to you! You now had to guard a section of the front line all night. No sleep yet again. I have to say I want to really wring the neck of this man. You stood there in the darkness until the sun came up and then you collapsed on the ground. Grief is complicated when someone has to pay for the captain's own bad judgement. Within two weeks you were all told that your colonel, Shakoupatov wanted all of you from the 5th frontier battalion to move from Olty to Gahgzevan. Now you discover something even more evil than bullets and knives. You are the victim of a bomb. You had never seen, nor heard of one before. Out of 20 soldiers you were the worst hit. Nine serious injuries throughout your body. Your commander came and stood above you and wept. He told you who could he trust to go out into the night to deliver messages across rivers and do the hardest tasks that he had always trusted you with? He prayed for you and left.

You were then transported to a train station which would take you to a hospital. In your diary you speak of Kemal, the Turks, and the communists being responsible for destroying your republic. You are eighteen now, suffering from nine wounds. All the wounded soldiers were laying on the grass. You remember you were the only one on a stretcher. You were transported to Leninakan (renamed Gyoumry in 1991). Once you were there you were assisted by nurses and helped the best they could. It is still 1920. The morning came for your operation to remove fragments of metal from your abdomen. A worker in the hospital pulled your severely wounded leg and you reflexively struck him from the excruciating pain. He caused you more injury. You apologized and he asked for your forgiveness as well. They put a mask over your nose with drops to put you to sleep. You were to be out by 5. You counted to 55. You were strong and possessed a steel will. They operated and you awoke too soon. You had never experienced such things and were very bewildered.

Unfortunately the helpers had no training as to the fragility of moving a patient. They were very rough and you shouted in agony. One piece of shrapnel in your leg could not be removed. You called it a souvenir of your Motherland. To the day you left this earth you could see it move around then disappear.

Word came once again that the Turks were descending onto Leninakan. Everyone was warned in the hospital to get up take their military bags and flee. You couldn't move. You were in such a weakened state after the surgery. You watched another Armenian take your military bag. You didn't want to accuse him in case you were wrong. He put on your clothes, took your things, and even took your military jacket with holes in it. You asked him if he would return them to you and if he didn't refuse then you knew for sure. You held on to your jacket and told him to please look in the pocket. Inside was a little book that you wrote things down in. He finally felt remorse and went and found some other clothes. Everyone was leaving. They took the most seriously afflicted patients and put you all in one room. Then the doctors and nurses and everyone else left.

You grew thirsty but no one was there to help you quench your thirst. It became way too quiet again. You all laid there anticipating the Turks charging in. You write Grandpa of "polygons." I try to understand the word. You speak of it often while in Leninakan. An Armenian soldier comes into the hospital and warns you all that the Turks have mobbed the "polygons" and that they are on their way to the hospital. You tell him why he came to die with you all? He wept that the roads are closed and that he was a stranger to this region. By morning more Armenian soldiers came and told you all to sleep because the Turks were nowhere near you all.

The night before you had broken two slats of wood from the center portion of your bed to use as crutches when you would try to escape again. You created four crutches, two for you and two for you friend Yervand who was lying next to you for days now. On your knees you crawled into a room with old clothes you crawled back and helped dress your friend. He thanked you for all that you were doing for him. He prayed that one day he could return a favor. (You write what an ungrateful person he was in the end. You helped save his life, and five months later when you went to his house he didn't even offer you bread.)

A doctor finally showed up at the hospital and they had brought back two carts to help transport the seriously wounded! You gave a man 250 rubles to move you and your so-called friend to the front spot so that your legs could have room to rest outwards. To date you had 25 of your family members slaughtered. You were all that was left. The doctor tried to make you walk and I thank God you fought back. You told him that you were all that was left. That these wounds are from fighting for your people, and now the doctor wants to leave you behind so that the Turks slaughter you off too. The doctor left you alone after that.

You were all taken to the train station and left there because the roads were closed. There was no one to put you wounded boy soldiers on the train. A wagon came by but there was still no way to get on it. A short man was walking by and you asked him to help you get into the wagon. He said he would if he and his wife could join your group. This was a military wagon. You were clever enough to tell the wife to hide under the benches for safety. There was no room for a needle you write. But the Turks were coming and the roads were closed by these lascivious slithering pariahs. I say this because it would take volumes of writing to accurately tell how many times you write that the Turks would walk into a dwelling start beating the men and boys and ask for Armenian girls like they were their pastry. You write that heavy fighting was going on so much so that a mother would forget their child. What a way of showing us the level of frenzy every mind was in. A whole night passed and the train began to move. You were all freezing and hungry, but the train was finally going in the direction of Yerevan, Armenia.

It would be four days before you received 300 grams of bread. I can't even relate to these figures Grandpa. Your group ate borshcht (Russian vegetable soup). Growing up I knew we would be eating borshcht when I saw the huge deep pot my mother would use to make this Russian soup. We had meat in it. I knew that was it for a week. Today I look forward to a bowl because it feels like I am home as I smell it, taste it, and sadly remember how great my mother's recipe was. All gone now. Food takes you home, food reminds us of those we have lost along the way. In the hospital in Yerevan you saw many visitors come and hug the soldiers that were laid up. No one came for you. You quietly wept for being all alone. "My heart would bleed and feel like it was bursting into pieces but nobody came to me."

One day a couple came and asked for you! When they came by they reminded you that you helped them many months ago by secretly bringing them meat. She showed you the ring you gave her as a wedding gift to the boy that was so certain that you stole her from him. She was so beautiful at the time yet in five short months you write she changed into a woman much much older and unrecognizable.

Then your corporal Dzarouk Horomtsi from the time you served at the front in Meternik arrived at your bedside. He showed you a newspaper with a story about you! Colonel Shakoupatov who was the division commander wanted to reward your valor and courage by giving you a military cross. "He wants you to recover and return to your battalion to receive your cross."

During your stay at the hospital, some came and took money to bring you bread and never returned, but one man was so good to you that he became your closest friend. His name was Janipek. He would take your money and bring you tobacco, and food. Sometimes he would sneak the doctor's food to you. The other patients thought he was your brother. You continued to recover until fate changed things again.

It was January 1921. These strange men came into the hospital and sat down near you. You had a cigarette but no matches. These slick men remind me of slimy conmen acting kind but with a big stick ready to hit. You greet them by saying "Sir." They tell you that "Sir" went up the donkey's ass.

That their names were comrades. That they were your comrade, and that tomorrow you would get white bread not black, and food to fill your belly.

Grandpa this sounds like a cult to me. You had no idea of what communism was or what it looked like. They were reeling you in. I remember going to Armenia during communist rule and within two days I was as paranoid as the people. Soldiers with rifles yelled at me because I stood too close to the base of Stalin's statue. I would sit in an Armenian's house and they would look behind them before they would whisper. My phone was tapped, my taxi driver was KGB, and I have never felt like the walls in a room were watching me. I had to hand my key to a burly woman on my floor before I left my room from hell. I had one handkerchief they claimed was a bath towel.

God bless America. We are so spoiled by our freedom that we give it away on the internet daily. No one cares about privacy. People talk without thinking, chattering every word that comes to them. They look like people who have toilet paper stuck to their shoes. It galls me. They will never understand that freedom takes a ton of work. A ton of young people die for us to walk around in our tunnel vision staring at our phones with the entitlement to boot that when we are choosing to walk into people because we are playing with our "thing" others should lovingly step aside. Then the sound bites are as much as we want to hear. Don't bum me out, let others take care of the bad people. Bad people never recognize themselves in others. That their stupor of self-involvement is making others suffer unnecessarily. So, when I kiss the ground in thanks of my motherland I think of all those who just walk around like they deserve to cut out in front of everyone because they are special.

In Russia years ago, under communist rule, I was truly shocked to hear American music everywhere. People walking around with American themed T-shirts. When they found out I was from America they would look up to the sky and say, "Ahh America, if only I could go." I found this sentiment the most in Armenia's larger cities.

Grandpa I know how insidious communism is. It always comes in when people are hungry. Most often when there is chaos after a war. It promises order and then the order becomes a high wire everyone walks in line on for the rest of their miserable lives. During your stay in the hospital documents were signed by the Ministry of the very broken Republic of Armenia. You write how at first you were all so glad that food started arriving from these comrades, that they convinced the leaders of Armenia that they would never use violence, and most of all never arrest leaders of the Republic. They broke every promise. They promised so much to the tired Armenian leaders in Yerevan. They asked one condition that the word "Republic" be dropped and changed to "Soviet Armenia." Then it began. Each night commanding staff, generals, captains, ministry staff, officers were arrested and put in prison. You and your boy soldiers were powerless to help. They used axes to kill their innocent prisoners.

"Every night, they would take and axe and assassinate them. They hit the captain, Hamazasp, with an axe and split his body into two pieces. It was happening again; the Armenians were being slaughtered like lambs, only now by the communists. Captain Goryoun and Karkin Nzdeh, fellow Armenians, encouraged the people to revolt in Yerevan, Nzdeh encouraged from outside the city from Aznkezour.

"They established contact with each other so that both sides trusted each other. In 1921 late at night they sieged the city. War began between the people and the Bolsheviks. The same Bolsheviks that stole everything from my father along with his mother. These ruthless beasts from hell were everywhere now. The Armenians fought with all their might. They won against the Bolsheviks and they threw them out of the city. They went and broke the doors of the prisons and released the innocent Armenians. They saved and took out their loved ones, along with the parliament staff of Armenia."

Grandpa you were still in the hospital and all of you were confused. The Dashnaktsoution (Armenians) occupied the city. The next morning they brought the wounded and dead to the hospital. You saw your brave captain Smbat from the Greek village: he was dead. This brave man was buried the same day. At least he got a grave.

Your wounds wouldn't all heal. You were still considered the most wounded and the most seriously injured. You couldn't even turn on your side. The fibula wound worsened each day. All they could do was wash it and bandage it. It continued to get very infected. You prayed every day for healing. You didn't want to be a burden to anyone else. You even found a way to go to the bathroom on your own. I love you Grandpa. It got really critical at one point. You had been at the hospital for five months now. The others who couldn't heal were sent to relatives. You had no one. You write of how the director of the hospital got annoyed with you still staying there and wanted to amputate. You protested. You were terrified that in the middle of the night they would do it so you had Janipek come and sit with you. He had been asking you for large sums of money and behaving strangely but he was there when you needed him. In the end he gave you every ruble back. He just liked to gamble. Your luck changed when a new doctor came from Istanbul. It was a woman! You don't write how a female doctor from Istanbul arrived in Yerevan but she admonished everyone for their negligence in treating you properly. She said there was no reason to amputate. She got this medicine that was like white wax; she melted it on the wound. You were then placed in bed for three days with that leg tied down. After that it was surgery. You told the doctors that your intuition felt strongly that the leg would heal completely. It did.

A beautiful thing happened: a doctor from Tbilisi and the female doctor from Istanbul fell in love and married. It is the end of 1920 and you are free from the military you had served above and beyond the call of duty. You never did go back to get your military cross. But, I better understand why you told me you didn't know what to do if your legs got too weak. I would just say something like "Oh, Grandpa you're fine." How could I know the depth of your comment? I was ignorant of all this. I would carry you on my back to the summit of Mount Ararat if I could be so lucky.

In February 1921 you were free from the army but a Bolshevik revolt broke out in Yerevan. They came back for blood. You escaped Yerevan with the same words you described in the Turkish massacres. Rape, mayhem, murder: in late April 1921 Yerevan had fallen again. Only this time the precious race of tired souls fell to communism.

Conclusion

I SPOKE TO A friend today and she told me that the Smithsonian
Institute had done a piece in the July/August 2015 issue about the 100th
anniversary of the Armenian genocide. That a woman was over 100 and
had survived the genocide and was interviewed and shown a large picture
of her homeland before the blood raid. I resisted at first but felt I should
honor Smithsonian and look. I made the mistake of going online to their
site to see the haunting pictures, even one by Walter Morganthau depict-
ing rows and rows of murdered Christian Armenians. How callous I have
become: instead of shunning the picture I was relieved they still had their
clothes on. They were spared the constant nudity and rapings that my
Grandfather witnessed.

As I scrolled down it happened. My blood boiled with rage and I could
hardly control myself. There it was all over again. Grown Turkish men,
plants for sure by officials. They were coolly talking about the silliness of
Armenians going on and on about something that didn't happen!! Why do
I care what these little minds think? I don't care, yet I do. I forced myself
to read their rhetoric to strangers that were coming to the site to honor
the few people left on earth who were actually there. One Armenian man
survived because a Turkish family hid him. I lay roses at their feet. The site
said "Please join the discussion!" There was no discussion, only the circular
argument that led me to write this book in the first place. One small man
talked about the Armenians using stories from their "Grandmas." I began
to write: well, if my Great-grandma wasn't slaughtered like a wild animal
I would gladly quote her. That perhaps his Grandma and other relatives
never experienced such a mass extermination. Maybe if he had he would
stop his tin can speech of all the organizations of his that claim it never
happened. Getting back to the most touching part of the Smithsonian
exhibit on line was one haunting picture.

An elderly Armenian man is still alive! He was the one hidden by a Turkish family. The photographer put a huge picture of his homeland out for him to touch while he stood in the middle of field in Armenia. He asked her to please find his church and put his picture there. The photographer hired a Turkish guide and when they found the rubble the guide broke down and wept. There I saw a picture of the old Armenian man waving while his photo sat inside the rubble of his beloved church. On the site once again were Armenian youths arguing appropriately with these two plants that seemed to be enjoying tormenting them—very arrogant in their choices of words. Two men stinking up the moment once again. After a hundred years some people finally were enjoying a photo exhibit which was a loving gesture by a photographer. One Turkish plant was claiming that Mount Ararat is of course Turkey's. He kept coming back taunting the other writers to keep defending the Genocide. I watched the bullies who were grown men having fun tormenting once again. How bizarre humans can be. Poor Turkish plants working hard to stir the pot. They couldn't even grasp each time he wrote "Ararat" that he was stating a pure Armenian word over and over again. The Bible took dictation a long time ago, and the bloodbath makers can never change the Armenian name of the Holy Mountain that is the cornerstone of the Armenian people.

Never was I so grateful for my Grandfather's diaries as this moment. He charts clearly how each time the Turks decided to lurk and demand any hidden Armenians to be released (he being a simple man and guileless repeated what was said at the time) they said the words the present government denies: "Turn them over to the government." The reason this feels so salient is that these two little men kept trying to dissuade people on the internet by saying the government had nothing to do with it. Perhaps in 2015 this is the catchphrase for the rhetoric makers. I felt twelve years old again, pushing through the crowd of people circled around that hired man to hold a sign that said Armenians killed too. Same pathetic behavior. It actually helps to hear the empty murderous words. Because it sounds so defensive that it helps the truth rise above the filth of denial. Souls must rest, so let there be one funeral without your kind of people coming and pillaging where you are not welcome because even with a tiny gesture of reverence that others give to those you murdered you still have to come and try and destroy the sacredness shared by so few so late. Ask yourselves why. This brings me full circle again. That it wasn't what the Turkish government did. It was how they did it. As Lord Bryce simply said, "Worse than any other." Wow you guys must really know the truth to work so hard to deny the obvious. So thank you once again for giving me the strengh to write and not step into your ignorant babble from your own officials that still can't figure out how to use the best political maneuver on planet earth.

Taking responsibility makes your government shine in the public eye. Please don't hurt the Turkish guide that wept and apologized. If it wasn't written in the Smithsonian article I would not have felt safe to rewrite it. To this day we shudder from your brutality. No matter your slick suits and flat expressions in the face of countless documents, audio histories from the victims themselves and the sad and horrid pictures. This, along with the numerous countries that don't fear you anymore and recognize the genocide. You won't budge. This would mean you have not evolved and that your regime is hiding a lot of evil under the earth that we pay for each year in America. What will happen when no great country needs anything from you anymore? Including your harbors where the cruise ships dock and play exotic for the tourists.

I have come back to my senses Grandpa. One hundred years and the vacuum of denial is as big as a black hole.

Eureka! It takes me 60 years to arrive to the most obvious reason why I am up before the dawn. I am remembering once again a comedy show I watched that discovered the key ingredient for a successful show. They called it the "Third Heat:" what is missing in these circular bullies pouring more blood-oil on our wounds are the Turkish people! Not these little plants that expose the most mutilating positions which are always the same. Where are you all? All you Turkish individuals, the thousands of you who know, who have Armenian friends that live in America, that live and know the truth. Why don't your words on how you feel knowing and living with such a shameful past ever reach newspapers? Or the pseudo-quote discussion page on the Smithsonian site? There are the usual grateful Armenians, the countless Armenians defending the truth, and two pathetic grown men babbling as usual.

Germany has taken responsibility for the horror of a small disenfranchised sick group that began as hooligans passing out pamphlets. Genocides are nothing new. What is new and forever amazing is the airtight vacuum that the Turkish government still has its tentacles in all the way to America. Wow, that is what makes these discussions nothing more than shouting at each other from across the mass open graves that never were covered with the tears of the new generation of Turks that are still being told nothing happened, when something beyond their comprehension started off the 20th century. Just as it had in the 19th century, and the 18th century, but this time because of World War I foreign people were nearby. So many people from all walks of life saw the slaughters. Some died themselves. The innocent people's cries were heard on the front page news around the world. Countless Turkish people young and old know the truth and their feelings are never captured in the same newspapers that will honor the 100th Anniversary of the Armenian Genocide. The pathetic Turks defecating on the beautiful short piece that was shown at the Smithsonian site actually were right about one thing. The Turks will not speak about their culpability. Most Turkish people have relatives in their homeland which was once my homeland too. They fear for their own lives.

Countless Germans were slaughtered by Nazis: no one ever talks about that. Turkish citizens who know the truth don't want to be killed just for speaking up. Why is it that the few Turkish scholars that had the courage to say that it was best to admit that the Turks massacred the Armenians had to escape their own country? They live in America now. God bless you dear brothers and sisters. Why don't we have the "Third Heat?" The German people began writing, and speaking out on behalf of the Jewish citizens that were slaughtered. Time for you Turks hiding out to come forth and be the third heat. Talk about how it feels to come from such a barbaric heritage. Maybe Turks need to connect the dots that have to do with the pattern of victim/victimizer. In ancient times Turks were horribly massacred. Perhaps that fed your hatred and capacity to kill like no other. But to deny annihilating your neighbors in the 20th century makes you worse than all that has happened to your own people in the past. Your people are our people we are all the same underneath. The problem with "victim/victimizer" is the mere fact that many nations have suffered massacres. In rebuilding their lives they didn't come back and annihilate innocent people.

So during this new marker of the silent killers with a hundred years in between is that no Turkish people, regular normal people, spoke online. Not even from America. Talk about airtight! There was mass silence even on a Smithsonian web page. When the day comes that normal Turkish people are unafraid to say "I am Armenian." "I am one of the people who died." When we get one million and five hundred of you to come forth it will cleanse the corpse stains all over your nation. That is the third heat.

Sigmund Freud said that the definition of insanity is doing the same thing over and over again trying to get a different result. Are you listening Turkey? Dr. Freud help me not to do it over again. Help this be different. Help this be true.

I feel better this moment. Never did I think as the sun began to rise that I would lay the corpses down at your feet, my Turkish neighbors. Please step forward and have the courage to speak up after a hundred years. You know why your government won't speak? It is because soon all of us will be gone. Then the few of us living will just be silly old people talking about their dead relatives long ago.

I am sitting with the early sunrise and sipping strong English tea. The candle went out that was on by itself for days. I feel somewhat unsure as to what to do next. I quietly asked deep inside my soul, how can it be over? How can I be done? I distinctly heard a quiet voice inside my being comfort me and say that my job was to start something, not to end it.

My Grandfather's life was a masterpiece of prevailing against all odds. He survived the Russian army; he made his way as a youth. He made all his own decisions and he was fueled by faith. He would have walked my aunt's dog by now and returned to his humble apartment. Just like in the Russian army where he awoke every morning on hay pillows and mattresses, did his exercises, then did his military exercises and gained the trust of his foreign commanders that were occupying his homeland. He did the same at age 88 and in perfect health. Up at 6.30 a.m., walk two miles, take her dog to the park and run him, then walk back two miles while the rest of us slept. He read, he wrote, he celebrated every important holiday and personal triumphs in every one of his seven surviving children's lives, along with his countless nieces and nephews. When I opened my first mental health clinic, he informed me he was coming to give his blessing. I didn't give him the directions and he didn't drive. One day there he was with a beautiful plant. He had taken the bus all the way to my clinic. He sat with great respect and regard and quietly got up after his blessing and left. There I was alone with my plant. Within six months there were five other clinicians and the clinic flourished just like his plant. When I look back to the miracle of his life's journey I reflect on my own as well. He fell in love with an Armenian girl from Van. "Van" was like saying "the Holy Land" to an Armenian. Old genes ran through the veins of those that survived there. He met the Grandmother I never knew. He fought for her. He had no loved ones and the customs to win an Armenian girl were complicated. After the extermination of his race the customs were even more rigid and demanding. In his day if a young bride had a baby she could not touch anything directly with her hands until the baby was baptized. Why I will never know? When he saw Aghavni he fell in love. He wanted so much for her to be his wife but her brothers would not let him. He asked a man to represent him to the family since he had no one to assist him in the tradition of asking for her hand and he was met with a beating, perhaps by the brothers. He got his bride and she bore him ten children but three died. He named all of them after his loved ones that had perished. During World War II they were living in Russia. Once again they were in hell. This time the German soldiers would occupy their land and if the Russians got the land back they would kill the ones who stayed during the German occupation. It went back and forth so many times that all my loved ones were psychologically affected whether they knew it or not. My mother would say how they ate once a day at midnight. They had to bury their food under dirt otherwise the German soldiers would smell the food and take it. Once they made my Grandmother cook the food and would not let her give a piece of food to her dying three year-old daughter. The commander made her cook the food then gave it to his horse. So the horror stories continue how during the cloak of war humans regress to subhuman behavior while calling their victims subhuman. Poor Grandpa, he went through so much all over again. Lost everything. Then the Germans made him dig ditches for their war effort. Then they put all my loved ones into German labor camps. They were not slaughtered like the Jews for some reason. Mainly because the psychotic Hitler seemed to think they had some Aryan bloodlines. But my mother worked in the snow barefoot and Grandpa worked in ditches and somehow at the end of the war Armenians in America sponsored them to come to America. They were on a huge ship crossing to America when Grandpa learned they were being sent to Mississippi to be cotton pickers on an African American owned farm. This was the last omission I found out. I learned that an African American family sponsored them all to come to America. No one spoke of it. That family ran out of money and could not pay for the tickets from Rhode Island to Mississippi, and there my mother and Grandfather and all my aunts and uncles sat on the ship waiting to go back! They were not allowed off the ship because back in the day America actually followed their own rules which was no one came into our country who was not sponsored and medically checked out before they left their country. This is the proper way to come to the land of the free. "Illegal" is now called "undocumented." An Armenian woman from the local Armenian Organization council came aboard the ship and found them all. They were brought out and allowed to go on land under the care of Armenian families. My parents couldn't speak the language but found work and never took a cent from America. Instead they gave back every year. That is how a country flourishes, not the other way around. My poor Grandmother was not so lucky. She was only 39 years old when she learned she was pregnant again. Instead of this being a sign of good things to come, neighbors shamed her, saying that a woman her age was too old to have a child! These women were Armenian. My Grandfather only learned much later what cruelty his wife suffered in the hands of these sadistic, primitive women. I will never understand why evil lurks in the hearts of people. My mother and her sister were saving their pennies to by the baby a gift when the birth arrived. Instead these women led my Grandmother to believe they were saving to run away from the shame of having and elderly mother giving birth. Now I see hundreds of women going to fertility clinics in their late 30's to try and get pregnant. These Armenian women gave my Grandmother a potion to drink. She became violently ill instead. When she did have her baby, she gave birth to a beautiful little girl. She hemorrhaged to death. Grandpa was devastated. My mother, being the eldest of girls at age 18, had to become the matriarch of the family.

Once again that baby girl was given the name of a loved one who died: this time it was her own mother.

My mother worked two jobs, sewed in the middle of the night, washed all her siblings' clothes and lost her youth forever. Grandpa you used to say my mother was your arms. As I drove you around in my little car you would raise your arms and show me from your underarms down with opposite hands pointing that "Your mother is my arms." You said it with love. I was 17; I didn't quite grasp the significance of the gesture. I knew it was in gratitude but I didn't know the degree of sacrifice my poor mother made in her frenetic life. She worked all day, washed all night my whole life. She told me proudly that she couldn't stop, that if she did she feared she would go crazy. You see Grandpa I never felt her arms around me as a child. I felt she cooked, and cleaned, and led, and demanded, but she could not be, she could not rest. She couldn't find inner peace until the last few years. I knew you well, so I thought. There was a calmness with the two of us. I loved your company; I looked forward to it, and now looking back your worry beads that you held and used almost daily prove to have been the clue I missed. Only now do I put it all together. I would take your worry beads as a good luck icon with me whenever I lectured or was in front of a large group of people. I took it with me when I was talking on the radio to give me strength. I never saw that it was your outward sign of the worry you still carried inside. I thought it was a habit, a touchstone of some kind. I thought it was being Armenian. Now they are around the neck of our Goddess of Mercy, a statue. When I need strength or need you near I still carry them Grandpa and so does my husband, so thank you for bringing him to me.

I love you, and I look at the picture of us with my arms around your shoulders and you smiling, and notice I was always reaching out to every-one I loved for the hug that I had to initiate in order to feel close.

I have been blissfully with my soulmate for over 24 years. The man who changed my life and who has quietly supported me Grandpa in every endeavor of my life has never asked for anything in return but to love and respect us. He supported me as I started my dissertation on treat-ing Post-Traumatic Stress Disorder using art therapy with the children in Armenia after the devastating earthquake in December 1988. Then he stood by me as I pondered having children while I helped countless kids and their families. Then he was there for me when my loved ones got sick and slowly died one by one. He supported me when I chose to do the funerals in the Armenian tradition, which is long and complex and has many steps that go on for several years. He stood by me as I gave lectures, did the radio coverage of Armenia and then helping children in America after the devastating earthquakes we had here. He stood by me when I wrote a children's book that took forever to complete. He made my lunch every morning as I headed out to work and help families with atypical and autistic children. He stood by me when I would be on the phone late into the night helping families in crisis. He stood by me when I had to take over the family business after you, my father, and then my dear mother all died suddenly. He stood by me every day of my life from the moment I heard his voice on the phone in March of 1991. Here's the kicker: he is German. The only other race my mother told me to always avoid. "These people are the coldest people on earth." Thanks to my pure-hearted husband you healed your heart mother and would tell me how much you loved him and that he was your son.

When the 100th anniversary of the Armenian Genocide finally happened on April 24, 2015 he saw that look I get. I had successfully pushed away my Armenianism for a good while since my mother died three years ago. But the truth was I am always carrying the flame high above my head with tired arms for my ancestors and my parents and for you Grandpa.

My beloved husband has read every book possible about the Jewish Holocaust: even though Hitler was Austrian not German he has felt a responsibility to understand all that he can about the subjugation of innocent people. He knew more about being Armenian than my Armenian friends. He is a scholar in his own right and stood by me since I began this journey of translating the 400 page diary of yours Grandpa, and now 22 years later he stands by me while I am writing about it. That is love. This man has given me a true partnership from his heart and soul which is all humanity's bloodline. I continue to fall deeper and wider in love with my husband. In 24 years I have never cried a tear because I didn't feel heard or loved. He taught me to be patient that this day would come. He kept saying the world will understand but it will be a slow process.

Grandpa, he was the "*Gagad a Ger*" you told me about. My beloved soulmate came, while I searched for you in the ruins of Armenia.